MW01256090

Estate Planning Strategies

COLLECTIVE WISDOM, PROVEN TECHNIQUES
of WealthCounsel® Attorneys

Copyright 2022 by WealthCounsel, LLC

All rights reserved. No part of this book may be reproduced or transmitted in any form or by any means, electronic or mechanical, including photocopying and recording, or by any information storage or retrieval system, except as may be expressly permitted by the 1989 Copyright Law or in writing from the publisher. Requests for permission should be addressed in writing to:

WealthCounsel
P.O. Box 71188
Salt Lake City, UT 84171

ISBN: 978-0-578-39955-3

This book is a collection of general legal essays written and edited by attorneys from across the United States. In the preparation of this book, every effort has been made to offer the most current and correct information possible. Nonetheless, inadvertent errors can occur, federal tax and estate laws often change, and probate, estate, and property laws vary from state to state.

The information in the text is intended to afford general guidance to the public. The impact of estate and tax laws varies greatly based upon the unique facts of the individual. Accordingly, the information in this book is not intended to serve as legal, accounting, investment, or tax advice. The authors, editors, and publisher disclaim any responsibility for positions taken by taxpayers in their individual cases or for any misunderstanding on the part of the readers. The editors have reviewed the book for stylistic and grammatical consistency and disclaim any responsibility for the accuracy or originality of the author's contributions.

The publisher is not engaged in rendering legal, accounting, or other professional service. If legal, accounting, tax, investment, or other expert advice is required, readers are encouraged to consult with professional advisers. This book is sold with the understanding that the authors, editors, and publisher are not offering such advice in this publication.

TABLE OF CONTENTS

Introduction to Estate Planning

Why Estate Planning Is Important

By Sarah L. Ostahowski (Clare, Michigan)

As the kind older gentleman looked across the table at me, he held his wife's hand, patting it lovingly. He explained, "My wife has dementia and can't remember much anymore. She still remembers me, most of the time. It is time to get estate planning documents in place for her so she will be taken care of in case I am not here anymore." I had already spoken to his wife for several minutes, but it was clear that she had no memory of our conversation and did not know where she was or why she was there. With a heavy heart, I explained to my new client that at this point, it was too late for his wife to create estate documents. We would need to move through a court process to have his lovely wife placed under a guardianship and a conservatorship. I explained that because she no longer had the capacity to make decisions for herself, she did not have the capacity to create and sign those documents. Her husband cried, distressed because he did not want a judge to deem his wife crazy. I assured him the process would be done with integrity and grace.

These conversations are some of the hardest I have in my practice of law. Many people put estate planning on the back burner because there will always be time later to do it—then suddenly, there is no more time. Estate planning gives you a chance to leave a path for your family. It does not need to be difficult. Many clients tell us that if they had known it would be so easy, they would have done it a long time ago.

Estate planning is the process of creating a plan in advance to help your family know what to do when you pass away or become incapacitated. A plan allows you to choose who you want to be in charge of your care and your assets if at some point you are not able to make your own decisions. But only you can put that plan in place. If you do not plan, the details will be left up to the court system and state law. Your family will be left trying to put together a puzzle with no idea what the picture is supposed to look like.

Estate planning allows you to plan for tax issues or for divorce and creditor protection for your kids. It allows you to plan for the unexpected, like children dying before their parents or a sudden injury resulting in the need for long-term care. It allows families to plan for children with special needs to ensure that they are properly cared for throughout their lives. Estate planning gives you the peace of mind that comes from knowing you will not leave behind a mess for your kids or spouse.

Did you know that if you do not put a plan in place, your state already has one for you? That's right, your state has already decided what it thinks you would want to happen. Some people think this plan will work fine. If you are not sure what your state has in store for you and your heirs if you do not create your own plan, you should meet with an estate planning attorney to find out. The attorney can also walk you through the differences between a will and trust, and explain how powers of attorney and other estate planning documents work. After meeting with an estate planning attorney, you can make an educated decision about which plan will work best for you and your family.

Estate planning is about so much more than death, money, and taxes. It is about more than a will or a trust. It also enables you to plan ahead for medical and financial decision-making, your minor and adult children, charitable giving, and the unknowns of long-term care. Most importantly, it is about passing along your stories and heritage and keeping your family together after you leave this world. Estate planning is about planning for life to go on when you are no longer there. What legacy do you want to leave?

Sarah's Law Firm specializes in estate planning and elder law. Their focus is helping people decide if they need a will or a trust, drafting powers of attorney and other planning documents, and helping families navigate long-term care.

Sarah Ostahowski

2

Goals of Estate Planning

By Nicole D. Warmerdam (San Mateo, California)

Contrary to popular belief, estate planning is not a one-size-fits-all proposition. Your estate plan should reflect who you are and what is most important to you. It should be tailored to your specific goals and take into account your particular circumstances. A carefully considered estate plan will give you the peace of mind that your final wishes will be faithfully executed.

When it comes to estate planning, the first and most important thing you can do is prepare. Your estate planning attorney will ask you to make some important decisions as you develop your plan. Many of these decisions require a good amount of thought, discussion, and possibly compromise. Thinking through some of the critical issues ahead of time will allow you to formulate your main estate planning goals. This in turn will enable your attorney to tailor their advice for you and draft a portfolio of legal documents designed to accomplish your goals.

Planning your estate may seem daunting at first, and you may not even know where to start. It is often helpful to think of your planning in terms of three stages: setting up your plan in the present, planning for the possibility of your future incapacity, and planning for the eventual distribution of your estate after you are gone.

The first stage is what you are doing right now. You are attempting to articulate what you want to happen if and when certain things occur in the future. Because none of us has a crystal ball, you should prepare not only for the things that will inevitably occur but also for the unexpected. It is also important to build flexibility into your estate plan to allow for changes in your circumstances and in the law. Additionally, you should consider how your plan fits into your current lifestyle: do you like to keep things simple, or are you willing to accept some complexity in order to better accomplish your goals?

The second stage involves paving the way for your loved ones to step up and manage your personal care and finances should you become unable to do so yourself. No one wants to think about becoming incapacitated, but statistically, disability is more common than most people think. An effective estate plan should provide for your care and protection in the event that you suffer a long-term illness or injury at some point and are unable to handle your own affairs. Whom do you want to manage your assets for your benefit if you cannot? How do you ensure that your loved ones and dependents will continue to be provided for? Whom do you trust to make decisions about your medical care, housing, and quality of life? Do you want to leave specific instructions regarding your care or wishes, addressing issues such as life-sustaining treatment, autopsy, cremation, and organ donation? Without proper planning, the local probate court will supervise your estate and determine who will decide what type of care you will receive.

The third stage involves ensuring that all of your assets are transferred to your intended beneficiaries in an efficient and cost-effective manner upon your death. Without proper planning, state law will dictate who will receive your assets. These default rules often create unexpected problems, particularly if there are former spouses, children from another marriage, minor children, or estranged children in the picture. An effective estate plan starts by addressing who will inherit your assets and whether they will inherit them outright or in a trust. The latter might be preferable if you want to limit a beneficiary's access or control the timing of their access to their inheritance. You might want to consider such protections if a beneficiary is a minor, is disabled, has trouble handling money, has creditor issues, has substance abuse issues, may be getting divorced, or is highly susceptible to bad influences. If you are a business owner, you will need to create a succession plan for the continuation of your business. Are one or more of your children interested in taking over the business (and how will you equalize the inheritance for the children who do not want to run the business)? If you have co-owners, under what conditions and terms can they buy your share of the business from your estate? Additionally, many estate plans should include provisions to avoid probate and minimize taxes for those who inherit your assets.

Once you have spent some time brainstorming about your planning, you can start to formulate the goals you want to accomplish and identify those that are the most and the least important. Prioritizing your goals will help you avoid feeling overwhelmed by directing your attention to what matters the most to you. The *Estate Planning Goals Worksheet* following this chapter can assist you with this process.

Think of this book as a trusted resource on your estate planning journey. It contains the collective wisdom of some of those I consider among the best estate planning attorneys in the country. As members of WealthCounsel, a national organization of estate planning attorneys, they have assembled a comprehensive guide on a wide range of estate planning issues, including strategies and techniques to help you identify and achieve your estate planning goals.

Nicole D. Warmerdam is a California certified specialist in estate planning, trust, and probate law. She counsels clients regarding a variety of estate planning and estate administration issues.

Nicole Warmerdam

ESTATE PLANNING GOALS WORKSHEET

Rate each of the following goals on a scale of 1 to 5 to reflect their importance to you (1 being the most important and 5 being the least important):

_____ Avoid a court-supervised conservatorship if I become incapacitated

_____ Leave instructions for my personal care and the support of my spouse or dependents if I become incapacitated

_____ Avoid a court-supervised probate when I die

_____ Reduce administration costs

_____ Preserve the privacy of my affairs

_____ Avoid complexity for me

_____ Avoid complexity for my beneficiaries

_____ Provide financial security for my spouse or children

_____ Fund educational expenses for my children or grandchildren

_____ Leave gifts to other family members

_____ Leave gifts to charity

_____ Disinherit certain family members

_____ Protect my spouse from lawsuits or creditors

_____ Protect my children's inheritance from my spouse's remarriage or incapacity

_____ Safeguard the assets of minor, disabled, or fiscally irresponsible beneficiaries

_____ Protect my children's inheritance from divorce, lawsuits, or creditors

_____ Plan for the transfer and survival of my business

_____ Reduce estate taxes for my spouse and my children

_____ Reduce income taxes (on a later sale of inherited assets)

_____ Retain the ability to stretch out retirement plan benefits for my spouse and my children

_____ OTHER:

3

Estate Planning Team

By Rosanna Chenette (Novato, California)

Estate planning encompasses more than just a set of legal planning documents. A comprehensive estate plan designed to protect you and your loved ones should involve an estate planning team. Although you are in full control of your estate plan, this team will help guide you in the many decisions you will make during your life that may impact your plan. Your estate planning team should consist of trusted advisors who work collaboratively to design and maintain an estate plan that will achieve your wishes, goals, and objectives.

Your team will help you create an estate plan that will enable your affairs to continue to run smoothly if you are unable to manage them yourself. For example, if you become incapacitated, your estate plan should ensure that the trusted individuals you have appointed in your plan are properly authorized to care for you and guided to make decisions on your behalf.

An estate planning team may include your estate planning attorney, financial advisor, tax professional, insurance agent, and spiritual advisor.

Your *estate planning attorney* plays a pivotal role in your team. Your attorney will typically start the engagement by prompting you with questions and listening attentively to your answers to capture your planning goals. The attorney will take the lead in coordinating your estate plan to harmonize your legal affairs. Your attorney's lead role on the team helps to achieve a plan that is properly implemented so the appropriate trusted individuals and professionals are authorized to care for you and to make decisions on your behalf when you are unable. After your passing, your attorney facilitates the distribution of your money and property to the loved ones and individuals you have selected as beneficiaries.

A *financial advisor* is a key player in the management of your financial and investment goals. While some choose not to include a financial advisor on their estate planning team, with today's uncertainties in the financial markets, it is ideal to have a trusted financial advisor involved. It is also important that the financial advisor be an informed participant who can help manage your financial affairs should you become incapacitated. When a financial advisor is part of the team, your estate planning attorney will ensure the plan documents authorize your appointed agent to work directly with your financial advisor, if needed.

An *insurance professional* manages your insurance policies and provides a thorough analysis of your current and future coverage needs. It is important to evaluate your automobile, disability, long-term care, and life insurance needs, and doing so in connection with an estate plan can help achieve a highly integrated and comprehensive plan. Having proper insurance is crucial, and coverage amounts must occasionally be adjusted. Many estate planning strategies rely on insurance to provide for your beneficiaries. For example, if you are the sole breadwinner in your family, life insurance proceeds will be necessary to care for your beneficiaries if you are no longer around to continue working or running your business.

A *tax advisor* or a *certified public accountant* (CPA) brings tax planning expertise to the team. Estate tax and income tax planning strategies are more important than ever today because of the possibility of future tax law changes. Currently, the federal estate tax, also known as the death tax, does not affect most people because the exemption amounts are high. For example, in 2022, the federal exemption amount is $12.06 million per individual. However, this amount may decrease in the future. A lower exemption could subject more people's estates to estate taxes. Even if your estate is exempt from estate taxes, it is always prudent to implement tax strategies designed to reduce income taxes. Having a tax professional on your estate planning team is essential to helping you navigate the changing tax landscape.

A *spiritual advisor* can guide you on how to pass your values down to the next generation. This can be accomplished through written or recorded stories. Sharing your values and philosophies about life is a great way to show love to your beneficiaries. This planning can also be a means of encouraging the continuation of your family values and traditions. For example, if charitable contributions are important to you, you can demonstrate that in your estate plan.

An estate planning team that includes an estate planning attorney, a financial advisor, an insurance agent, a tax advisor, and a spiritual advisor can help you design a cohesive life plan and provide strategies for holistically achieving your goals and objectives.

Each team member brings crucial expertise to the table necessary to optimize your estate plan.

The Law Offices of Rosanna Chenette, P.C. is an estate planning and elder law firm located in Marin County, California. We provide the compassion and knowledge necessary to protect your interests.

Rosanna Chenette

4

Relationship-Centered Planning

By Chris Rippy (Conway, Arkansas)

O ne of the most challenging yet enjoyable parts of practicing estate planning is truly getting to know the ins and outs of clients, their family members, their businesses, and all of the other variables that make them unique. No matter how many "standard" American families I meet with, I am amazed at each one's interesting dynamics.

The process during which your estate planning attorney gets to know you is an intimate one: the one- to two-hour initial consultation is just the beginning of the relationship. Keeping your estate planning attorney in the loop about major and minor life events is critical to relationship-centered planning, which is accomplished over years and even decades.

My new clients are constantly amazed at the depth and thoroughness of my questions regarding their family members, in-laws, careers, assets, and other aspects of their unique circumstances. Building this kind of relationship is key for your success in crafting an estate plan that passes down not only your worldly goods, but also the legacy represented by the values and memories that you want to leave. As Ruth E. Renkel once said, "Sometimes the poorest man leaves his children the richest inheritance."

With newer marriages or blended families, clients often desire more concrete terms in their estate plans with the goal of ensuring that their heirs will be entitled to receive some of their financial assets while providing their surviving spouse with the income or resources they need to maintain a certain lifestyle or meet their monthly expenses. Thinking through the what if's with your spouse and estate planning attorney is key to creating a successful estate plan, especially in blended family situations.

Another extremely important aspect of your estate planning journey is adequately conveying your family's unique needs and dynamics, especially regarding your children, to your estate planning attorney. In consultations with new clients, our law firm spends a significant amount of time discussing their children and grandchildren. Because you are the decision maker regarding the estate plan, we must rely on you to describe your heirs' particular circumstances, that is, their marriages, children, occupations, and any other circumstances that may assist us in making planning recommendations. Common questions and topics regarding your children or other heirs may include anything from your child's relationship with a spouse; ability to handle small or large amounts of money; current occupation and earning capacity; history with any sort of legal problems or substance abuse issues; and any health concerns or special needs. A well-crafted estate plan might not distribute assets directly to that child, but instead utilize the assets to protect them from themselves. The answers to these questions are necessary to the creation of a proper estate plan that is truly unique and tailored to your individual circumstances.

In addition to understanding the entirety of the circumstances underlying your family dynamics, an estate planning attorney can also provide guidance aimed at supporting and leaving a legacy in the other important aspects of your life, which may include your church, favorite charity, or any other important person or entity.

Americans are quite charitable. In 2019, Americans gave $449.64 billion to 1.54 million charitable entities. This represented a 5.1 percent increase from 2018. If you would like to provide for a church or charity in your estate plan, this is an important conversation to have with your estate planning attorney. Even a modest monetary gift or transfer of personal property can make a significant impact on a charity. The first of my clients to pass away donated her car to a local homeless shelter in 2011. Ten years later, on almost a weekly basis, I see the director of the charity utilizing the vehicle to benefit the charity. Even small gifts can go a long way for the charities you have supported throughout the years.

Many clients come to an estate planning consultation under the impression that we will focus mainly on their financial assets and are surprised when that is not the main topic of our discussions. Your financial situation is an important aspect of your estate plan, but complicated estate tax planning is typically not necessary for most clients. In 2022, generally only estates worth a minimum of $12,060,000 may be subject to federal estate taxes. The estate tax exemption amount varies at the state level, though only seventeen states have their own estate tax. Even though estate taxes are not currently a significant concern for the majority of clients, it is still extremely important to share your financial situation with your estate planning attorney.

Although it may not be necessary for the initial consultation, you will eventually need to provide your estate planning attorney with detailed information on all of your financial assets, including real estate, bank accounts, retirement accounts, brokerage accounts, term or permanent life insurance policies, and any other significant assets that you have. In addition, you should provide your estate planning attorney information about any future assets that you may acquire, for example, from a family member who will likely predecease you. Planning not only for the present, but also for the future, is a key aspect of your estate plan.

Building a close relationship with your estate planning attorney is key to the successful creation of an estate plan that not only efficiently passes down your financial assets, but also takes into consideration your circumstances and ensures that your needs and goals are adequately met.

Chris Rippy is the managing partner of Rippy, Stepps, & Associates, P.A. and focuses his practice almost exclusively on estate planning, business planning, and family planning matters.

Chris Rippy

5

Integrated Estate Planning: Wills, Living Trusts, and Asset Protection

By H. Van Smith (Richmond, Virginia)

W hen training new staff members at our law firm, I sometimes listen in on their phone calls with new clients. Two frequently asked questions are "Does your law firm do wills?" and "How much do they cost?" Many clients are initially unaware that estate planning typically involves more than simply drafting a will.

When I was growing up, my mother used to listen to Paul Harvey, the late radio personality. Harvey always ended his broadcast with the familiar line "And now you know the *rest* of the story!" Everyone should have a will, but I would like to share the rest of the story—estate planning strategies that complement a will.

Years ago, in the midst of a consultation, I heard a familiar story. After the death of her mother, my client sat in our conference room and explained her situation:

> *I'm the eldest daughter and the executor of my mother's estate. Your law firm came highly recommended for estate work. My parents were good savers and*

> *lived frugally, but by the end of my mother's life, the long-term care facility and unreimbursed medical expenses had gobbled up much of their savings and retirement. The house, the car, and some funds in the bank are all that is left. Probate should be pretty straightforward.*

I did not want to ruin her day, but I thought to myself, "Had her mother come to see me six or seven years ago, I could have saved her family $275,000-$320,000 or more with proper estate planning."

THE FOUNDATION OF GOOD ESTATE PLANNING

At a minimum, everyone should have a will. A will, simply put, enables us to legally say, "Here is my stuff, and here is who gets it when I die." If you have minor or special needs children, additional protection and guardianship language will be included in the will.

Most folks think that estate planning is simply specifying "when I die, X." But the foundation of good estate planning also includes providing guidance for managing your finances and health before you die. Statistically speaking, you will have many good years in retirement. However, for 52 percent of U.S. residents, there will be a period of years during which a family member or other agent manages your care and finances in part or in full.

As a result, a solid estate plan should also include a financial power of attorney, a health-care power of attorney or advance directive, a HIPAA authorization, and memorial instructions. These documents provide a rulebook for your agent to guide their decisions while they are acting on your behalf, reducing the likelihood of innocent or intentional mishandling of your finances or care when you can no longer act for yourself.

Keep in mind the following issues that you will face with a will-based estate plan:

- **Probate.** This is the process of inventorying and accounting for your assets and debts when you die, in the county or city of your residence. In Virginia, as in many states, it often takes two to three years and can cost more than 3-5 percent of the total estate. If you must face probate, rely on a law firm to assist you. As our clients know, skilled attorneys can save time and money in probate.

- **Compliance with state law.** A will is drafted to comply with the laws and require-ments of the state in which it is written. Thus, if you move to another state, you must have your will reviewed and possibly updated to ensure that it complies with the laws and requirements of the new state.

- **Outright inheritance.** Most wills provide for heirs to inherit money and property outright, assuming they are of appropriate age. Statistics indicate that 87 percent of adult children will deplete their inheritance within eighteen months of their parent's death, whether by divorce, litigation, bankruptcy, business failure, debt, or extravagant spending.

We can do better. Once our clients understand the rest of the story, they experience a far better outcome.

CONSIDER ADDING A REVOCABLE LIVING TRUST TO YOUR ESTATE PLAN

Imagine that you are the conductor of your own estate planning train. The first car on the train is the will. Now, imagine adding a second car to your estate planning train—the living trust. What is a trust? What are the advantages to adding this second car to your estate plan?

A revocable living trust is simply an invisible legal bucket that holds your assets. You can put assets in and take assets out. *Revocable* is a legal term that means "take-it-outable." In other words, a revocable living trust does not restrict your ability to spend your money or use your assets in the manner you did before you had the trust.

A revocable living trust provides the following key advantages:

- **Avoidance of probate.** By adding the second train car, the living trust, your assets held by the trust avoid the potentially lengthy and expensive court proceedings known as probate. Why? If your estate plan consists of only a will, then the probate process empties your "pockets" of all the stuff you own. By adding a living trust to your plan, the legal bucket (and not your pockets) now holds your assets. When you die, you simply let go of the bucket. The trust survives your death, and your assets are distributed according to its terms rather than through probate.

- **Portability.** A living trust that was validly formed in one state will be recognized as valid in other states. By adding a living trust to your estate plan, you gain portability, which saves time and money if you move to a different state.

- **Asset protection for heirs.** A skilled estate planning attorney can build asset protection into your children's trust, which springs to life upon your death. Asset protection planning serves to protect their inheritance from potential divorce, bankruptcy, business failure, litigation, and other future creditors.

Many clients ask whether they still need a will after establishing a living trust. Importantly, a trust does not replace a will. When you add a living trust to your estate plan, your will should be a *pour-over* will. This means that any assets that may have been left out of your trust will be poured over from the will and into the trust when you die, potentially saving time and resources in the administration of your estate.

ADDING AN ASSET PROTECTION TRUST TO STRENGTHEN YOUR ESTATE PLAN

Going back to our railroad analogy, imagine adding a third car (a caboose) to your estate planning train—the asset protection trust. If established and funded properly in advance, an asset protection trust provides one key benefit: it will protect your assets from loss in the event of future litigation, long-term care, or unreimbursed medical costs. However, you must establish and fund the asset protection trust prior to any incident that leads to litigation. In other words, you cannot wait until you are served in a lawsuit or are involved in an accident and then rush to your lawyer's office to create one. Asset protection trust planning must be set up in advance of the need and will typically require you to endorse an affidavit of solvency to avoid allegations of fraudulent intent.

The current requirement is that the asset protection trust must have been in existence for five years for U.S. citizens and three years for veterans (defined as those who served ninety days or more, including at least one day of wartime service, and who were honorably discharged). It must also have been properly funded (the process of ensuring that your assets are added to your trust by change of title or beneficiary designation), which your qualified estate planning attorney will facilitate. If these requirements are met, and if you meet the needs basis for care, you may then become eligible for Medicaid (for citizens) or the Veterans Affairs Aid and Attendance program (for veterans and their spouses) to pay for or assist you with expenses associated with in-home care, assisted living, or nursing home care.

Many clients ask if they still need a living trust after they form an asset protection trust. The answer is yes. You need all three cars—the will, the living trust, and the asset protection trust—in your estate planning train to create an integrated system. You live out of your living trust and protect your assets with your asset protection trust. The living trust is like your wallet, and the asset protection trust is like your safe in the basement.

The pour-over will, living trust, and asset protection trust work together to provide a solid and effective estate plan. There is so much more to learn and appreciate about each of these components, but I hope that now you, too, will know the rest of the story when you contact a law firm to begin your own estate planning.

H. Van Smith practices estate planning and estate litigation at Smith Strong, PLC in Richmond, Virginia. He has received both the Super Lawyers' Rising Star and Virginia Business Magazine's Legal Elite designation for the years 2014 through 2021.

H. Van Smith

6

Estate Planning:
An Evolving Process

By Glenn Busch (New York, New York)

Socrates once said, "death is a very narrow theme, but it reaches a wide audience." Our inevitable demise is not something we like to think about; however, it is part of the human experience. Planning for it, while not fun, is something we all must consider. As our life evolves and changes, our estate plan must also be adjusted to ensure our wishes are satisfied.

You have worked hard throughout your life to save and care for your family. You may feel a sense of accomplishment after executing your last will, trusts, powers of attorney, healthcare directives, and funeral plans—and you should. Estate planning, however, is an evolving process. Updating your estate documents from time to time will ensure a smooth transition for your heirs and beneficiaries when certain life events occur. An estate plan checkup every few years will ensure that your plan reflects changes in your life and your family.

These changes may involve your family, financial circumstances, a divorce, opening a new business, an inheritance, or an investment in a new economic venture, to name a few. Perhaps you or a family member relocated to another state, or you have purchased property in another state. You will need to update your plan to reflect those changes.

If you have lost a spouse or child, your estate documents may need to be updated. Are you getting married? If this is the second marriage, you should consider how best to address children from the prior marriage and property rights. Have you experienced the birth of a child or grandchild? Perhaps you want to protect the child's inheritance or provide for a grandchild: if so, specific asset protection strategies to accomplish these goals should be reflected in your estate plan. Are there circumstances in your family that require further review of your will and trust, such as a child with special needs, a health concern, an addiction, or a change of economic or marital status? If any of these situations have arisen, you should revisit your plan, review your options, and possibly redraft your estate documents.

Often clients decide to replace or change a named executor, trustee, guardian, or agent. Are you still happy with the parties you have named? Did they relocate or have you lost touch with them? Have circumstances changed, causing you to feel dissatisfied with your original choices? Have your children matured, so that you feel more comfortable adding them to the documents as your executor, trustee, or agent? Have you considered executor fees and commissions? Perhaps you would like to rename a trustee or executor in light of these considerations.

Addressing your children's needs is one of the essential issues you will face in estate planning. Are you satisfied with your child's guardian? You should make sure that the proper guardians are named. Have you reviewed the trusts you established in your will for the benefit of your minor children in the event you and your spouse pass away? Have you discussed your wishes with your named guardians and informed them about any changes or guidelines you want them to follow?

Have you updated your healthcare directive, power of attorney, do not resuscitate order, and living will to make sure they reflect your current wishes and concerns? Do these documents reflect recent changes that should be considered in light of the COVID-19 pandemic to permit your healthcare agents to communicate with medical professionals electronically through Zoom, FaceTime, WhatsApp, or other methods? Are your named healthcare agents up-to-date, and do your documents provide their correct phone numbers? Do the parties you named have a copy of your power of attorney, healthcare proxy, and living will? If they do not, do they know where they are kept in the event of an emergency?

You should review the beneficiary designations on your bank, brokerage, and retirement accounts to ensure that the proper parties are named and that they coincide with your estate plan. Have you transferred and titled your assets to implement the plan you just executed? Is a further update warranted? Additional steps are often required to implement your estate plan. Have you taken those steps?

Will Rogers once said, "The only difference between death and taxes is that death doesn't get worse every time Congress meets." Our tax laws consistently change, so it is important to review your estate plan regularly to make sure it reflects recent tax law changes. For example, the Setting Every Community Up for Retirement (SECURE) Act eliminated many beneficiaries' ability to withdraw an inherited retirement account over their life expectancy and now requires a ten-year drawdown in most cases. Additional changes in our tax laws are almost inevitable.

As you review your estate plan with your attorney and financial adviser, your life circumstances will impact how your estate plan works to accomplish your goals. You may also consider discussing your estate plan with your family from time to time to share your intentions with them—after all, they will be the ones most affected by your plan. Consider annual family meetings to discuss your plan.

Consider an update under the following circumstances:

- Increases or decreases in family assets
- Relocation to or purchase of a second home in a different state
- Death, illness, or disability of a beneficiary, family member, guardian, executor, or trustee
- Birth or adoption of a child
- Changes in federal or state tax laws that affect taxes or investments
- Marriage or divorce involving you or a beneficiary
- Health concerns, addiction, special needs, or other issues that may affect beneficiaries or family members
- Changes in assets that need to be retitled to reflect the estate plan you want to implement

Glenn Busch, Esq., BSBA (Accounting), JD, and LLM (Tax), focuses his law practice on estate planning, business planning, estate administration, real estate transactions, and wealth preservation.

Glenn Busch

7

Considerations As You Begin Your Estate Planning

By J. David Meredith (The Woodlands, Texas)

Congratulations! You have called the attorney's office and have scheduled your initial appointment to begin planning your estate. You may be wondering, "What do I do now? Should I do something to prepare for this meeting?" Your attorney will probably have some paperwork for you to complete to help identify any issues that should be discussed. However, if your attorney does not provide guidance prior to your initial meeting, then you may find it helpful to start thinking through some things on your own.

WHERE ARE YOU HEADED?

Think of the estate planning process as a journey. Just as you would plan for an upcoming trip, you should take some time to consider what you want to accomplish with your estate plan. When preparing for a trip, most people start by deciding where they are ultimately headed and identify any stops they want to make along the way. In the estate planning context, I see this as identifying your goals and objectives. Some simply want a plan in place in case of an emergency or untimely death, but others find it important to ensure that there are guidelines and instructions to help their family and heirs continue their legacy.

WHAT ARE THE PROBLEM AREAS?

As you plan for a trip, you might consider whether there are any places you want to avoid going. In the estate planning context, this is analogous to any concerns or worries that you might have. I have found that there are three main areas that generate concerns for many clients—family, money, and assets. The following are common concerns in these areas:

1. **Family issues:** Do you have a blended family? Is there a difficult situation with a child or other beneficiary? Is there any unresolved family conflict?

2. **Money issues:** Do you have a spouse or a child who does not do a good job of managing their finances? Are there any tax concerns?

3. **Asset issues:** Do you have property or assets in multiple counties or states? Do you have unique assets or things you want to keep in the family, mineral interests, rental or vacation properties, classic vehicles, or collections?

WHO WILL HELP?

The people you name to help are called fiduciaries. A fiduciary is someone who works on behalf of another person and has certain duties to act in that person's best interests. You and your estate will need an agent, trustee, and executor—all of which are fiduciary roles—to serve in the event you are incapacitated or at your death. As a result, you should identify the person or persons who can help you, your family, and your heirs. Undoubtedly, they should be people you trust and who have the skills and knowledge to make good decisions. It is no coincidence that the first five letters of the word *trustee* spell *trust*.

WHO WILL BENEFIT?

Prospective clients often say that they just want to keep it simple. There seems to be a perceived relationship between complexity and cost—many think that a simpler plan is less expensive. If this is your opinion, I encourage you to consider this: do you want it to be simple for you, or do you want it to be simple for your family and loved ones?

If you want to keep things simple for yourself, then you may not need to do anything. Not having an estate plan is called intestacy. Each state has its own laws to determine who will take over your affairs if you are incapacitated, who will inherit your assets, and who is eligible to be in charge of your estate upon your death. In other words, your state has a default estate plan that will be put into effect for you unless you do something to override it. If cost is a factor in your desire to keep things simple, then you are in luck! It will not cost you any money or time if you choose to do nothing; it cannot get cheaper than that! But be aware that if you do nothing, then you are very likely leaving a big mess for your family that may end up costing *them* a lot of time and money. By not doing anything, you may inadvertently be creating the most expensive estate plan of all.

If you take on the responsibility of going through the process of carefully creating your estate plan and putting in the time, effort, and money now, your family and loved ones will have a much easier path ahead.

Type of Planning	Work Required during Your Lifetime	Consequences, Benefits, and Results upon Your Incapacity or Death
Intestate (you do nothing now)	None	▪ A court-supervised guardianship if you are incapacitated ▪ Very likely a lengthy, complicated, and expensive court probate process upon your death ▪ Assets distributed to your heirs based upon your state's intestacy laws ▪ Gifts to your heirs likely made to them outright, which means the inheritance will be subject to your heirs' creditors, spending habits, and lifestyle actions
Will-based planning (including a will, power of attorney, and healthcare documents)	▪ Creation of the will, powers of attorney, and healthcare documents ▪ Updating beneficiary designation forms	▪ Probate of the will through the court upon your death, which may include public disclosure of your assets and net worth ▪ Assets distributed according to the terms of the will and beneficiary designation forms

Type of Planning	Work Required during Your Lifetime	Consequences, Benefits, and Results upon Your Incapacity or Death
Living trust-based planning (including a living trust, power of attorney, and healthcare documents)	• Creation of the living trust • Funding the living trust (Note: this will require some time and effort on your part.) • Updating beneficiary designation forms • Creation of powers of attorney and healthcare documents • Thoughtful consideration of how the trust will be established and how assets will benefit your family and loved ones upon your passing	• Enhanced management and control of your assets by your successor trustee if you are incapacitated • Trust administration upon your death; no probate through the court if your assets are transferred to the trust during your lifetime (no probate = no public disclosure) • Assets distributed to your beneficiaries based upon the terms of the living trust

David Meredith is Board Certified in Estate Planning and Probate by the Texas Board of Legal Specialization. His firm specializes in estate planning, probate, and trust administration for individuals and families in Texas.

David Meredith

8

Protecting Those You Love and All You Own

By C. Dennis Brislawn, Jr. (Bellevue, Washington)

This chapter—whose title states a pretty broad goal—is aimed at helping you to adopt a process leading to a plan designed to accomplish it. Starting with the end in mind allows you to select the best tools to use with the resources you have available and even to consider adding or refining them.

You can start the planning process before you hire an estate planning attorney. Work through the following general concepts but do not get stuck if you are not able to provide an instant answer. Put anything that you cannot quickly resolve on the shelf to deal with later.

Your planning information includes goals, people, and assets. Do the best you can—perfection is not required at any step. You can come back later and update steps as you work on your plan.

GOALS: WHAT YOUR PLAN SHOULD ADDRESS

Here is a short list of common goals. Feel free to add your own. If you are married, both spouses should rate their goals individually before comparing notes. You may be surprised at what you learn. Rate them as H (high concern), S (some concern), L (low concern), or N/A (not applicable).

Level of Concern	Goals
	Maintain control and organize my affairs
	Maintain my lifestyle
	Reduce taxes
	Provide for and protect my spouse
	Protect children's inheritance in the event of a surviving spouse's remarriage
	Provide for and protect the inheritance of children and grandchildren
	Plan for a child with disabilities or special needs, such as medical or learning disabilities
	Plan for or disinherit a family member
	Provide for the care and disposition of pets
	Protect assets from courts, government, creditors, failed businesses, or divorces
	Plan for continuation, transfer, or survival of a family business
	Build character in family members or help my community (plan for charity)

PEOPLE: CRITICAL "WHO" QUESTIONS

The people identified in your inventory are what this process is all about. Create a list of individuals, starting with yourself and your significant other. Consider the following roles to create a master list:

- Who are the individuals that you are legally required to provide for during your lifetime? (This includes minors or others you deem to be dependent on you in some manner or for a period of time.)

- Who are the individuals (including charities) that you would choose to benefit if you pass away?

- Who are the individuals or entities (trust professional or trust company) you trust to faithfully invest, manage, and apply your assets for you if you become legally disabled?

- Who are the individuals or entities (trust professional or trust company) you trust to manage your assets for you and to faithfully carry out your wishes if you pass away?

- Who would be the guardians of your minor children?

- Who would make your healthcare choices, coordinate your care, and possibly make a decision as to whether to continue heroic care if you have a terminal illness and are unable to make the call for yourself?

ASSETS: CRITICAL "WHAT" INFORMATION

You should organize your asset inventory into two parts. Part A is your list of key assets and related debts, organized by category. Part B is your list of income by source and your ordinary monthly expenses. There are forms available online that you can use for your asset inventory. You can also ask your advisor to provide one or design your own.

Part A includes the following categories of assets and debts:

- Personal cash accounts (e.g., bank, savings, credit union, money markets, certificates of deposits, etc.)

- Personal real estate (e.g., primary residence, vacation home)

- Business real estate (real property held in your name and not by a separate business)

- Businesses (e.g., a sole proprietorship, LLC, S corporation, partnership) (Note what each business does and what it owns, for example, bank accounts, real estate, etc.)

- Loans or contracts payable to you

- Investment accounts (not retirement)

- Stocks and bonds (held by you and not in an account)

- Oil, gas, and mineral interests

- Stock options

- Retirement plans

- Qualified tuition plans

- Life insurance policies and annuities (include the death benefit, not the cash value)

- Personal effects

- Anticipated inheritances, gifts, or lawsuit judgments

Once you have completed your list, calculate the subtotal for each category and then add them up to obtain a total. The total of the assets less debts is your net estate.

Part B starts with the income you receive each month and where it is from. Estimate income you receive occasionally as if it were received monthly. This may include alimony or child support payments. Next, list your regular and ordinary monthly expenses. Finally, identify any extraordinary expenses you may have, such as alimony or child support, lawsuit judgments, etc.

Your income received, less expenses paid, provides a baseline amount necessary to maintain your current lifestyle. It is not necessarily the amount you would like to have.

PROCESS

This process is a pathway to an outcome. Most of us benefit from working with one or more experienced, professional advisors. The primary advisors on your estate planning team generally include an estate planning attorney, a financial advisor, a certified public accountant (CPA), and a life insurance advisor. You can start with one advisor and add others as needed. Your advisor will gather your information and apply it to their process to move your plan forward.

An estate planning attorney will help you design a will or living trust plan with all of the documents required to protect you and your loved ones. It uses your financial and insurance resources to fund the plan. A financial planner will help you determine your goals and review your resources and then will advise you about the resources you need, both now and in the future. A CPA will help you examine your tax and other compliance issues to lower your risk, waste less, and keep more. Your insurance advisor will help reduce your risk by providing a safety net to use if it is needed.

During your planning process, you and your team will evaluate one or more "toolkits" to determine which of them apply to your situation. Each of the planning disciplines has a role to play. The actual tools selected, whether legal, financial, tax, insurance, or some combination, will depend on your personal, financial, tax, and risk fact pattern.

PLANNING TOOLKITS

Core planning involves all disciplines and is your primary toolkit. Your attorney builds your will-based or trust-based plan to control and apply the resources you acquire with the help of your financial planner and insurance advisor, while your CPA ensures that the plan works properly for tax purposes. This part of your plan deals with your current life, any period of incapacity, and death. Each of your advisors brings a unique perspective to preserving your lifestyle and protecting others whom you love. But you might consider additional toolkits if necessary to accomplish your goals.

Wealth transfer planning is about sharing wealth with others on your terms and on purpose. Once you have completed your core planning, the next goal is to use your power to make gifts to reduce your taxes and to protect your assets from taxes, lawsuits, and other risks. You could use one or more irrevocable trusts with financial and insurance tools for this purpose.

Business entity planning may involve an active, for-profit operating business, such as a bakery, or a passive business focused on investment in the market or real estate. Business planning can reduce income and estate taxes, provide training for your successors, establish your nest egg, and more.

Philanthropic planning uses charitable planning as the alternative tax system. There are many opportunities to benefit a charity, create a legacy, and receive income and estate tax benefits that keep more of your assets in your pocket, as well as that of the charity you choose, while reducing the share paid to the government in the form of taxes. Your legacy can be more than financial. This area is complex and often overlooked, but it provides creative options that work extremely well in combination with your other planning.

SUMMARY

Adopting a process is key to both getting started and crossing the finish line. This process harnesses your information and allows you to leverage what you know and care about so your team can help you achieve the best possible result.

Oseran Hahn, P.S. is a comprehensive wealth-planning law firm focused on protecting those you love and all that you own.

Dennis Brislawn

.

Property and Probate Concepts

9

Real Property and Personal Property

By Heather Parker (Mesa, Arizona)

There are two basic types of property from a legal perspective: real property and personal property. The distinction is important because ownership of these types of property is established in different ways, and therefore, they must be addressed differently in estate planning.

REAL PROPERTY

Real property is generally thought of as land and structures permanently attached to the land, such as a house, office building, or driveway. Real property also includes things below the earth's surface, such as minerals, oil, gas, or similar valuable resources. If we could look at the earth from space and cut a sliver down to the core of the earth, this sliver would encompass both land rights and air rights above the surface. The degree to which air rights extend above the land can vary and may involve a different area of law, but suffice it to say that rights can exist for real property both below the earth's surface and above it into the sky.

Earth layers cross section

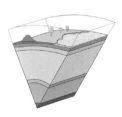

Real property rights extend beyond ownership and include a right to occupy real property—for example, an apartment lease or a contract for a dormitory. They may also include rights to travel across land, such as an easement or a right of way. Utility companies often have an easement over a piece of property to gain access for the expansion of services to an area. A right of way is used when a property owner's neighbor is granted the right to access their property by crossing over part of the owner's property.

Ownership of real property is shown through titling. Title to real property is usually acquired by a deed (i.e., a warranty deed, quitclaim deed, or beneficiary deed), which legally documents the transfer of ownership from one party to another. These deeds are recorded within the land records of the city or county in which the property is located to provide public knowledge of the real property's owner. The purchase and sale transaction for real property typically includes a title insurance policy, which insures the buyer's ownership rights in the described property against any other possible claims against the property.

One of the first steps to consider in estate planning is the way property is titled, because this may direct how title will change upon the death of one of the property's owners. For example, assume John and Sally Smith purchase their house together, taking title as joint tenants with right of survivorship. If John Smith dies, his interest automatically goes to Sally and she becomes the sole owner of the property.

You can take additional steps to plan for the disposition of real property through estate planning using the titling process, by transferring your ownership into a revocable living trust. A trust enables a designated person (the trustee) to manage the real property for you if you are incapacitated. The trustee also has the right to sell the real property, if appropriate. In some states, a deed can designate a beneficiary for your real property so that the title to the property automatically transfers to the person you name, upon your death. If you do not transfer your real property as part of an estate plan, what happens to it upon your passing will be determined by the laws of the state in which the property is located; depending on those laws, court involvement—referred to as a probate case—may be required. That is why it is so important to understand the process and create a plan to be sure that your property will go to your intended beneficiaries upon your passing.

PERSONAL PROPERTY

Things we can move around and take with us are referred to as personal property. I often describe it to clients as their "stuff," that is, the items inside their homes. For example, if you were to take the roof off a house and tip it upside down, the items that fall out would be personal property. These items do not typically have any title document that shows proof of ownership. This type of property can be further broken down into two categories: tangible and intangible.

Tangible personal property is what we can touch and feel, such as clothing, furniture, jewelry, or electronics. Even our pets can be considered tangible personal property (although we often think of them as family and should plan for them when considering what will happen upon our passing).

Intangible property includes things we cannot touch or pick up, such as life insurance, investment accounts, or a debt someone owes to us. These types of property usually have related paperwork that show they are of value to you—for example, a life insurance policy, an account statement, or a promissory note. Cryptocurrency, trademarks, and copyrights are additional examples of intangible personal property, and there is generally some method of evidencing your rights to those assets as well.

As often happens in the law, there are plenty of exceptions to the rules to keep us on our toes. Motor vehicles are one of those exceptions. They are technically tangible personal property, which makes sense because they are movable objects. However, there is a titling process for cars, so they do not fall within the general rule.

It may seem like a mobile home should be considered real property. However, they are movable (although they rarely are moved) and are often treated as vehicles. As a result, they are deemed tangible personal property and have titling documents similar to a vehicle.

Your estate planning attorney can help you determine what will happen to your personal property upon your passing or during your incapacity. You can use a beneficiary designation or a list referenced within your will or trust. As a result, it is important to know what you have and generally what it is worth, and to be aware of how your state will allow you to plan for its management or distribution.

Heather L. Parker has been an attorney since 2000. She and her staff in Mesa, Arizona, take great pleasure in helping families and business owners create plans to be sure their loved ones are cared for through estate planning and business formation.

Heather Parker

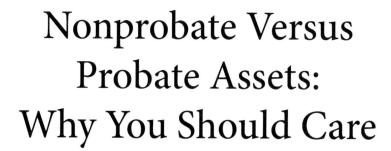

Nonprobate Versus Probate Assets: Why You Should Care

By Danielle Feller (Statesville, North Carolina)

W hen considering your estate plan, you should categorize all of your assets into two groups: probate and nonprobate. Knowing the difference between probate and nonprobate assets will help you take the appropriate steps in your estate plan to ensure that your belongings are distributed according to your wishes when you die.

NONPROBATE ASSETS

Nonprobate assets typically have a named beneficiary, are owned as joint tenants with right of survivorship (JTWROS), or are payable on death (POD) or transferable on death (TOD). Neither your will nor state intestacy laws control the distribution of nonprobate assets. Instead, they pass according to contractual obligation or by state law upon your death. The executor or administrator of your estate has no control over nonprobate assets, and they are not subject to probate court administration. Real property and personal property can be nonprobate assets. Below is a list of common nonprobate assets:

- Property held in the name of a revocable living trust
- Bank accounts with POD or TOD designations
- Bank accounts held as JTWROS
- Real property held as tenants by the entirety by a married couple
- Real property held as JTWROS
- Life estate interests
- Retirement accounts, including 401(k)s and individual retirement accounts (IRAs) with named beneficiaries
- Life insurance policies with named beneficiaries
- Personal property that is titled as JTWROS

PROBATE ASSETS

Probate assets are typically held solely in the name of the decedent and do not designate beneficiaries. They are distributed based on a person's valid will and controlled by the executor or administrator of an estate, who must follow specific steps before transferring the assets. For example, probate assets are generally used to pay creditors and other debts of the estate, including the decedent's personal credit card bills, medical bills, and estate taxes. The debts of the estate must be paid before any assets can be distributed to the designated heirs. Additionally, the court oversees the probate administration process, and the executor or administrator often must account to the court for these assets. If a person dies without a will (that is, they die intestate), then the state intestate succession laws will determine how the assets are distributed. Examples of probate assets include the following:

- Bank accounts in your name with no designated beneficiaries
- Real property held solely in your name
- Real property owned by two or more people as tenants in common
- Vehicles, motorcycles, boats, and watercrafts that are not titled as JTWROS
- Personal property such as jewelry and household furnishings
- Interests in a partnership, corporation, or limited liability company
- Life insurance policies or retirement accounts that either list the estate as a beneficiary or do not list any beneficiary
- Shares of stock

HOW ASSETS ARE TRANSFERRED ON DEATH

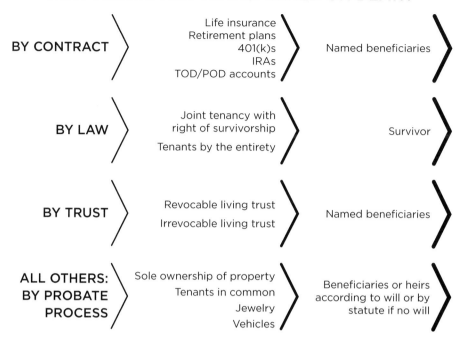

BY CONTRACT	Life insurance Retirement plans 401(k)s IRAs TOD/POD accounts	Named beneficiaries
BY LAW	Joint tenancy with right of survivorship Tenants by the entirety	Survivor
BY TRUST	Revocable living trust Irrevocable living trust	Named beneficiaries
ALL OTHERS: BY PROBATE PROCESS	Sole ownership of property Tenants in common Jewelry Vehicles	Beneficiaries or heirs according to will or by statute if no will

WHY DOES THIS MATTER?

Distinguishing between probate and nonprobate assets is important when considering your estate planning needs. If you are trying to avoid probate, you may want to consider placing all of your assets into a revocable living trust or ensuring that your bank accounts are set up as JTWROS or are POD or TOD. You may also want to talk to an attorney about owning real property with a spouse or other family member as JTWROS. Additionally, if you own property and later get married, you may need a new deed indicating that you and your spouse own the property as tenants by the entirety.

One of the most common questions clients ask is what they can do to speed up the process when administering an estate. Unfortunately, it usually takes six months to a year to fully administer an estate. The executor or administrator must follow statutory requirements, file inventories and accountings, file notices to creditors, pay estate costs to administer the estate, pay off all estate debts, get beneficiaries to sign receipts for their distributions, keep meticulous records, and more. As a result, it may take up to a year or longer for beneficiaries to receive their distributions from the estate.

On the other hand, if all of a decedent's assets are nonprobate assets, then an estate administration is not required, and the named beneficiaries will receive their assets right away. For example, if you designate a beneficiary on your IRA, the beneficiary will receive the money from the account immediately after your death. However, if you do not name a beneficiary on your IRA, then the money in the IRA will go to the estate. The money from the IRA will be used to pay off any debts of the estate before being distributed to your heirs. Thus, it can take six months to a year for your heirs to receive what is left of the IRA funds.

It is also important to keep privacy in mind when considering probate versus nonprobate assets. When an estate is probated, it becomes public record. In contrast, if all of your assets are set up to avoid probate, then no one will know whether you died with $400 or $4,000,000.

The overall goal is to make sure that when you die, your wishes are carried out as smoothly as possible and that all of the assets that you worked so hard to acquire during your lifetime are disbursed according to your plan.

Example: You are a single mother with four children: three biological (C1, C2, C3) and one step-child (C4) from a former marriage. You do not have a will. You have checking and savings accounts and both accounts name you and C4 as JTWROS; C4 lives closest to you and helps manage your finances. You also have a 401(k) plan that does not list a beneficiary. You assume that when you die all of your assets will be evenly split among your four children. Unfortunately, because you do not have a will, when you die C4 will receive all of the money in the checking and savings accounts as the surviving joint tenant. The 401(k) proceeds will go to the estate because no beneficiary was listed, and it will be considered a probate asset. Thus, it will be used to pay debts and estate administration costs. After the debts and costs are paid, C1, C2, and C3 will be entitled to split the remaining amount equally.

NEXT STEPS

Schedule a meeting with your estate planning attorney to review your assets and determine whether each one is a probate or nonprobate asset. Review your insurance policies and retirement accounts to determine whether the beneficiary listed on the policy or account still reflects your wishes. Additionally, ensure your will is up-to-date and reflects your current intentions. If the COVID-19 pandemic has taught us anything, it is that we never know what life may throw at us. Give yourself and your family the peace of mind of knowing that your estate plan is set up appropriately.

Daly Mills Family Law works closely with clients to understand what is important to them and help them establish an effective estate plan. Daly Mills Family Law also assists clients in estate administration and guardianship.

Danielle Feller

11

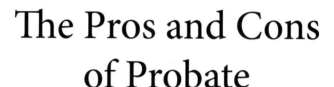

The Pros and Cons
of Probate

By Courtney Medina (Upland, California)

Your financial advisor or accountant may have recommended that you set up a revocable living trust so that you can avoid probate. What is probate and why do some seek to avoid it? In short, probate is the process whereby a state court[1] oversees the administration of a decedent's estate. This process can include, but is not limited to, determining a document to be a valid will, establishing a decedent's rightful heirs, ensuring that creditors are paid, and determining what percentage of the decedent's estate each heir or beneficiary should receive. This chapter covers the most commonly cited reasons some opt to avoid probate and instead establish a revocable living trust.

PROBATE OF YOUR ESTATE CAN BE COSTLY

Probate costs often include compensation of the personal representative and attorney, court costs, probate referee's fees, bond, and the cost to publish required notices.

Personal representative is the general term used for the executor or administrator of

---

1   Probate proceedings are governed by the state courts, and each state determines fees and costs differently. This chapter focuses on probate law in the state of California and provides only general information; there are nuances in the law not detailed in this chapter.

an estate. In California, a personal representative receives a percentage of the estate as compensation for their service. For example, for a $600,000 estate in California, a personal representative's compensation would total $15,000, as detailed below:

4% on the first $100,000 =	$4,000	
3% on the second $100,000 =	$3,000	
2% on the next $400,000 =	$8,000	
Total =	$15,000	

A personal representative may retain an attorney to represent them throughout the probate process. An attorney representing the personal representative receives the same percentage of the estate as the personal representative. Therefore, the combined compensation for the personal representative and attorney would total $30,000. This $30,000 compensation comes off the top, that is, before any distributions are made to the heirs or beneficiaries. In some cases involving matters outside of a typical probate, additional compensation can be requested by the personal representative or the attorney.

Court-related expenditures can also be costly. If you file a petition to initiate a probate action of a decedent's estate in California, you will pay a $435 filing fee and a $30 court reporter fee, depending on the county. To close the probate, you will again pay a $435 filing fee and a $30 court reporter fee.

In California, the court will appoint an appraiser, called a probate referee, to assign a value to certain assets such as real estate or investment accounts. The fee paid to the probate referee is one-tenth of 1 percent of the total assets that are valued by the probate referee. For example, if the probate referee appraises a $400,000 house, they will receive a fee of $400 plus expenses such as mileage, photos, and maps.

In many instances, the court will require the personal representative to post a bond. A bond is simply a financial guarantee to the heirs or beneficiaries and creditors that the personal representative will act properly in handling the estate's assets. Generally speaking, the court determines the amount of the bond based on the value of the assets and the gross annual income of the estate. Even if all heirs or beneficiaries waive the bond requirement, the court may still order that a bond be posted.

If the court orders a bond, then the personal representative must post the bond before acting in that capacity. A bond company bases its qualification on the credit score of the personal representative, the types of assets in the estate, and the level of authority the court grants to the personal representative. The annual premium for a $300,000 bond for someone with a good credit score may be $1,000 to $1,200.

Publication costs vary depending on the type of notice published as well as the newspaper publishing the notice. Publication costs are paid directly to the newspaper and typically range from $200 to $800. At the beginning of the probate process, the court will require proof of proper publication. Depending upon the circumstances involved in the probate action, other notices may require publication as well.

PROBATE CASES MAY BE VERY LENGTHY

With California probate cases, a court order is required before you may distribute assets to the heirs or beneficiaries. In many instances, you must also obtain permission from the court before you can sell or liquidate assets. For example, the court may require a hearing and court order before real property can be sold to the buyer you have selected. This potentially slows down the sales process and may result in the loss of a buyer. Moreover, the requirement for court hearings and orders means that often one or more years can elapse before the heirs or beneficiaries receive any portion of the estate. Alternatively, administration of a trust can be a much swifter process, and therefore, a better option for some.

PROBATE PROCEEDINGS ARE OPEN TO THE PUBLIC

If you die with only a will and no trust, or if you die without either a will or a trust, depending on the value of your estate, a probate action will be required to distribute your assets to your loved ones. Probate matters are open to the public. For this reason, some see a revocable living trust as a more favorable choice.

In general, the administration of a trust is private, and no court involvement is required. Therefore, the assets titled in your trust's name and the identity of your trust beneficiaries do not become public. Furthermore, only certain individuals are entitled to a copy of your trust document upon your passing.

IN SOME INSTANCES, STATE LAW DETERMINES WHO INHERITS YOUR PROPERTY

If you die without a will or a trust, state statute governs who is entitled to inherit your assets. For example, imagine that you pass away without a will or trust, and you leave a California residence titled as your sole and separate property. Generally, the court will divide your residence as follows: if you are married, among your spouse and issue (i.e., your children, grandchildren, and so on); if you are unmarried, among your issue; if you are unmarried and leave no issue, between your parents; if you have no living parents, are unmarried, and leave no issue, among your siblings; and so on. As you can see, it may be beneficial to draft a will or trust so that you can determine who receives your property, how much property each beneficiary receives, and when the beneficiaries receive the property (e.g., 50 percent at age twenty-five and 50 percent at age thirty-five, as opposed to an outright distribution).

On the one hand, some see court oversight as a benefit of probate. With this oversight, the court makes decisions that are binding on the heirs and beneficiaries. On the other hand, the probate process is public and may be lengthy and costly. Moreover, probate is based on a predetermined set of rules. A favorable alternative for those seeking to avoid probate is a revocable living trust.

In summary, these are the pros and cons of probate:

- Pro: The court oversees the administration of the estate.

- Cons:
  » Probate is a costly process.
  » Probate cases can take a very long time to complete.
  » Probate proceedings are public.
  » If you die without a will, state law—not you—determines who receives your assets.

C Medina Law, Inc. is a southern California firm whose practice encompasses probate (decedent's estates), trusts, wills, conservatorships, and guardianships and assists clients throughout San Bernardino, Riverside, Orange, and Los Angeles counties.

Courtney Medina

12

Five Common Methods to Bypass Probate

By Carla Miramontes and Michelle A. Booge (Phoenix, Arizona)

L et us take a quick look at five methods for transferring ownership of assets after death without the hassle, cost, or delay associated with probate court proceedings.

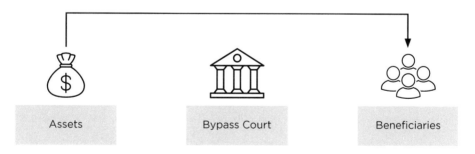

1. PAYABLE ON DEATH AND TRANSFER ON DEATH ACCOUNTS

When you establish a bank or investment account, you have an opportunity to name an individual to whom you want the assets in the account to be payable when you die.

This type of account transfer is commonly referred to as payable on death (POD) or transfer on death (TOD).

2. RIGHT OF SURVIVORSHIP ACCOUNTS AND DEEDS

When two or more persons are listed on a bank or investment account or on the title to real property with a right of survivorship, ownership transfers to the surviving owner or owners upon the death of one of them.

Tip: Inquire whether your financial institution permits multiple-party accounts with a right of survivorship, and then add a POD or TOD authorization effective upon the death of the last surviving owner.

3. DESIGNATED BENEFICIARIES

Life insurance, annuity contracts, and qualified retirement plans such as 401(k) plans, 403(b) plans, and individual retirement accounts (IRAs) are designed so that the individual owner of the policy or account can name beneficiaries to receive the death benefit or account proceeds upon the owner's death.

4. BENEFICIARY DEEDS

Some state laws allow you to record a deed with the county recorder's office that, upon your death, will transfer ownership of your real property (e.g., house, office building, ranch) to your chosen beneficiary or beneficiaries without court involvement.

5. TRUSTS

By creating a trust and retitling your assets to the trust or designating your trust as the beneficiary of your accounts, you can not only avoid probate but your beneficiaries can also receive distributions in the manner and timing that you determine.

UNEXPECTED DISADVANTAGES OF NONPROBATE TRANSFERS (EXCLUDING TRUSTS)

- You could unintentionally overlook tax planning.
- Creditor protection for beneficiaries may be lost.
- A beneficiary with special needs may be ineligible for needs-based government benefits.
- A beneficiary incapable of managing assets may squander an inheritance.
- You could lose an opportunity to preserve asset principal for future generations.
- You could add a family member or fiduciary as a joint owner of an account **rather than as a signer** for the convenience of assisting you in managing your affairs but

without intending that the family member or fiduciary become the owner of the account upon your death.

- Some people transfer all of their assets to a single person, typically an adult child, via nonprobate transfers, trusting that the child will give each sibling a fair and equal share. This seemingly simple do-it-yourself estate plan results in disharmony or litigation more often than not because the "sharing" does not occur or is unequal.

TEST YOUR KNOWLEDGE: TRUE OR FALSE QUIZ

- Every account requires you to list a beneficiary.
  False. However, adding account beneficiaries is often part of the process to ensure the estate plan works as intended.

- If a beneficiary dies before the account owner, the probate court must administer the account.
  False. However, it is important to list contingent, or secondary, beneficiaries because, without a contingent beneficiary, the account custodian's contract determines whether the account will pass to the account owner's estate via probate or their heirs at law.

- An account owner can change beneficiaries only once per year.
  False. We recommend that you review your account beneficiaries at least every couple of years and more often if your circumstances change—for example, if there is a marriage, divorce, legal separation, or death of a loved one.

- Only individuals (living, breathing people) can be beneficiaries of accounts or deeds.
  False. Charities, trusts, nonprofits, and social enterprises are examples of other commonly designated types of beneficiaries.

TIPS

- It is important to contact the financial institutions that hold your accounts to request written verification that the beneficiary designation on file is accurate.

- Often, you can make updates to beneficiary designations online via the financial institution's website.

- Each individual's situation is unique. Consult an experienced estate planning attorney and a certified financial planner to create a comprehensive estate plan that meets your goals.

- Estate planning attorneys and certified financial planners have a duty to advise their clients of the options available given the nature of the client's estate, family dynamics, and ultimate goals. Invest a bit of time and funds now to set up a plan that will serve you and your beneficiaries in the event of your incapacity or death.

Review your plan yearly, and contact a professional to discuss changes in your situation and make updates when needed.

- The five methods for bypassing probate discussed here are only a small sampling of available tools that you should discuss with an experienced professional.

Carla Miramontes *Michelle Booge*

Accomplished attorneys, caring individuals, and devoted to their clients, Dyer Bregman & Ferris, PLLC, offers estate and special needs planning; probate, trust, and guardianship/ conservatorship administration; and related services such as real estate and business transactions and personal injury law to help individuals, families, and businesses reach their goals.

13

Intestate Law Overview

By Yasmin Adamy (Jacksonville Beach, Florida)

I f you pass away and do not have a valid last will and testament, the assets in your estate will go to the people designated by the laws in the state where you reside or where you own real property. This set of default rules is called the *laws of intestacy.* The people who inherit your estate are your *heirs,* and they are typically those of your kin who have the first right to inherit from you.

Sometimes, the people who inherit under the laws of intestacy are not the people you would want to inherit your estate. The laws of intestacy are not always fair; they are simply the state legislature's best guess about what most people would want. In some states, the probate court will formally determine who your heirs are and the share that each heir is entitled to receive based on intestate succession law. When interpreting who counts as your heir and what share of your estate they should receive, the court has to adhere to the laws of intestacy. Because you are no longer alive, you can give the court no insight about your preferences. The court cannot make exceptions on a case-by-case basis.

To ensure that the people you want to inherit from you actually receive what you want them to have, you can opt out of the laws of intestacy by having a valid last will and testament or avoiding probate (e.g., by establishing and funding a trust). Your last will and testament or trust provides your instructions about who should receive your property when you die. By executing a valid last will and testament or avoiding probate, you are choosing not to leave it up to the state to determine your heirs; rather, you are choosing who will inherit from you.

Below is a flowchart showing how intestate succession works in Florida. Keep in mind that every state has its own intestacy law.

FLORIDA INTESTATE SUCCESSION FLOWCHART
WHO RECEIVES THE ESTATE WHEN SOMEONE DIES WITHOUT A WILL?

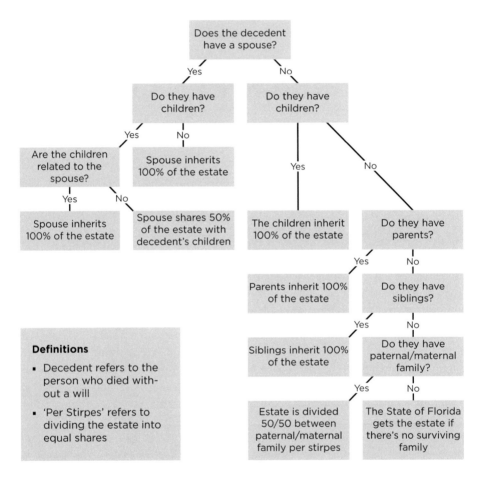

Disclaimer: This chart represents a simplified format of Florida intestacy laws. The chart is for informational purposes only and should not be considered professional legal advice

THE BASIC MECHANICS OF THE LAW OF INTESTACY IN FLORIDA

- The decedent's (deceased person's) surviving spouse receives the entire estate if the decedent has no surviving lineal descendants (children, grandchildren, great-grandchildren, etc.).

- The decedent's surviving spouse will also receive the entire estate if the decedent had descendants that are also the surviving spouse's descendants and neither the decedent nor the surviving spouse had any other children.

- If the decedent is survived by both a spouse and lineal descendants and not all of the lineal descendants are also the spouse's descendants, the spouse is entitled to one half of the estate, and the descendants share the balance, per stirpes (any amount left to a descendant that predeceases the decedent will be passed down to that descendant's own heirs).

- If there are lineal descendants but no surviving spouse, the estate is shared by the lineal descendants.

- If there is no surviving spouse and no lineal descendants, the estate passes to lineal ascendants (parents, grandparents, great-grandparents, etc.) and collateral relatives (siblings, aunts, uncles, etc.). This means that, if the decedent's parents are alive, they are entitled to the estate. If the parents are not alive, the estate passes to the decedent's brothers and sisters and their descendants, per stirpes.

- If none of the above heirs survive, the estate passes one-half to the decedent's maternal relatives and one-half to the decedent's paternal relatives, starting with the decedent's grandparents and otherwise going to the grandparents' descendants, per stirpes. If there are no relatives on one side, the entire estate passes to the other side.

EXAMPLES OF HOW THE LAWS OF INTESTACY COLLIDE WITH YOUR INTENTIONS

A first example involves the laughing heir. A laughing heir is legally entitled to inherit your property when you die, even though that heir is only distantly related to you and therefore may not have any personal connection to you; in fact, this person could be a total stranger. Some states have a laughing heir statute that cuts off the right of inheritance when the remaining relatives become too remote. In those states, if no relative falls within the limitation set by the law, the property passes to the state. This makes sense, because it is unlikely that you would want a stranger or the state to inherit from you!

A second example involves the child who is not a blood relative. Under most state laws, unless an individual has been legally adopted, the law does not consider them an heir.

Even if you raised and cared for this child as your own and consider them to be closer to you than a blood relative, state law would not consider them your child unless you have legally adopted them. Stepchildren are not considered your children unless you legally adopt them. You could even be a child's legal guardian, but without a formal legal adoption, the child would not inherit from you.

A third example involves your life partner. For someone to inherit as your spouse, you must be legally married to them. If you do not legally marry them and you die intestate, the state will not recognize them as your heir and they will receive nothing from you. Even if you cohabit with this person for thirty years and run a household together, if you are not married, they have no spousal status and will not inherit from you.

A fourth example involves the heir who receives too much. During your lifetime, you provide a substantially greater amount of money to one of your children. The rest of your family members understand that the child who received the greater amount of money during your lifetime has already received their inheritance. You do not intend to include that child as an heir upon your death because you wish to treat your children equally. You are confident that everyone understands your intention to equalize the total monetary amount each of your children will receive (during your lifetime and at your death). It seems logical and it is fair. However, you die intestate. Under the laws of intestacy, each of your children receives an equal amount of your estate, so your intention for equalization fails. The court must follow the plain letter of the laws of intestacy and cannot infer your preferences because you did not leave your instructions in a valid last will and testament or trust. This situation can result in one child getting double the amount you intended!

HOW TO AVOID THE LAWS OF INTESTACY

You can opt out of the laws of intestacy by making a valid last will and testament or by establishing and funding a trust or otherwise avoiding probate. Your will or trust serves as your legal instructions regarding whom you choose as your beneficiaries, the amount each beneficiary will receive, and when each beneficiary should receive it. In contrast to the laws of intestacy, which are generic and inflexible, your estate plan can be tailored to effectuate your intentions fluidly and dynamically.

Adamy Law, PLLC, in Jacksonville Beach, Florida, is a boutique law firm that concentrates on the areas of estate planning, probate, wealth preservation, business succession, and estate administration.

Yasmin Adamy

14

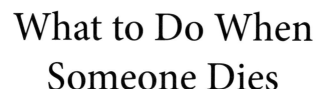

What to Do When Someone Dies

By Mark John M. Ignacio (San Diego, California)

A loved one's passing is one of the most difficult experiences we encounter. Memories of the joyous times flood our mind, our feelings for our loved one fill our hearts, and tears inevitably swell in our eyes and streak our cheeks. The emotional pain is heavy, yet the litany of things that must be done is equally daunting. The questions can be endless:

- Whom should I call?

- How do I pay for things?

- How can I find out if there is a will?

- Are there burial or cremation instructions?

- When can I transfer the house?

- Am I responsible for bills and invoices?

- How do I get access to bank funds if I am not an owner of the account?

Let's consider a scenario that will provide a practical guide for addressing these questions. Drew, a military retiree, was a widower in his early seventies who lived alone in the family residence. Drew and his wife, Wendy, executed separate wills, each naming the other as the beneficiary of their estate, with their children as equal contingent beneficiaries. Drew had a fatal heart attack. He is survived by two adult children: Al, who lives nearby and is named in the will as the executor, and Belle, who lives out of state. Chester, the family dog, lived with Drew. Drew and Wendy owned the family residence and are the only borrowers listed on the mortgage note. Drew also owed outstanding balances on two credit cards. He owned investment accounts and a life insurance policy.

IMMEDIATE TASKS
(WITHIN TWENTY-FOUR TO FORTY-EIGHT HOURS)

1. INFORM IMMEDIATE FAMILY MEMBERS AND OTHERS

Al should call Belle immediately and tell her the sad news. He should also call anyone else related to Drew, such as siblings and other relatives, as well as Drew's close friends. In addition, if your loved one was employed, a union member, or a member of an organization, you should contact the appropriate department to inform them of the death.

2. IDENTIFY THE DECEASED'S FINAL DISPOSITION WISHES

Drew had told his children that he wanted to be buried beside Wendy. Since Drew was a military retiree, Al should notify the Department of Veterans Affairs to arrange the burial. However, if your loved one had created an estate plan, you should check the documents to determine if your loved one wanted to be cremated or buried or to donate their body for scientific purposes.

3. DELEGATE TASKS

Delegating tasks to other family members is beneficial. For example, Al could ask an uncle to write Drew's obituary, and Belle could start creating a list of people to invite to the funeral or memorial service. If the loved one died leaving minor children, you should seek help to make immediate arrangements for the children's care until guardianship matters have been resolved.

SHORT-TERM TASKS (WITHIN THE FIRST TWO WEEKS)

1. ORDER DEATH CERTIFICATES

Drew's death must be legally documented, and a death certificate is typically used to establish it. The funeral home can assist you with obtaining death certificates, or you may order them directly from the appropriate government agency. You should generally order at least five copies of the death certificate and an additional one for each parcel of real property or life insurance policy the deceased owned.

2. GAIN ACCESS TO AND SECURE THE DECEASED'S RESIDENCE

As Drew's adult child who lived nearby, Al already has the keys to his father's home. Al should visit the residence regularly to ensure that the doors and windows are secured and the contents are safe. In addition, Al should take Chester in or find shelter for him. If your loved one rented their living space, you should notify the landlord to arrange for access to the residence and secure their belongings.

3. CONTINUE TO COLLECT IMPORTANT INFORMATION

Al should collect Drew's vital information, such as his full legal name, date of birth, and Social Security number. Locating contact information for your loved one's trusted advisors is imperative. Finding important documents such as a will, trust, recent income tax return, and personal letters is also helpful. You may need to have technical support assist you with accessing your loved one's personal computer or cell phone if you do not already have the passwords.

4. IDENTIFY BILLS AND CANCEL UNNECESSARY SERVICES AND CREDIT CARDS

Al should begin reviewing Drew's papers for any credit card statements and other bills. He should identify and immediately cancel Drew's personal services, such as online streaming, subscriptions, cable TV, and internet, or notify the providers of those services of Drew's death. Al should do the same with Drew's two credit cards. It is important to note that unless you cosigned an account with the deceased, you are not personally responsible for their debts.

MEDIUM-TERM TASKS (WITHIN THE FIRST ONE TO TWO MONTHS)

1. MAKE AN APPOINTMENT WITH AN ESTATE ATTORNEY

Al needs to know how to fulfill Drew's final wishes. The best way to do this is to review Drew's will with a local estate attorney who is well-versed in his jurisdiction's laws. Finding the appropriate estate attorney to aid you is important. Ask for referrals from family and friends, consult with the local bar's legal referral service, or conduct an online search. This attorney will determine if your loved one's estate falls within the state's probate jurisdiction or if the estate settlement can proceed without court involvement. The attorney will guide you through the requisite mechanisms for notifying the appropriate beneficiaries, appraising assets, handling creditors, and ultimately, closing the estate.

2. MAKE AN APPOINTMENT WITH A TAX PROFESSIONAL

Al will need to consult a seasoned tax professional to file the tax returns for both Drew as an individual and Drew's estate. Because Drew has passed, his Social Security number should not be used for any subsequent transactions; rather, if and when he is formally appointed as the executor by the probate court, Al will need to obtain an Employer Identification Number from the Internal Revenue Service to transact business on the estate's behalf. When your loved one passes away, the executor (or personal representative) must address several tax consequences, especially if the sale of any high-value assets will result in a capital gain. Seek assistance to determine which state and federal forms you should file, as well as the tax consequences of inheriting a deceased person's retirement plan.

3. IDENTIFY ASSETS

What else did Drew own? Did he own a vehicle? Did he have a safe deposit box? What tangible personal items are at Drew's home? Identifying the deceased's assets can be a laborious process because you may discover more assets as you dig through what is often a morass of documentation. Identifying assets is an important step because you must determine how your loved one's assets can ultimately pass to the intended beneficiary. Further, you must determine whether death benefits can be obtained by filing the appropriate claims.

4. CONTACT THE THREE CREDIT BUREAUS

Drew owes balances on his two credit cards, and Al wants to ensure that no one can make further charges, even after he has canceled them. To limit identity theft, it is important that you inform the three credit bureaus (Experian, Equifax, and Transunion) of your loved one's passing. You will need to complete a form with each credit bureau and present a death certificate.

LONG-TERM TASKS (WITHIN THE FIRST YEAR)

1. FINALIZE REAL ESTATE ISSUES

Al and Belle have sentimental ties to their father's home, but they recognize that selling it and dividing the proceeds will be easier. However, not all real estate issues can be easily resolved. Sometimes, one beneficiary wants to live in the home and needs time to buy out the other beneficiaries. On the other hand, real estate may have high earning power, so renting it and dividing the income may be beneficial to all involved. Regardless of the issue, you should finalize any real estate matters within the first year after the deceased's death.

2. IDENTIFY, NEGOTIATE, AND SETTLE ALL LIABILITIES

Although Al knows he is not personally responsible for the estate's liabilities, he does not want creditors to initiate collection proceedings against the estate. Understanding the two types of debts—secured and unsecured—is important. Secured debts are created with a lien, such as a mortgage; unsecured debts such as most credit card bills are not subject to liens. Negotiating a reduction of the liabilities is typically easier for an unsecured debt than for a secured debt.

3. SEEK GUIDANCE FROM ADVISORS

Settling Drew's estate may involve resolving several tax issues, such as capital gains, past-due personal taxes, and estate taxes. Likewise, legal issues related to estate accounting, incorrect beneficiary designations, and probate proceedings require the constant assistance of the estate attorney. Until the estate is settled, tax and legal matters will require attention, so remaining in communication with your trusted advisors is important.

4. DISTRIBUTE REMAINING ASSETS

With the sale of the home and payment of all administrative expenses, Drew's estate has been liquidated and the proceeds placed in a single estate bank account that Al and Belle can divide between themselves. If your loved one had created a trust, the successor trustee should distribute the assets pursuant to the trust instrument. If the estate was administered using your state's probate mechanism, the executor or administrator must follow the court order or other required procedure for the distribution. Upon the successful distribution of assets, the executor or administrator should be discharged to conclude the estate settlement process.

Mark Ignacio is a California solo practitioner who engages in estate planning and estate settlements.

Mark Ignacio

SECTION 3

The Documents

15

Estate Planning Documents Overview

By Ashley E. Sharek (Wexford, PA)

Although most people dislike thinking about death, the estate planning process allows you to think about death with a view toward protecting the ones you love. By implementing an organized strategy in the form of a well-conceived and properly executed estate plan that carries out your wishes upon your death, you can avoid leaving loved ones with a financial mess.

When asked to describe an estate plan, most people identify a will as the key document, which they assume only an elderly or wealthy person needs. Although a will is definitely part of a well-designed estate plan, the elderly and the wealthy are not the only people who need one. There are additional components that work alongside the will to ensure that nothing falls through the cracks when you pass away. What most people fail to realize is that estate planning is something that everyone needs: it is just a matter of which documents make the most sense for your specific situation.

At a minimum, you should have what I like to call the "Big Three" documents: a will, powers of attorney, and a healthcare directive. If you do not have all three of these documents in place, you will leave gaps in your plan that could cause conflict among your loved ones that may require court intervention. Let's walk through these documents in the order in which you might need to use them so that you can better understand the purposes they serve.

HEALTHCARE DIRECTIVE

Depending on the state in which you live, a healthcare directive may be one document with several parts or several individual documents. Either way, the following components work together to protect your healthcare interests.

A *HIPAA authorization* allows you to name a family member, loved one, or friend who can access your medical status or records from a doctor's office or hospital. This authorization also gives the named person the authority to call the doctor or hospital to inquire about your condition or treatment. Essentially, your doctors and other medical personnel are allowed to discuss your medical situation with the person you name in this document.

A *healthcare power of attorney* is a document that names the healthcare agents—preferably your first choice and an alternate—who can make medical decisions for you if you cannot make them for yourself. The agent's powers include making medical decisions for treatment or care, authorizing admission or discharge from a healthcare facility, allowing or withholding medical care or treatment, hiring or firing medical staff, and signing a do-not-resuscitate (DNR) order. You grant all of these powers to your healthcare agent to authorize them to step into your shoes and make these types of healthcare decisions if you cannot make them for yourself.

Completing a *living will* is the most challenging part of the healthcare decision-making process. It communicates detailed instructions for others to follow if you are ever in a permanent vegetative state due to irreversible brain damage or suffer from an end-stage medical condition and no longer have the capacity to voice your own opinions about your medical care or treatment. Though difficult, making decisions about your healthcare outcomes for yourself in advance leaves you with peace of mind and relieves your healthcare agent or loved ones of the burden of making these decisions on your behalf.

DURABLE POWER OF ATTORNEY

A *durable power of attorney* grants another person (your agent) the power to make some or all of your financial and legal decisions on your behalf. Simply put, if you cannot do something for yourself, then you can empower your agent to do it for you. These powers can be significant, such as the ability to make decisions about banking and investments, change beneficiaries on policies, obtain credit cards and life insurance, or file taxes. They can also include less consequential powers such as opening mail or canceling a gym membership.

Most people assume that they only need a durable power of attorney if they are elderly or incapacitated. Clients often say, "Oh, I don't need that document. My parents have one of those to help my grandma." While that may be true, a durable power of attorney can also be a convenient tool for spouses. For example, if one spouse has an irregular schedule or travels extensively for work, their partner could act as their agent to close on a house in their absence.

This powerful document gives great financial and legal power to your agent. Typically, when you name a trusted spouse as your agent, the durable power of attorney takes effect immediately when you sign it. To protect yourself, you can elect for the durable power of attorney to go into effect only if you become incapacitated, which is called a *springing power of attorney.* As its name suggests, the power of attorney springs into action only when you need it.

WILL

A *will,* or more formally, a *last will and testament,* is the document most commonly associated with estate planning. We have all seen the dramatic scenes in movies where an attorney comes to read the last will and testament of a recently departed client in the presence of their grieving family. Spoiler alert: that only occurs in Hollywood and is not something that happens regularly!

In reality, your last will and testament spells out how you wish for your assets to be distributed through probate after your death. In order for this to happen, you also need to name an executor of your estate. An executor takes on a fiduciary role to collect your assets and pay any final bills, funeral expenses, attorney's fees, or other debts owed. The executor then distributes your remaining assets according to your wishes. In your will, you can make a specific gift to an individual or a charity, as well as a residuary distribution. The residuary is everything remaining in your estate after all final bills are paid and specific gifts are made. For example, you may want to leave everything to your spouse, but if your spouse predeceases you, you may wish for your assets to be split equally among your three children.

Though a will is necessary, having only a will does not avoid probate. Probate mandates that your will becomes part of the public record and involves the payment of taxes and amounts owed to creditors. This process generally costs an estate about 5 percent of its value. One way to avoid probate is to also use a trust.

TRUSTS

There are two types of trusts: revocable and irrevocable. Let's consider the revocable trust first. I liken a revocable trust to a treasure chest where you store all of your assets during your lifetime, but you do not close the lid or lock it. By leaving the lid open, you can continue to put new assets into the chest or take them out as you wish. For example, when you sell one house and buy another one, you can simply add the new one to your treasure chest and remove the old one. A revocable trust allows you, as the creator and original trustee, to maintain absolute control of the assets in the trust during your lifetime. Likewise, you can also revoke or dissolve your revocable trust at any time you choose.

Most people create a revocable living trust to avoid probate. They may want to keep their assets private. They may also want to protect their children by preventing them from inheriting a large sum of money outright. A revocable trust can be drafted to include a *lifetime asset protection trust* to protect the assets that you leave to your heirs from their creditors during your heirs' lifetimes. Your children can access the assets they may need for their own maintenance, education, support, or health. They may also receive discretionary distributions, but you can determine when those distributions begin and how much money can be distributed to them when you create the document. A revocable trust is usually the best tool for someone who has children, owns a business, owns property such as a vacation home or timeshare in another state, or wants to avoid the public probate process.

An irrevocable trust serves different purposes: it can be used either to mitigate the tax burden of high-net-worth individuals or to prevent assets from being counted for Medicaid qualification purposes. Either way, an irrevocable trust, once formed, remains irrevocable. Consequently, once you transfer assets into this type of trust, the lid of the treasure chest is closed and locked. Irrevocable trusts are effective because you essentially give up ownership of the assets in the trust. As the trustmaker, you appoint an independent trustee (someone other than you) who controls the trust and the assets it holds. There are several types of irrevocable trusts, each of which functions because the original owner no longer has a legal right of possession or access to the assets. Though giving up ownership and control of assets can be difficult, the significant benefits of a properly drafted and funded irrevocable trust make this document a powerful tool.

Each type of trust serves different purposes, and each can be a useful estate planning tool when it is created to meet your specific needs. But you must fully fund your trust for it to work. Merely signing a trust document is not enough to protect your assets. You must transfer your assets into the trust by retitling deeded property or updating beneficiary designations on financial policies to name the trust as the beneficiary. Without a fully funded trust, you simply have a useless stack of paper that has no effect on your estate plan.

Sharek Law Office, LLC serves all Pennsylvania residents with a practice that aims to minimize the obstacles associated with traditional estate planning. We meet with clients where they are, at a time convenient for them, so estate planning no longer needs to be pushed to the back burner or added to the never-ending to-do list.

Ashley Sharek

16

Designating Fiduciaries

By Joel R. Beck (Lawrenceville, Georgia)

Regardless of the type of estate plan you choose, you must designate people to serve in the many important roles in your plan, among which are the executor (also called a personal representative), healthcare agent, agent under a power of attorney, trustee and successor trustee, and guardian for your children. The people who serve in these positions are called *fiduciaries,* because they generally have a fiduciary obligation to act in your best interests (or the best interests of those you leave behind) and in accordance with the law. Given the importance of their obligations, you must be sure to select the right people to handle the responsibilities outlined in your estate planning documents. Your fiduciaries will be responsible for following your estate plan, fulfilling your wishes and instructions, and making decisions about you and your affairs along the way, so it is in your best interest to choose these individuals carefully.

For many people, these fiduciary roles take on a sense of honor, sentimentality, or tradition. For example, some clients tell me that they want to name their oldest child to key roles in their plan or to handle the responsibility of settling their estate. Others want to include all their children as fiduciaries, even having multiple children or other loved ones serve jointly in one job to avoid excluding anyone or hurting anyone's feelings. In these situations, I have a serious discussion with the client and share these three pointers for designating fiduciaries:

1. You are not bestowing an honor by selecting someone to serve as a fiduciary; rather, you are hiring them for an important and perhaps difficult job.

2.   Consider their skills, abilities, and capacity to serve when evaluating a candidate for a role in your estate plan.

3.   Remember that it may be in your best interest to specifically exclude certain individuals from serving in your plan.

With so many factors to consider, choosing your fiduciaries can be a tough decision. Incorporating these three pieces of advice into your selection process will help ensure that you hire the right people for the right job and that your plan will function as intended when needed. Here is how it works.

Remember that you are giving someone a job—an important job, at that—in your estate plan. Fiduciary roles are not symbolic positions that require no work and that merely honor the person chosen because of their relationship with you. Indeed, under state law, the fiduciary generally has an obligation to carry out the elements of your estate plan in an expeditious, diligent manner, adhering to your instructions in the plan as well as applicable law. Even for simple estates, hard work may be necessary to carry out your plan. For example, regardless of the size of your estate, after you die, your executor will have to marshal your assets, pay your creditors, keep an accounting of funds, and ultimately distribute assets in accordance with your plan. I recommend that my clients view the task of designating fiduciaries as if they are a business owner and are hiring employees for different jobs in their business, which leads to the next point…

Recognize that not everyone is suited for each position. We all have different skills and abilities. We may excel at one task but be unable to perform another task well. I did not do well in college algebra. In fact, I was invited back to take the class a second time! Therefore, hiring me to teach college algebra would be a terrible business decision, even if I am a nice guy that you generally like. When we hire someone for a job in our business, we focus on the skills and abilities required for the duties of each position. Different jobs require different abilities: wise business owners recognize this and act accordingly when hiring employees.

> *"If their financial life always resembles a train wreck, that person is likely not a good choice to oversee your assets, and you should consider other people for such a role."*

What does this mean for designating fiduciaries in your estate plan? It means that your goal is to select people with the right mix of skill, ability, and capacity to serve well in the various roles you must fill. Of course, each person should be trustworthy, but beyond that, they should have the right aptitude for the position in which they will serve. When choosing someone to manage your assets under a power of attorney or through a trust, you should ensure that the person is able to manage those assets wisely and understand some basic financial principles. If their financial life always resembles a train wreck, that person is likely not a good choice to oversee your assets, and you should consider other people for such a role. When selecting a guardian for your minor children, take into account the candidate's parenting style, values, relationship with your children, and other related factors. When choosing your healthcare agent, assess their ability to understand and evaluate medical diagnoses and treatment options and their capacity and willingness to make difficult decisions. For example, if your desire is to not have your life prolonged by artificial means in certain conditions, your healthcare agent needs to be willing and able to honor your wishes by making the choice to stop treatment or remove life support.

One more point on considering a potential fiduciary: their location is generally not as important as it used to be. It is typically easy to carry out many fiduciary tasks and responsibilities from a remote location. Further, most states allow you to appoint fiduciaries who live outside your state, but some states do impose certain requirements or limitations, which you can discuss with your estate planning lawyer. In short, in most locales, choosing people who are in your area is far less important than choosing trustworthy people with the right mix of skills and abilities to serve in various fiduciary roles.

Remember that you may need to specifically exclude some individuals from serving in your plan. Let's face it, there may be some people in your family that are simply not good candidates, and you cannot trust them to serve as a fiduciary. Or perhaps family dynamics and relationships are such that you want to ensure that a certain person is not involved in your plan. That is okay. I recommend discussing this concern with your estate planning attorney to determine if you should explicitly address the issue, and if so, the best method for doing so. For example, it may be appropriate to make specific statements in your documents that it is your express wish that a certain person (or persons) not fill any fiduciary role. Alternatively, a letter documenting your wishes and held by trusted family members or your attorney may be beneficial. Those entrusted with the letter can reveal it later if necessary. Remember, no one is entitled to a role in your estate plan, and it may be in your best interest to exclude certain people.

A valuable benefit of completing your estate plan is the ability to designate trusted fiduciaries to act on your behalf or in the best interests of those you leave behind. Following the points in this chapter will help you select the right individuals to carry out your plan.

Joel R. Beck is the founder of Peach State Wills & Trusts, a division of The Beck Law Firm, LLC, which provides estate planning services to people across Georgia.

Joel Beck

17

Ancillary Documents:
The Unsung Heroes
of Estate Planning

By Felicia Acosta-Steiner (Wichita, Kansas)

Ancillary documents are the "belts and suspenders" of a comprehensive estate plan, used by estate planning attorneys to reinforce and support your main will or trust document. These unsung heroes work hard alongside your main document to cover all of your bases by addressing as many life and aging events as possible. Used for incapacity planning, ancillary documents are important tools to have ready if you become unable to handle your affairs because of an unexpected short-term disability or legal incapacity.

When you begin the estate planning process, you may be thinking only about what happens at your death, but it is equally important to include the documents necessary to handle your affairs while you are still alive should the need arise. By having ancillary documents in place, you are taking the necessary steps to allow someone to quickly step into your shoes, typically without the need for court approval and oversight, if you become unable to act on your own behalf. This aspect is extremely important because, absent a well-drafted power of attorney, your family may be forced to endure a formal court proceeding before they can take any actions involving your assets and attend to your medical and healthcare needs.

> *An ounce of prevention is worth a pound of cure.*
>
> *-Benjamin Franklin*

Though there are several helpful documents you may wish to include in your estate plan, typical ancillary documents used in the event of a disability or legal incapacity include financial and healthcare powers of attorney and an advance healthcare directive, also known as a living will.

FINANCIAL AND HEALTHCARE POWERS OF ATTORNEY

A power of attorney is like a permission slip that allows you to name someone to do things for you who will be available when you cannot do those things for yourself. In the document, you are typically referred to as the principal, and the person to whom you are assigning the power is your agent or attorney-in-fact. You can assign this power to one or more individuals who act together or separately depending on your preference or your state's law. However, you may also find it useful to list a successor agent if your first choice is unwilling or unable to act. A power of attorney is a voluntary assignment, so you, as the principal, can replace your agents or revoke the power at any given time, as long as you are legally competent.

Depending on your unique situation, a power of attorney typically allows your agent broad power to address as many life and aging events as possible. Your attorney can also draft the document to limit your agent's power to a single act or for a specific purpose such as closing the sale of a home in your absence. However, for estate planning purposes, you generally create durable powers of attorney that become effective when you sign your document, continue to be effective through any period of incapacity, and end only at your death. A durable power of attorney is different from a temporary power of attorney, which usually terminates if you become incapacitated. A springing power of attorney may grant your agent power at some point in the future when a specific event, such as your incapacity, occurs. If you use a springing power of attorney, a well-drafted document will usually provide guidance about how to determine whether the specific event has occurred. A power of attorney can be created by statute, in which case your estate planner may be guided by state law or required to use a form prescribed by your state's legislature.

Once you have executed the document (and any specified events have occurred), your agent will typically be authorized to act on your behalf regarding matters including, but not limited to, buying and selling real and personal property, arranging for your personal care, negotiating medical or nursing care agreements, obtaining life or health insurance policies for you, employing tax professionals, and managing and handling your financial affairs.

Although the powers described above are typically distinct from decisions about your medical and healthcare needs, in some states, you, as the principal, may be able to assign power to your agent for such decisions in the same document used for your finances. Note, however, that most states require separate documents that distinguish a business and financial power of attorney from a medical one.

In general, a medical or healthcare power of attorney grants your agent access to your medical records and power to make decisions on your behalf about your medical treatment, medications, and surgery if you are unable to speak for yourself because of loss of consciousness, coma, stroke, Alzheimer's disease, or other form of dementia.

Your agent will generally be able to act for your healthcare or finances without court intervention or supervision only to the extent you have authorized such actions. While the law does not require an agent to act for you, if the agent chooses to act, they must comply with your wishes under an agent's fiduciary duties to act with loyalty, good faith, care, and prudence.

ADVANCE HEALTHCARE DIRECTIVE OR LIVING WILL

A living will allows you to express your wishes with respect to withholding or using life-sustaining or artificial means to prolong your life if you have a terminal condition or are in a persistent vegetative state or an irreversible coma. A living will directs your healthcare provider regarding how you wish your life to end and details which kinds of treatments you want or do not want if you are unable to express your wishes. Generally, at least one physician must verify a patient's terminal condition.

> *Under Kansas law, two physicians are required to certify a patient's terminal condition, one being the attending physician.*

As with a power of attorney, a living will is important because it provides clarity to your family and your healthcare providers if there is conflict or disagreement regarding your wishes. A living will, like a power of attorney, remains in effect until you revoke it, as long as you are legally competent. If you change your mind after executing a living will, it is best practice to destroy the original and notify anyone who knows of the document or possesses a copy, including your family members and healthcare providers, that it is no longer valid. Also, note that a living will is different from your last will and testament, which expresses your wishes for the distribution of your assets at your death, and a do-not-resuscitate order (DNR), which instructs healthcare providers not to perform cardiopulmonary resuscitation (CPR) should you stop breathing or if your heart stops.

ACTION ITEMS

Check with your estate planning attorney to learn which ancillary documents fit your specific needs. If you have an existing estate plan, check the language to determine whether you have granted springing or immediately effective powers to your agents. In addition, the best practice is to revisit each of your choices for designated and successor agents and consider whether the people you selected are still the best choice. Think about current relationships and circumstances that may affect whether you want to modify your prior decisions, and consider any healthcare issues that may prevent you from updating or revoking these documents in the future. Then meet with your estate planning attorney to discuss your wishes and prepare and execute documents that accurately reflect your wishes.

Felicia Acosta-Steiner is an attorney at Legacy Legal, LLC. She was drawn to the law by a passion for giving back to her community. Licensed in both Colorado and Kansas, Felicia focuses on probate, estate planning, trust administration, and adoptions.

Felicia Acosta-Steiner

18

Planning for Incapacity

By Ashley Ryan Sorgen (Medina, Ohio)

I ncapacity is a legal standard that is met when you can no longer manage your own financial or healthcare affairs. The capacity to handle your financial affairs includes knowing what bills you owe and when they are due, recognizing the fairness of a deal or opportunity, and managing a checking account to avoid spending more money than you have. The capacity to handle your healthcare affairs includes taking medication at the correct time, recognizing when you need to see a doctor, and ensuring that you live in a sanitary and accessible environment.

HANDLING INCAPACITY IN THE ABSENCE OF AN ESTATE PLAN

If you have no plan for incapacity, you must rely on state law to determine the process for appointing someone else to legally act on your behalf. Such legal processes are called guardianships or conservatorships, depending on the terminology used in your state. If you are subject to a guardianship, you are called a ward or incapacitated person.

There are two general types of guardianships: guardianships of the estate (which grant the guardian the authority to manage your finances and are called conservatorships in some states) and guardianships of the person (which grant the guardian the authority to manage your healthcare). A guardian may be appointed for the estate, the person, or both.

Before a person can be formally appointed as guardian, they must file an application in the probate court in the county where you reside. Each state has its own requirements that the guardianship applicant must meet, including

- an accounting of your next of kin (all family members who would inherit from you under state law if you die without a will),

- a statement of expert evaluation (a physician's opinion on your inability to manage your own affairs), and

- a criminal background check.

Most states also require that information (or notice) regarding the application for guardianship be shared with your family. Courts also typically require proof that notice was delivered, such as receipts for certified mail, documents signed by family members acknowledging receipt, or documents waiving notice and consenting to the appointment.

After receiving the application, the court sends an investigator, sometimes called a guardian *ad litem,* to meet with you to assess whether the application for guardianship is appropriate and whether a less-restrictive alternative is available for managing your affairs. The court ensures that you are kept informed about the legal process to the greatest extent possible, and some courts will help you locate an attorney to represent your interests during the guardianship appointment process.

If more than one person applies for guardianship, state law guides how the judge should prioritize one applicant over another. Further, the judge may require the guardian to buy an insurance policy (or bond) to prevent the loss of your assets. The guardian must also undergo training in some states and make regular reports to the court, some of which may become a matter of public record. Although a guardianship may terminate if you regain capacity, many guardianships remain in force for the rest of the ward's life.

Although guardianships are useful if a ward has no estate plan, there are certain restrictions on guardians' actions; for example, in some states, a guardian must obtain the court's permission before spending a ward's money.

ALTERNATIVES TO GUARDIANSHIP

You can use legal tools such as trusts, financial powers of attorney, and advance health-care directives to control who makes decisions for you if you become incapacitated. Separate rules govern whether and how someone may assist you with federal benefits, such as Social Security, Medicare, and Medicaid. For example, the agency may appoint a representative payee or you may appoint a representative to assist you. Both roles are subject to rules similar to the guardianship reporting requirements.

TRUSTS

Trusts are beneficial in a number of ways, including situations in which you plan to leave a portion of your estate to an incapacitated individual. There are numerous different kinds of trusts that are used for a variety of purposes. Because trusts are private agreements between the trust's creator (called a grantor, trustor, settlor, or trustmaker) and the trust's manager (the trustee), the terms of the trust govern how the trustee uses assets owned by the trust for the benefit of a beneficiary. Assets you own outside of a trust are managed separately.

POWERS OF ATTORNEY

A financial power of attorney (POA) is a legal document governed by state law that you may use to manage assets titled in your name alone and to facilitate other personal business matters, such as filing income tax returns and accessing digital assets. As the POA's principal, you grant one or more agents the legal authority to act on your behalf but only to the extent that you allow. Some financial POA documents grant an agent broad authority that begins immediately (general POA). Others more narrowly address specific purposes (limited POA) or become valid only if you become incapacitated (springing POA).

State law may require the use of specific language in the POA for your agent to have certain authority, such as making gifts on your behalf, or to qualify the financial POA as durable.

You may name a primary agent and alternates or even coagents (multiple individuals to work together); however, some financial institutions have restrictive internal rules about honoring financial POA documents. For example, some institutions refuse to honor a financial POA that requires more than one person to authorize a transaction.

ADVANCE HEALTHCARE DIRECTIVES

Advance healthcare directives address healthcare decisions. Such documents typically include a healthcare POA and a living will declaration. In some states, the healthcare POA and a living will declaration are separate documents, rather than being combined in an advance healthcare directive. A healthcare POA (also called a healthcare proxy or designation of healthcare agent) works similarly to a financial POA; the agents you name have the authority to make healthcare-related decisions on your behalf.

It can be helpful for your healthcare POA to contain language authorizing medical providers to release your protected health information in accordance with the Health Insurance Portability and Accountability Act (HIPAA), even though HIPAA and state law may already provide that authorization.

A living will declaration communicates your wishes for treatment if you become totally and permanently unconscious or have a terminal condition. Total and permanent unconsciousness depends on whether you are aware of yourself and your surroundings and the physician's degree of medical certainty in making the diagnosis. A terminal condition is an untreatable condition from which you cannot recover and which will result in imminent death.

In addition to living will declarations, some people choose to have physicians' orders for life sustaining treatments and other directives that instruct medical professionals to provide, withdraw, or withhold life-supporting measures. Such directives are typically revocable (you may change them) and generally remain private.

ACTION ITEMS

If you have an existing trust, financial POA, or advance healthcare directives, confirm whether the language in the documents reflects your wishes and current state laws. If you have no existing estate plan, think about whom you trust to manage your affairs as you would manage them for yourself. Meet with an estate planning attorney to document and properly execute a plan that empowers those you trust to advocate for you if you are unable to do so for yourself.

Edmonds Sorgen, LLC is a boutique estate planning and elder law firm customizing approachable, family-friendly estate plans and cultivating peace of mind for an easy transition of wealth to loved ones.

Ashley Sorgen

19

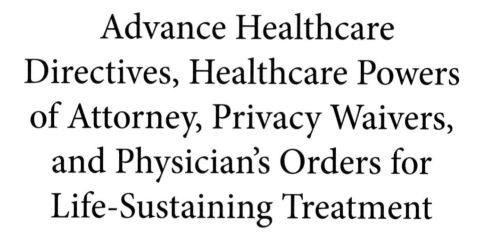

Advance Healthcare Directives, Healthcare Powers of Attorney, Privacy Waivers, and Physician's Orders for Life-Sustaining Treatment

By Marty Burbank (Fullerton, California)

Complete estate planning packages comprise many documents, including wills, trusts, and financial powers of attorney. These documents address money, taxes, who will oversee your estate, and who will receive your belongings. Much of estate planning addresses what happens after you have passed away. However, some of the most important estate planning documents are related to your healthcare. Healthcare estate planning documents are strictly about you, the quality of your life, and the quality of your death.

Before law school, I worked in the healthcare field for twelve years. My experience working in the intensive care unit influenced me to become an elder law attorney. I stood at the bedside of loved ones with many families who were struggling with end-of-life decisions. I have faced these decisions in my own family. As an elder law attorney, I have helped thousands of people plan and draft their healthcare documents.

When we refer to healthcare documents, we mean four separate but interrelated documents: an advance healthcare directive, a healthcare power of attorney, a Health Insurance Portability and Accountability Act (HIPAA) privacy waiver, and a physician's order for life-sustaining treatment (POLST).

ADVANCE HEALTHCARE DIRECTIVE

Most people are familiar with the advance healthcare directive, sometimes known as a living will or directive to physicians. The form's name is not as important as the form's purpose, so do not be alarmed if your attorney uses a form with a different name.

An advance healthcare directive is important because it lets you express what is important to you and how you should be treated. The document may be essential at the end of your life, but it is also crucial if you become unconscious or are otherwise unable to communicate. People often think of this document as guidance for end-of-life support, but it can involve much more.

An advance healthcare directive may define what life support means to you. Most people consider advanced cardiac life support, cardiopulmonary resuscitation, and a ventilator to be life support, but it may also involve tube-feeding, intravenous fluids for hydration, antibiotics, and blood transfusions.

It may also address nonmedical wishes. Do you want to be surrounded by family and friends? Would you rather have peaceful time alone with your spouse? Would you like for a chaplain or other clergy to be available? What music would you like to hear? Do you find the smell of flowers or freshly baked bread comforting? I was blessed to witness a remarkable moment of clarity and awareness in one of my clients after several days of nonresponsiveness when a hospice chaplain sang for them.

It is crucial to put these thoughts in writing and sign the document correctly. In most states, an advance healthcare directive must be signed and witnessed by two disinterested people or acknowledged by a notary public.

HEALTHCARE POWER OF ATTORNEY

Sometimes the healthcare power of attorney is a separate document, and other times it is included in the advance healthcare directive. The healthcare power of attorney allows you to designate someone as your agent to make healthcare decisions on your behalf when you cannot do so for yourself.

Like the advance healthcare directive, the healthcare power of attorney may be needed at the end of life or after an accident or other sudden health issue. For example, one of my clients was in a horrible plane crash. Immediately after he touched down, a larger plane landed on top of his aircraft. He was struck by the propeller of the larger plane. My client's injuries were so severe that first responders ran past him, believing he must be dead. He spent a week in a coma. Because a healthcare power of attorney was in place, his agent could discuss his treatment options and make healthcare decisions on his behalf. He has recovered and is now able to fly again.

You can also authorize your healthcare agent to make decisions about your living arrangements, such as whether you will receive care at home with full-time caregivers or in an assisted living or memory care community.

Without a healthcare power of attorney, it may be necessary to go to court to establish who will have the authority to make these important decisions.

HEALTH INSURANCE PORTABILITY AND ACCOUNTABILITY ACT (HIPAA) WAIVER

HIPAA became law in 1996. Among other things, HIPAA puts rules in place to protect the privacy of patients. Protecting privacy is important, but it can lead to some unintended consequences. For example, one of my clients called my office in a panic when her mother had been taken to the hospital. Without a HIPAA waiver, my client was not able to get any information about her mother's condition.

A nurse told my client that because her mother was married, the healthcare providers could only talk to her husband. It was true that her mother was married, but her husband had lived in another state with his girlfriend for more than sixteen years. My client's only option was to call her estranged father and persuade him to contact the hospital to get information about her mother's condition. This situation could have been avoided if my client's mother had signed a HIPAA waiver authorizing the healthcare professionals to provide information to my client.

PHYSICIAN'S ORDER FOR LIFE-SUSTAINING TREATMENT (POLST)

The POLST is a relative newcomer as far as healthcare documents go. Unlike the other documents, it is not something that a lawyer can draft. The POLST is a physician's order that should be honored by any first responder, nurse, or other physician who may provide medical care. It is filled out by your doctor, often after you have developed a terminal illness, and specifies your end-of-life care decisions.

CONCLUDING THOUGHTS

While these documents are essential, I always make sure my clients know that conversations about the documents and how one wants to be treated are more vital. Of course, the dialogue between the principal and the agent is critical, but you should have similar conversations with those who will be there to support your agent when faced with tough decisions. It is not uncommon for a family member or loved one who feels they have been left out to create a big disruption at a very sensitive time. Clear communication of your wishes to the important people in your life will ensure that you receive your desired care as well as maintain the peace between your loved ones at a difficult time.

OC Elder Law helps older clients and their families plan for the legal and care issues related to aging, including estate planning and administration.

Marty Burbank

20

$\approx$

Your Net Worth Includes Far More Than Dollars and Cents

By Doug Coe (Wichita, Kansas)

During the first estate planning meeting, clients routinely say something like "I have a net worth of $1.5 million and two grown kids. I want to transfer everything to them when I die, and I want to keep things as simple as possible. I don't need anything fancy." Though a simple estate plan may end up being the correct strategy, it is very important to broaden your perspective about what constitutes your true net worth—what you really want to leave to your children.

It is true that you cannot take it with you when you go. However, there are some things many clients care deeply about leaving to their beneficiaries—things they would not take with them, even if they could. Consider the following hypothetical: You have money, education, work ethic, values or faith, and family harmony. You can give any four to your beneficiaries. Out of these five items, which four do you choose? Many clients say they would give items two through five to their beneficiaries because the money is less important to them and the money will come naturally if they have the other four. Questions like this help you understand your true net worth and what you most want to transfer to your beneficiaries.

> *"[T]here are some things that many clients care deeply about leaving to their beneficiaries—things they would not take with them, even if they could."*

Another key question is "When you think about the impact of your estate plan, what would you consider to be a grand slam home run?" Put differently, if you could accomplish any one thing in your estate plan, what would it be? Clients rarely respond, "I want to give every single penny I possibly can to my beneficiaries. My only goal is to give them as much money as I possibly can." Instead, clients routinely express the following types of goals:

- "I want my middle son to develop a work ethic. I want him to be able to stand on his own two feet."

- "I want to make sure my son-in-law does not have any access to the money that is left after I die."

- "My deepest desire is for my youngest daughter to put her faith in God, as I have."

Of course, it is harder to transfer something like faith in God with an estate plan than it is to transfer money. However, if you have not determined the target, you are far less likely to hit it. Identifying the primary goal is extremely important: it is the first step in designing your estate plan. Developing a strategy to accomplish that goal is the second step.

> *"However, if you do not even know what the target is, you are far less likely to hit it."*

With creative thinking and a good estate planning attorney, you can develop a strategy unique to your circumstances and desires. Though it is often impossible to know with certainty if your strategy will work, you can dramatically increase the odds of success if you think creatively and wisely. For example, consider the following goals and proposed strategies:

Goal 1: "I want my kids to get a high-quality education. I do not want them to waste the time they spend in college. Frankly, I would rather them get a job if they are just going to party their way through college."

Strategy 1: In your trust agreement, offer to pay for up to 75 percent of any postsecondary education expenses. Your beneficiary will need to come up with the other 25 percent on their own. This requires them to have skin in the game and will reduce the odds that they will waste the opportunity to learn. Of course, the percentage you contribute is a judgment call. Clients often include ceilings or reference points, such as "The trustee may pay for the first $5,000 of tuition per year. After that, the trustee may pay for 75 percent of any tuition expenses up to a maximum of $50,000 per year for four years."

Goal 2: "I just do not want everyone fighting when I am gone, and I do not want to cause a big headache for my family to deal with."

Strategy 2: "[T]here is a one-third risk of significant family discord in the post-death administration of an estate or trust in the circumstance where there is more than one then-living adult child and a child or children serves as financial fiduciary."[1]

Just because one of your children is smart, hardworking, professional, and honest does not mean they are qualified to be a trustee, and it most certainly does not mean your other children will be grateful for the work that child does as a fiduciary. Even if your responsible daughter executes her duties as trustee perfectly, your son might have a poor understanding of what should or should not happen under the trust agreement. Despite flawless execution as trustee, your daughter may still find herself dealing with a complaint (or lawsuit) from her ungrateful brother. Of course, the risk only grows in blended families or families in which harmony is already compromised.

Using a neutral, third-party trustee, executor, or fiduciary for financial matters dramatically reduces, if not eliminates, the risk of family disharmony. Though there are expenses associated with using a nonfamily fiduciary, preserving family harmony is an enormous benefit.

Goal 3: "I do not want to force my kids to go down the traditional four-year college path. College is not for everyone, you know! What if they want to start a business? At the same time, I do not want to just give them a pile of money."

Strategy 3: Offer to pay for up to 50 percent of the start-up costs of a business. If the business idea is good, a bank or other investor or lender will fund the rest of the costs. Alternatively, the beneficiary will come up with the other 50 percent on their own, and they will have quite a bit of skin in the game. The trust funds will help the beneficiary launch the company, but the risk of throwing money away on a bogus business is dramatically reduced.

| *"Start by identifying your goals beyond the simple transfer of financial assets."*

Though you undoubtedly have goals that are not addressed in these examples, you now have a framework to begin with. Once the larger goals are identified, think strategically and creatively about how you might accomplish them through your estate plan. Think big!

Doug Coe is an estate planning attorney in Wichita, Kansas. He is passionate about CHANGING LIVES THROUGH ESTATE PLANNING™.

Doug Coe

1   Timothy P. O'Sullivan, *Family Harmony: An All Too Frequent Causality of the Estate Planning Process,* 8 Marq. Elder's Advisor 253, 260 (2012).

21

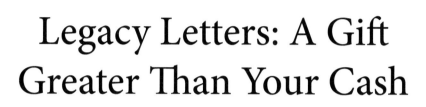

Legacy Letters: A Gift Greater Than Your Cash and Property

By Jennifer Elliott (San Clemente, California)

I magine saving your money all your life to create a legacy for your family. You work hard so they can live comfortably after you pass away. You establish an estate plan that clearly defines your wishes for the assets you would like to leave your loved ones. You spend hours properly funding that plan to make sure your trustee has all the tools they need to access your assets and carry out your wishes. You update it regularly to be sure it is current and written in accordance with local laws, thus avoiding estate tax, capital gains tax, and litigation. After your passing, your trustee properly handles their duties, keeping your estate out of court, and ensuring that your spouse is secure in the family home and that your investment accounts are distributed to your children. Your family is financially set for life because of your careful planning. This is the ideal situation, right? What more could your spouse and children want than financial security? What could be more valuable than money after you are gone? The answer may surprise you. It costs nothing but is priceless.

Your loved ones want *you*. They want memories of you in your own words and hand-writing. This written expression is called a legacy letter, and it is more precious than the real estate and cash that you spend your lifetime acquiring. In less than an hour, and with no investment, you can give your loved ones the most cherished gift of all.

Legacy letters are called ethical wills in the Jewish faith. The Catholic Foundation of Central Florida has resources to assist with creating a Catholic legacy letter. Regardless of whether the letter is faith-based, it allows you to share your story with your loved ones and future generations. You can include family stories and traditions that you wish to pass on to your children and grandchildren and disclose sentiments to the special people in your life after you are gone. Passing down the stories and challenges of previous generations gives a sense of identity and self-esteem to your loved ones, their children, and generations to come.

Who receives a legacy letter? Anyone who is important to you: your spouse, child, grandchild, or friend. You may also give a letter to those from whom you have been estranged to heal the relationship so all may be at peace. You can write one letter to everyone, but your loved ones may prefer to each receive their own reminder of you. You can create a video or recording instead of a letter, but consider how quickly technology changes—for example, VCRs are now extinct—so a written letter may be the most reliable medium.

What do you write? Consider your audience. Remind your wife about the first time you knew you loved her. Write to your son about the times you were proud of him. Tell your brother you forgive him and wish to put an end to that long family feud.

Here are some suggestions for what to include in your legacy letter:

- How you feel about the recipient of the letter
- Accomplishments and relationships you are proud of
- Traits you admire in the recipient
- Your apologies or regrets
- Forgiveness
- Stories of your childhood
- Family traditions you hope to pass on
- Secret family recipes
- The meaning of personal belongings you are leaving behind
- Your favorite book, movie, song, or Bible verse
- Causes that are important to you and why
- Lessons you have learned in your life

- People who have influenced you during your life
- Your wishes for the recipient
- Your definition of success
- Feelings of love and gratitude

In addition to being an invaluable gift to your loved ones, legacy letters are also a gift to yourself. Taking time to recount your life and legacy can bring you peace. You may no longer be there to tell your children daily that you love them, but they will be able to read your words anytime they need to. The exercise of coming to terms with your own life and contemplating your ending can make you feel alive and renewed. It can also inspire gratitude for your accomplishments and the relationships you have built with your special people.

Write your legacy letter today while you are well. You can build on the letter over the years as you grow and reflect. If you are diagnosed with a serious illness after you have written the letter, your legacy letter will ensure you are always remembered. When a terminal client walks into my office to establish their estate plan, I suggest that legacy letters make their priority list. Several clients have told me how writing such letters brought them a sense of calm amid the stress of their condition. They no longer had to worry about leaving behind their loved ones because they now had a tool to relay their dearest sentiments. One client wrote a letter to be opened by her daughter on her wedding day and another to be opened on the birth of her first child. Though she could not be present at the events, she ensured that her daughter would feel her presence and love on those memorable occasions.

The biggest challenge may be the first sentence. Consider using something like: "Dear ___, I am writing this letter to let you know more about me, our family, and my hopes for your future." You may find inspiration by surrounding yourself with photos and mementos that are important to you. Just as the legacy letter writing process may trigger emotions and tears, it can also bring you great insight and clarity as you think back on your lifetime.

Keep your legacy letters in your estate planning binder with instructions to your trustee to deliver them after you pass away. After you are gone, the item your loved ones will cherish most is not the house or the stock account. It is you, in the form of a letter, expressing your love. It will be the most important gift you leave, and you will find that its creation is a gift to you as well.

RECOMMENDED READING

12 Great Tips on How to Write an Amazing Legacy Letter, Legacy Letters (Sept. 12, 2013), https://www.legacyletter.org/12-great-tips-on-how-to-write-an-amazing-legacy-letter/.

Catholic Legacy Resources, Catholic Foundation of Central Florida, https://www.cfocf. org/legacy (last visited Nov. 12, 2021).

Mark Goldfarb, Presentation at the Temple Beth Ohr in La Mirada, CA (2021).

Jennifer Elliott owns San Clemente Estate Law, P.C. in South Orange County, California. She devotes her practice to estate planning, probate, trust administration, and asset protection.

Jennifer Elliott

22

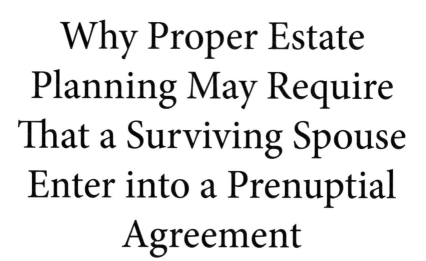

Why Proper Estate Planning May Require That a Surviving Spouse Enter into a Prenuptial Agreement

By Clifford Rice (Valparaiso, Indiana)

One of the most valuable and beneficial things an estate planning attorney can do for married clients is to design an estate plan that protects both the surviving spouse and the children from the effects of the surviving spouse's remarriage.

When a married person dies, their surviving spouse is often emotionally devastated. Losing a spouse is nearly always a shock, notwithstanding the age of the couple or the state of their health. After the funeral ends and the well-wishers drift away, loneliness can set in. The surviving spouse is left in the home alone with a silence that may seem deafening. They may not be eating properly or sleeping well, and it may be difficult for them to find joy in life. And little wonder… they have lost their life's companion of perhaps forty or more years. Then, the surviving spouse goes to church, the senior center, or on a cruise, and they meet someone. At some point, they want to remarry.

There is nothing wrong with remarriage after losing a spouse. Unfortunately, however, that new marriage may not last fifty years. It may not even last fifty weeks. While it is well documented that nearly half of all marriages end in divorce, it is less well-known that nearly 60 percent of all second marriages end in divorce. If there is a divorce, the new spouse and stepparent may want 50 percent of everything you and your first spouse worked for together over a lifetime. Additionally, the laws of many states provide that assets brought into the marriage can become part of the marital pot and can end up passing to a new spouse and stepparent rather than to your children.

If a surviving spouse remarries and then becomes the first in the **remarriage** to die, the laws in many states allow the surviving spouse in the remarriage to retain all of their own separate assets as well as one quarter to one half of the deceased spouse's assets, potentially leaving the deceased spouse's children with a reduced inheritance. In addition to this statutory share of the assets of the first spouse to die, in some states the surviving spouse in the remarriage may be entitled to a survivorship allowance. The money and assets accumulated by the couple in the first marriage could end up passing to the new surviving spouse and stepparent—a result that the spouses in the first marriage most likely did not intend. This does not have to happen.

For many married couples, good estate planning may include language in the will or trust of the first spouse to die that **requires** that the surviving spouse enter into a valid, written prenuptial agreement before they remarry. Language can be spelled out in the estate plan setting forth the precise requirements for the prenuptial agreement. The prenuptial agreement must be signed well in advance of the remarriage. Each party must be represented by independent legal counsel. In addition, each party must disclose, in writing, the nature and value of the assets they are bringing into the marriage. The language in the will or trust can also provide that the prenuptial agreement must require the new spouse to waive, in advance and in writing, their right to take away anything from the surviving spouse in the event of a divorce or if the surviving spouse dies prior to the new spouse. As an enforcement mechanism, the will or trust can specify that the assets left behind by the first spouse to die will no longer be accessible to the surviving spouse if the surviving spouse fails to meet the specific requirements in the trust for the preparation and execution of a valid written prenuptial agreement. It seems safe to say that a surviving spouse would be extremely reluctant to lose access to approximately half of all of the assets. If planning to remarry, they can honestly say to their soon-to-be-spouse: "Honey, I love and trust you; this has nothing to do with you or me. Many years ago, before I even met you, I entered into an estate plan that requires that I have a valid, written prenuptial agreement before I remarry. If we don't do this, I am going to lose almost half of everything I own! It's not that I don't trust you, honey. I really have no choice." This explanation will be true: the language can clearly be seen in the trust instrument created by the first spouse to die.

With this language in place, the likelihood that a surviving spouse will create a valid, written prenuptial agreement is greatly enhanced. The surviving spouse and the children will both win. There is only one person who will lose: a predator or gold digger who comes along and marries the surviving spouse after the first spouse dies. The language for this remarriage protection and prenuptial agreement has been in WealthCounsel's document creation software for more than twenty-five years, and practitioners have seen it work with great success. Experienced attorneys often include this language in the estate planning documents of married couples because it is such an effective, beneficial, and well-established safeguard.

A 2013 Pew Research study shows that previously married adults age sixty-five and older remarried 50 percent of the time.[1] Given the fact that nearly 60 percent of second marriages end in divorce and the possibility that your surviving spouse may die before their new spouse, the potential savings can amount to hundreds of thousands of dollars per family. Compare this to the well-established practices of avoiding probate admin-istration or achieving a second stepped-up tax basis following the death of the first spouse, which may save only tens of thousands of dollars. The remarriage protection prenuptial language, when drafted appropriately and incorporated in a married couple's estate plan, can ensure that your hard-earned assets stay in your family.

Clifford Rice has been practicing law for nearly fifty years. The practice of Rice & Rice is entirely dedicated to estate planning, Medicaid planning, and elder law. Clifford Rice holds the AV rating from Martindale Hubbell and has personally counseled over 17,000 families, helping them save tens of millions of dollars in probate fees and nursing home costs.

Clifford Rice

---

1   Pew Research Center, *American Community Survey (1% IPUMS)* (2013).

23

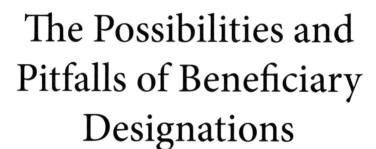

The Possibilities and Pitfalls of Beneficiary Designations

By Anthony G. Celaya and Meghan M. Avila (Napa, California)

Like it or not, you cannot take your property with you when you die. You can, however, direct where your property will go. In simple terms, there are only three ways to do this—with a will, a trust, or a beneficiary designation document. Because of the ease of designating a beneficiary, you may have opted to use this method for at least some of your accounts, but have you sacrificed certainty for simplicity?

Five common assets that include the option of designating a beneficiary at your death are (1) bank accounts, (2) investment accounts, (3) retirement accounts, (4) life insurance policies, and (5) real estate.[1] Typically, when setting up one of these accounts, policies, or special deeds, you fill out a form or other document that asks you to designate the individuals you would like to inherit your property. After you die, assuming

---

1   Some states allow for transfer-on-death deeds, which are essentially equivalent to beneficiary designation forms. When the homeowner dies, the property is transferred directly to the beneficiary without probate.

Figure 1 – You can't take it with you.

your designation is effective, the asset is transferred to those individuals directly, outside of probate or any government control.

THE LIMITS OF BENEFICIARY DESIGNATIONS

Choosing beneficiary designations to pass on your property seems like a no-brainer. It is easy, cost-effective, and simple. However, in many cases, beneficiary designations fall short and end up doing more harm than good. Consider the following scenarios:

Scenario 1. You name your only daughter as the beneficiary of your bank account, which holds your life savings of $250,000. When you die, she inherits the property seamlessly, as you wanted. However, she has recently experienced several financial reversals, including a failed business, and has incurred some debt. The moment she receives the money, several creditors lay claim to it.

Scenario 2. You have set up a retirement account with your two children as equal beneficiaries. Unfortunately, you and one of your children are in an accident, and both of you pass away. Now there is no beneficiary for the portion that would have gone to your deceased child, and that portion of your estate ends up in probate to be administered under the supervision of the court and distributed according to state law.[2]

Scenario 3. Your investment account is worth $100,000, your life insurance policy has a $100,000 payout, and your house is valued at $100,000. Since you have three children, you decide to designate each child as a beneficiary of one of your assets with the intent that they will have equal inheritances. However, when you die ten years later, your life insurance policy is still worth $100,000, but your investment account is worth $200,000, and your house is worth $150,000. The inequity causes a family fallout.

---

2   While some beneficiary designation forms allow you to include contingent beneficiaries, no form can accommodate all the contingencies life may bring.

ALTERNATIVES TO BENEFICIARY DESIGNATIONS

These scenarios illustrate that you may need to use more than beneficiary designations to ensure that your property goes to your chosen beneficiaries in the amounts you want and in a way that is protected from creditors. Consider how beneficiary designations stack up against outright dispositions under wills and gifts made in continuing trust:

Benefit	No Plan	Beneficiary Designation	Will	Trust
Power over who gets your property	No	Limited	Yes	Yes
Control over amount of final distribution	No	Limited	Yes	Yes
Probate avoidance	No	Limited	No	Yes
Privacy	No	Yes	No	Yes
Protection from creditors, beyond protections for certain types of assets under state law	No	No	No	Yes
Tax planning options	No	No	Limited	Yes
Creativity, incentives, contingent gifts	No	No	Limited	Yes

Many people use beneficiary designations to pass on their assets and property because avoiding probate is a primary goal. However, beneficiary designations alone fail to achieve other common goals.

ASSETS THAT REQUIRE BENEFICIARY DESIGNATIONS

Two of the five assets noted above—retirement accounts and life insurance policies—can only be disposed of (at least without adverse consequences) through beneficiary designations. Additionally, for some business bank accounts, beneficiary designations may be almost impossible to avoid. In these situations, owners who have created trusts can name their trust as the designated beneficiary, thus taking advantage of the benefits of a trust even for assets that require beneficiary designations.[3]

Scenario 4. You have created a trust to pass your property on to your children, but you cannot place your largest asset—a $400,000 retirement account—into your trust because the retirement account must continue to be owned by you and may be passed on only through a beneficiary designation. One of your children has special needs, so you are concerned that she will not be able to manage her inheritance if she receives it directly through a beneficiary designation. Consequently, you name your trust rather than your children as the beneficiary[4] of the account. After you die, the account will go into your trust. However, since your trust is set up for the benefit of your children, your

---

3   Naming a trust as a beneficiary of a retirement account has tax implications that should be discussed with your attorney.
4   You will need to find an attorney who knows how to craft a trust that can be a valid beneficiary of a retirement account.

children will still ultimately receive the money. In addition, the portion allocated for your special needs child will be protected inside the trust.

ACTION ITEMS

Because beneficiary designations are quick and easy, banks and other financial institutions may insist that you rely on them to accomplish your estate planning goals. However, they are far more nuanced than they seem and can both help and hinder your goals. Therefore, make a list of your assets and consult with an estate planning attorney to determine how each asset is currently titled and how it will be passed on to your beneficiaries—in court, by beneficiary designation, through a will, or with a trust. Your attorney will then be able to advise whether your current estate plan will accomplish your goals for your family and other loved ones or if modifications should be made.

Anthony Celaya   Meghan Avila

Celaya Law is a California estate & Medi-Cal planning law firm whose priorities are expertise, service, and relationships. Principal attorneys Anthony G. Celaya and Meghan M. Avila make a special effort to be accessible to their clients, and the firm's no-cost, lifetime client care program allows for a highly personal, service-oriented experience unique among law firms.

24

Types of Wills

By Erin Johnson (Rico, Colorado)

A will is a legal document that directs the distribution of your assets when you die. Wills state how you want to leave your assets to individuals or charities, and can address the custody of your dependents and transfer of your financial interests. There are different types of wills that can be used for different purposes. State laws vary regarding all aspects of wills, so be sure to consult a local attorney.

The terms *will, last will,* or *last will and testament* all refer to the same document. Historically, a will addressed real property and a testament addressed personal property, but modern usage shortens these terms to will. However, many wills still use the term *testator* (male) or *testatrix* (female) to describe the person making the will.

There are certain basic requirements that must be met regarding wills. You must be of legal age, usually eighteen years old, to create a will. If you are the person creating the will, you must clearly establish that you intend the document to be a legally effective disposition of your property at your death. This is called testamentary intent.

You also need to have *testamentary capacity* to create a will, that is, you must be of sound mind and memory. You need to be aware of the nature and extent of the assets that you own, know who your natural heirs are, understand the disposition you are making in the will, and be able to express how you want your assets to be distributed when you die.

Your will must be signed by you, which demonstrates that it is your will. You must do so voluntarily and without coercion. If you sign a will because someone has threatened you, the will could be considered invalid because it was made under duress or coercion.

Most modern wills are typewritten, signed, witnessed, and have a notarized affidavit attached. The witnesses are usually disinterested parties who will not benefit from the will. A will can be self-proving if it contains a notarized sworn statement attesting to the validity of the will.

A *holographic will* is one that is entirely handwritten, as well as signed by the testator. It should generally also be dated, though that may not be a requirement. Many states consider this type of will to be valid. It may be witnessed, which helps to establish its validity, and other requirements may also apply depending on your state's law.

Many people desire to have a *simple will*. This is not a type of will, but a person who wants a simple will is often seeking a basic will that meets the legal requirements of a valid will and directs the distribution of your assets, possibly also appointing an executor or personal representative who will administer your estate after you die. You can also designate a guardian for your minor children.

Wills that contain provisions to establish testamentary trusts, which I will refer to as *testamentary trust wills,* are wills that direct the establishment of one or more trusts after you die to manage your assets for the care of others. A trust that is created through the probate process from this type of will has a trustee who will manage your assets as you direct in your will.

If you establish a trust while you are living, you should have a *pour-over will.* A *pour-over will* directs the distribution of any probate assets that are not already in your trust. This type of will is simplified to minimize conflicts between the will and the trust and to address any assets that have not been transferred to your trust at the time of your death.

An *oral will* or a *nuncupative will* consists of a verbal expression of a person's dying wishes to witnesses. It usually is created in dire health circumstances and is sometimes called a *deathbed will*. It is difficult to prove the validity of an oral will, and they are not recognized at all in some states. A *video will* is an oral will; however, in practice, it is generally used as a backup and not as a substitute for a written will. A *video will* could be used as evidence to show that you are of sound mind and that you are not being manipulated. More often, however, it is used as extra documentation of the will signing ceremony.

A *joint will* or a *mutual will* is a single will signed by two people, usually married, which leaves all of one's assets to the other when they die and determines what happens to the remaining assets when the second person dies. This type of will is legally problematic and not often used. *Mirror wills,* that is, separate wills reflecting the same wishes made by two people, are more commonly used.

Some states now allow the use of *electronic wills* or *e-wills,* some of which are remotely signed and witnessed. Electronic wills statutes generally provide that certified paper copies can be used for probate in place of the original will documents. This is an evolving area of the law, and the statutes in the states that allow *e-wills* vary widely.

An *online will* is not the same thing as an *e-will.* An *online will* is a document that is downloaded from the internet, sometimes from online software or online estate planning service providers, and is modified and signed. While these types of wills may be valid (if executed as required by state law), the quality can vary greatly. You may end up with a will that does not reflect the law in the state where you live, even if the website claims it does.

A *living will* is not really a will at all. Instead, it is an end-of-life directive from you to your medical service providers communicating your wishes about life-sustaining medical procedures and other end-of-life care if you are unable to understand medical information or communicate your wishes.

If you are interested in creating a will, it is always best to work with an experienced estate planning attorney. An estate planning attorney has extensive training and experience with various techniques that apply to different family situations. Your attorney will interview and work with you to discern and achieve your objectives for your assets after you die. Based on your unique goals and circumstances, your attorney can design a customized and legally valid estate plan that will leave the legacy you desire.

Erin Johnson is an attorney practicing in southwest Colorado in the areas of estate planning, land use, real estate, and business. She has an extensive background in estate and succession planning, business, and real estate development. Ms. Johnson works creatively and effectively with families to help them realize their long-term goals–in life, business, and estate planning.

Erin Johnson

25

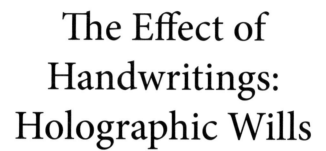

The Effect of Handwritings: Holographic Wills

By Sheena M. Moran (Littleton, Colorado)

Holograph: a manuscript handwritten by the person named as its author

Imalda Jean hires an attorney and drafts a trust. Imalda's assets are not held in the trust but rather are owned in Imalda's name. Imalda also has a pour-over will, which will transfer her assets into her trust upon her death. She has a heart attack and is scheduled for open-heart surgery. Prior to her surgery, Imalda writes a note that she declares to be her last will. The note states that it revokes any prior wills she drafted. This handwriting designates a number of gifts to individuals in specific amounts and states that the remainder (residuary) of the estate should be distributed to her children. Imalda signs and dates her note. What is the result? Imalda has just drafted a will. This will supersedes the will and trust that Imalda had previously drafted with the careful advice of her attorney. In many states, this handwritten note would unravel an estate plan in which a client had invested thousands of dollars in professional fees.

Many states recognize a handwritten will, also known as a holographic will, if the material portions of the will are in your handwriting and the document is signed. However, the laws vary by state as to whether the state recognizes holographic wills, and if so, the requirements for a valid holographic will. At least three jurisdictions, Maryland, New York, and the US Virgin Islands, do not recognize holographic wills except for those created by members of the US Armed Forces. Twenty-one states and Puerto Rico have statutes permitting holographic wills. Ten states do not recognize handwritten wills created by a resident within the state but recognize a holographic will as a foreign will when the holographic will was properly drafted under the laws of another state where the drafter resided at the time of the will's execution. Some states do not recognize holographic wills at all.

HOW TO USE A HANDWRITTEN WILL

Let me be clear: I never advise a client to draft a handwritten will as their only will, but in an emergency, a handwritten note can suffice to declare your last wishes if you have no other estate planning documents in place. For example, when a person without an estate plan calls from a hospital, a handwritten will may be better than having absolutely nothing in place. In anticipation of surgery, you may write a note to your family stating how you desire your assets to be divided. This note should also identify the person you want to handle the distribution of these assets.

As an example, the note could look like the following:

Will

Upon my death, please don't fight. I give the farm to my son, Andrew. Please divide the rest of my assets equally and give it to my children. I want Jamie to distribute everything and handle everything. She knows where everything is. I love you all.

Michael Timothy Thomas

Your state statute *may* recognize this writing as a holographic will because the material portions of this will are in the handwriting and signed by the decedent (person who died). I recommend dating the holographic will, but this is not always required by state law. However, a date may be very important if there are multiple estate planning documents and there is a conflict about which one is the most recent.

You may be thinking that you should just draft a holographic will and not spend money on a lawyer. However, it is very important to be aware of the common problems resulting from the use of a holographic will.

Disadvantages of Using a Holographic Will

Holographic wills are significantly more likely to trigger legal challenges. The following questions often arise:

- Is this the decedent's handwriting?

- Is the signature the decedent's?

- Is the name printed on the document a signature?

- Is the document in writing or typed? Is a typed document allowed by the relevant state statute?

- Is the holographic will dated? Does your state's law require that it be dated?

- Does the writing demonstrate testamentary intent?

- Was the document a draft?

- How should the provisions be interpreted?

Tip 1: When drafting a holographic will, you should ensure that it meets the requirements of *your* state's law. At the very least, it should meet all of the following requirements:

- You, the drafter, are at least eighteen years old.

- The writing is in your handwriting.

- It is labeled as your will.

- It revokes any prior will.

- It demonstrates testamentary intent by using language such as "At my death, I give the farm located in Lamar, Colorado to my son, Andrew."

- It is specific as to the property and beneficiaries.

- It is dated.

- It is signed by the drafter.

HOW TO ENSURE THAT YOUR NOTES DO NOT UNINTENTIONALLY ALTER OR REVOKE YOUR WILL

When preparing an estate plan, you must be careful to ensure that your handwritten notes will not undo your estate plan.

Scenario 1. When reviewing your original documents, which are executed, signed, and dated, you write your thoughts on the original documents. These handwritten notations are thoughts you want to share with your attorney. These notes include changes to distributions you are considering and want to discuss with your attorney. You are killed in a car accident on the way to the attorney's office. Your original will must be filed with the court.

In this scenario, the court reviews the will. Depending on your state, the court may treat your handwritten notes as a revocation of your original will or as an amendment to your will, regardless of whether that was your intention. Thus, your handwritten notes may be honored in a manner that you did not desire, may not be honored at all, or may cause your estate to be treated as if you had died without a will.

Scenario 2. *Let's return to Imalda Jean. Imalda survives her surgery. She makes an appointment and meets with her attorney. Her attorney takes the information from the holographic will and updates Imalda's trust. When updating the trust, the attorney and Imalda discuss her wishes and refine her instructions. This includes updating her specific gifts to percentage distributions instead of monetary amounts. However, Imalda did not give the attorney the original holographic will. Instead, she gave the attorney a copy. Imalda never revoked the holographic will. In addition, she did not execute a new pour-over will. Upon Imalda's death, her handwritten note is declared to be her will (a holographic will) because it was the most recent will.*

In this scenario, the court acknowledges the existence of her trust and her holographic will because it was dated after her pour-over will (which would have transferred assets into the trust). Because the holographic will disposes of all of her assets to specific individuals and was executed after the pour-over will, the holographic will controls in place of the pour-over will. Although the trust exists, it was never funded (no assets were transferred into the trust, and the trust was not named as the beneficiary on Imalda Jean's accounts). The holographic will controls the complete disposition of Imalda Jean's assets, as her trust does not hold any assets to distribute. Her holographic will does not direct that the assets should be transferred into the trust. In addition, it does not reflect the changes that she and her attorney discussed. The will makes specific gifts that exceed the value of her estate. As a result, her residuary beneficiaries (her children) will not receive any assets.

Tip 2: If you draft a handwritten note or write on your original will, make sure to take the following steps:

- Inform your attorney about it.

- Bring the original and all copies to your attorney.

- Appropriately revoke the note by executing a new will.

- Using handwritten notes can be dangerous to your estate plan. Make sure that any handwritten notes regarding your estate plan are carefully discussed with your attorney to ensure that they are given the effect you desire and do not invalidate or harm your estate plan.

Sheena Moran

Sheena Moran opened S. M. Moran Law Office, P.C. in 2009. The firm specializes in estate planning to address high net worth, tax planning, business interests, family farms, and real estate.

26

Trust Terminology and Types of Trusts

By Amanda Wood (Woburn, Massachusetts)

One of the most important aspects of my job as an estate planning attorney is to provide my clients with the peace of mind knowing that their goals and concerns are being addressed and their wishes will be followed in the event of their passing. For many clients, achieving this peace of mind means acquiring a detailed and thorough understanding of their estate plan. Trusts, which are particularly dense legal documents, prompt a significant portion of my clients' questions. In this article, I will define trust terminology and explain some of the most common trusts we draft in the plain English that my clients so often request.

TRUST TERMINOLOGY

First, what is a trust, and who are the necessary parties when creating a trust? A *trust* is formed when a grantor conveys property to a trustee, who in turn holds the property for the grantor's beneficiaries. A *grantor,* also known as a settlor or trustor, is the person creating the trust. A *beneficiary* is someone who benefits from the trust, typically in the form of monetary distributions. A *trustee* is the person the grantor designates to hold and deal with trust property. The trustee has duties to follow the terms of the trust, act loyally in the interests of the beneficiaries and for the trust's purposes, and more. The duties of the trustee are known as fiduciary duties.

Though not necessary, trusts also commonly include a *trust protector,* who holds powers beyond those of the trustee. Just as it sounds, the trust protector's role is to protect the trust and its beneficiaries. Common responsibilities of a trust protector include removing an errant trustee or amending a trust to account for changes in the law.

There are a few general classifications into which all trusts fall. First, all trusts are either inter vivos or testamentary. An *inter vivos trust* is one that is established during the grantor's lifetime, while a *testamentary trust* is formed through the grantor's will after the grantor passes away. All trusts are also either revocable or irrevocable. A *revocable trust* is one that the grantor can amend (change) or revoke (take back altogether) during the grantor's lifetime. An *irrevocable trust,* on the other hand, is one that the grantor cannot amend or revoke after it is established.

Looking specifically at trust property and distribution, the first distinction is between principal and income. The property that the grantor transfers into the trust is called *trust principal* or trust corpus, which can be anything from real property to cash or brokerage accounts. *Income,* on the other hand, is the value that the trust principal earns. As an example, imagine that you change the ownership of your house so that it is owned by the trust, and later decide to move and rent it out. The house itself is the principal, but the money earned when your tenants pay their rent is trust income.

When choosing beneficiaries, clients' most common request by far is to split everything equally among their children. That split is often accomplished in documents using the legal term *per stirpes.* Per stirpes distribution requires that the assets be divided into equal shares based on the number of children the grantor has, with one share being allotted to each surviving child and the share for a predeceased child being further divided among the children of a predeceased child (i.e., the grantor's grandchildren).

TYPES OF TRUSTS

There are many kinds of trusts used to accomplish any number of different goals a client might have. As attorneys and advisors, it is our job to suggest the type of trust (or trusts) that will best achieve these goals. Presented below are brief explanations of the trusts we use most frequently.

First is the highly versatile revocable or living trust, sometimes called a family trust. *Family trusts* are revocable when established but become irrevocable upon the grantor's death to ensure that the grantor's wishes are carried out even after the grantor's death. These trusts typically seek to distribute an inheritance over time rather than in a lump sum, which makes them especially beneficial for families with children who are minors or younger adults. Distribution schemes are determined by the grantor but usually allow the trustee to distribute trust funds for discretionary needs while the children are young, with the remainder of the funds distributed at a stated age or series of ages during adulthood. Grantors can also include conditions for receiving distributions, such as attending college or receiving other higher education. Finally, as with all trusts, the family trust is used to keep assets out of probate and simplify the process for family and loved ones left behind after the grantor passes away.

The *credit shelter trust,* also called the A-B trust, bypass trust, or CS trust, is created on the death of the first spouse, typically under the provisions of a revocable trust, and is designed to minimize or eliminate estate taxes for married couples. Often, the first spouse to pass away simply leaves everything to the surviving spouse. What couples do not realize is that, absent proper planning, they are not utilizing the estate tax exemption available when the first spouse passes, possibly resulting in higher estate taxes when the second spouse passes. The provisions are complicated, but the job of the credit shelter trust is basically to reduce estate taxes by ensuring that both spouses' tax exemptions are used.

The *supplemental needs trust,* sometimes referred to as a special needs trust or SNT, is commonly used when a beneficiary is receiving government benefits. Since most government programs have asset or income limits, you must be careful not to leave the beneficiary an inheritance that will result in ineligibility and a loss of benefits. These trusts are written so that anything you leave the beneficiary only supplements, rather than supplants, the beneficiary's government benefits.

Finally, there is what we commonly refer to as a *Medicaid trust,* which is used to protect assets, most frequently a house, from Medicaid liens and estate recovery. This trust is complex and requires meticulous drafting to ensure compliance with strict, ever-changing Medicaid rules and regulations. The assets in the trust are protected after Medicaid's five-year lookback period has passed, allowing Medicaid recipients to leave these assets to their families rather than having to repay Medicaid for long-term care benefits paid on their behalf.

While this is by no means an exhaustive list of trusts or their terminology, these definitions should help to provide an understanding of trust basics, allowing for greater focus on the full picture of the estate plan and less focus on the complicated legalese.

Monteforte Law, P.C. specializes in estate planning and elder law. The firm has been in practice since 2006 and is located in Woburn, MA, just outside of Boston.

Amanda Wood

27

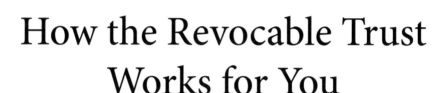

How the Revocable Trust Works for You

By Libby Banks (Scottsdale, Arizona)

The cornerstone of most estate plans is the revocable living trust (RLT). Contrary to what many believe, trusts are not just for the wealthy. RLTs provide benefits for most types of estates. In fact, there is no magic net worth above which a trust becomes the best plan for your assets. Rather, your family situation and the type of property you own are the two key factors to consider.

The following are a few of the advantages of using an RLT for your estate planning.

A REVOCABLE LIVING TRUST APPOINTS SOMEONE TO MANAGE YOUR FINANCES WHEN YOU ARE UNABLE TO

Wills and trusts both provide instructions about who should receive your assets after you die. However, an RLT also provides instructions for managing your assets and using them for your benefit if you are incapacitated. The trust names the trustee you selected and permits that person to easily step into your shoes to pay your bills, preserve your assets, liquidate properties, and generally ensure that your finances are managed and used for your benefit.

A REVOCABLE LIVING TRUST AVOIDS PROBATE, MAINTAINS PRIVACY, AND REDUCES THE COST OF WRAPPING UP YOUR ESTATE AT DEATH

A will tells the world who will receive your assets after your death. However, the will does not transfer the assets automatically. Instead, the person you appointed to wrap up your estate (your personal representative or executor) must submit the will, an application to be appointed executor, and other paperwork to the probate court to start the probate process. By contrast, a properly prepared and funded RLT will avoid the need for probate at your death. Since probate court filings are part of the public record, a trust also avoids the possibility of disclosing your assets to the public. With a trust, the person you selected to take charge of your estate will be able to step in quickly to gather, sell, and distribute your assets to your beneficiaries, very often without the need for court involvement.

Avoiding probate is usually a good idea. For example, in Arizona, where I practice, if you have specifically omitted one of your heirs from your estate plan, the probate court still requires that a notice be sent informing them that a probate has been filed—even though they are supposed to get nothing. As you can imagine, this may lead that person to contest the will in the probate proceeding.

Who are your heirs? If you have a spouse or children, they are your heirs. If you do not have a spouse or children, your heirs are your parents, siblings, and potentially any nieces and nephews, depending on the applicable state law that dictates the order of asset distribution.

HOW A REVOCABLE LIVING TRUST WORKS

I like to think of your RLT as your treasure chest. Your assets—that is, the things you worked and saved to accumulate—are transferred to your RLT. While you are alive and able, you manage those assets in your trust as the trustee and beneficiary.

How are assets transferred to the RLT? You title your home, bank account, stock brokerage account, and other assets in your name as trustee rather than in your individual name as owner. For instance, in Arizona, to transfer the home of a husband and wife (we will call them John and Ann Smith) to their trust, they prepare, sign, and record a deed to the house. The deed says that John Smith and Ann Smith, husband and wife, convey their house to John Smith and Ann Smith, Trustees of the John and Ann Smith Trust. You would follow a similar procedure for your other accounts and assets.

With an RLT, you control your financial affairs much the same as you do without a trust for as long as you are alive and competent. You can manage your assets, receive income, pay bills, buy and sell property, and so on. You have full control.

Your RLT also designates who will be in charge if you can no longer manage the trust assets because of death or incapacity. You decide who that will be and name that person in the trust document. The RLT tells the successor trustee how they should manage the trust assets and distribute money for your benefit if you are incapacitated. An RLT also contains your instructions for wrapping up your estate and distributing your assets at death.

My clients notice very little difference in how they handle their finances once they have the RLT in place and title their assets in their names as trustees. However, the person you have asked to be your successor trustee will certainly notice a difference in how much smoother it is to step in and take care of your financial affairs at incapacity or death with an RLT in place.

An RLT can also be amended, updated, and restated over time. It is not set in stone. For example, as your children get older or your designated trustees are not able to serve, you can amend the trust to address these changed circumstances.

A POUR-OVER WILL CATCHES WHAT IS NOT IN THE TRUST

When your estate plan is based on an RLT, you still sign a will, called a pour-over will. The pour-over will provides that any assets in your estate—in other words, assets that have not been transferred to your RLT before your death—and that do not have a named beneficiary, are to be transferred to the RLT by your executor or personal representative. If your RLT has been fully funded—meaning that ownership of all of the proper assets has been transferred to the trust before your death—then the will is never used. If the RLT has not been fully funded, then you may end up with a probate, during which the court will authorize your executor to transfer the property to the trust.

An estate plan using an RLT allows you to control your assets while you are able and allows your designated successor trustee to easily step in to manage your finances during incapacity and administer your trust at your death, all without probate and other costly court proceedings. It is easy to see why the RLT is the foundation of a good estate plan.

Libby Banks

The Law Office of Libby Banks is a boutique law firm focused on helping clients prepare estate plans that provide peace of mind. We always strive to establish relationships with our clients that are built on trust and mutual respect.

28

Joint or Separate Revocable Living Trusts

By Jerry D. Clinch (York, Nebraska)

Estate planning attorneys are routinely asked whether they recommend joint or separate revocable living trusts for married couples. The answer is not always cut-and-dried but may instead depend on a number of factors. For example, state law may dictate the advisability of a joint or separate revocable trust. A married couple's specific needs may also lead an attorney to recommend one over the other. In this author's opinion, the exclusive use of either joint or separate revocable living trusts for married couples—without careful consideration of the clients' circumstances—may not be advantageous unless, for example, the couple lives in a community property state where property is considered jointly owned by a married couple. In community property states, joint revocable living trusts may be your best (or only) option. Both types of trusts have a variety of advantages that should be considered in light of each couple's unique situation.

ADVANTAGES OF JOINT REVOCABLE LIVING TRUSTS

Generally easier for a married couple to fund and maintain. If all of a married couple's assets are held in a single joint revocable living trust, then the couple will not need to equalize the value of two separate revocable living trusts or decide which assets will be titled to each of them. When assets are jointly owned by a married couple, dividing the assets into separate revocable living trusts requires some additional considerations and steps to ensure proper funding of those trusts. For example, if a couple owns a second home jointly with right of survivorship, they will need to decide whether the second home will be placed fractionally into each spouse's separate trust (e.g., each trust owns 50 percent of the marital home), or if only one of the separate revocable living trusts will own the house entirely. If one spouse has a higher likelihood of being sued, such as a spouse who works as a surgeon, full ownership by the other spouse's separate trust may be advisable.

More streamlined tax filings during the spouses' lives. Joint revocable living trusts do not pay income taxes during the spouses' lifetimes; rather, the trust income is reported on the spouses' personal income tax return. On the death of the second spouse, the revocable living trust becomes an irrevocable trust. Unlike a revocable living trust, an irrevocable trust is treated as an entity that is legally independent of its grantors (i.e., the spouses) for tax purposes, and therefore, the trust must file its own return (Internal Revenue Service Form 1041). Because a joint revocable living trust often does not become irrevocable until both spouses have passed away, a Form 1041 often does not have to be prepared for the trust after the first spouse dies.[1] If the spouses had instead created two separate revocable living trusts, then at the death of the first spouse, the deceased spouse's trust would become irrevocable, and a Form 1041 may have to be filed annually. Further, a joint revocable living trust that does not become irrevocable at the first spouse's death would not subject a surviving spouse to the higher tax brackets associated with a deceased spouse's separate irrevocable trust. In contrast, separate trusts may result in additional tax liability for income generated by the deceased spouse's separate trust due to higher trust tax brackets.

Gives a surviving spouse complete control of the assets in the joint revocable living trust. A joint revocable living trust often does not become irrevocable upon the death of the first spouse. With separate revocable living trusts, a deceased spouse's trust becomes irrevocable at their death, and a surviving spouse will typically have limited control over those assets. In that situation, the trust instrument may restrict distributions to those necessary to provide for the surviving spouse's health, education, maintenance, and support.

Can simplify real estate transactions. When real estate, such as a house, is placed in a married couple's joint revocable living trust, it becomes owned by the trust. This can make it easier for the surviving spouse to sell the real estate and purchase other real estate. A bank may be less likely to issue a loan for a surviving spouse if real estate is held in a deceased spouse's separate irrevocable trust.

---

1 It is possible to have a joint trust with a separate share for each spouse, and the share of the first spouse to die becomes irrevocable upon their death. Such a trust functions more like separate trusts than the joint trusts described in this article.

ADVANTAGES OF SEPARATE REVOCABLE LIVING TRUSTS

May offer better protection from creditors. Upon the death of the first spouse, the deceased spouse's trust becomes irrevocable, making it more difficult for potential creditors to access the assets in the deceased spouse's trust while still providing the surviving spouse with access to assets held by the deceased spouse's trust to meet certain needs. Whether separate revocable living trusts may protect one spouse from the financial risks posed by creditors may depend upon the law in your state.

Can help provide for children from a prior marriage. Divorce is now common. Many people remarry after a divorce, often resulting in blended families in which one spouse is a child's biological parent and the other spouse is a stepparent. In a blended family situation, separate revocable living trusts can help ensure that a surviving spouse is provided for during life while also potentially ensuring that the children in a blended family will eventually receive the funds. Simply put, joint revocable living trusts do not work well if the spouses have different ideas about how money and property will be handled after the death of the first spouse.

Can simplify administration after a spouse dies. Separate revocable living trusts allow spouses to designate how they want the assets in their separate trusts distributed upon their deaths, with each spouse specifying who will inherit and what is left to the surviving spouse.

May help protect a spouse's inheritance or a prenuptial agreement. If a spouse is expecting to receive an inheritance that they wish to protect, or if a married couple has executed a prenuptial agreement, separate revocable living trusts can be of great benefit in keeping assets separate. This may simplify the process in the event of divorce.

May be a great option for farmers and their spouses. In Nebraska, farming is a common profession. It is not unusual for a husband to run the farm and a wife to manage the household. Statistically speaking, if a husband and wife are approximately the same age, the wife will likely outlive the husband. If the husband, who has been farming all his life, dies before his wife, and the wife is unable to continue the farming operation, separate revocable living trusts can be very valuable if set up correctly. In this scenario, it may be advisable for the married couple to place all farm equipment, livestock, and farm ground in the husband's separate trust. When the husband passes away, all of the farm equipment, livestock, and farm ground can be transferred to the surviving spouse's trust, which will receive a full step-up in basis, thereby enabling the surviving spouse to proceed with a tax-free sale of the farm if she will not continue the operation of the farm.

ESTATE TAX CONSIDERATIONS WITH JOINT AND SEPARATE REVOCABLE LIVING TRUSTS

Joint revocable living trusts and separate revocable living trusts, if properly drafted, can provide the same estate tax benefits. A joint revocable living trust intended to manage a situation in which the estate involved is worth more than the current federal estate tax exemption (in 2022, $12.06 million per individual) might be structured as follows[2]:

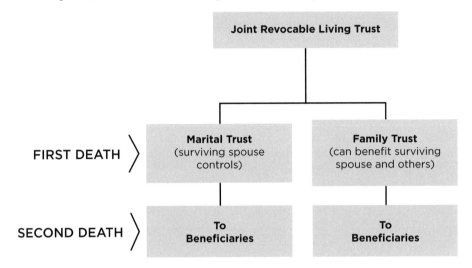

A WORD OF CAUTION CONCERNING SEPARATE TRUSTS IN COMMUNITY PROPERTY STATES

Separate revocable living trusts may not be appropriate in community property states. In those states (currently, Arizona, California, Idaho, Louisiana, Nevada, New Mexico, Texas, Washington, and Wisconsin), property acquired during a marriage is considered to be jointly owned by both spouses. A few other states, such as Alaska and Tennessee, are elective community property states, and married couples there may elect to treat certain property as community property. Thus, it may be advisable to use a joint revocable living trust in a community property state or elective community property state to preserve the status of the community property.

CONCLUSION

Joint revocable living trusts and separate revocable living trusts both have advantages and disadvantages. A qualified estate planning attorney can assist you and your spouse

---

2 This kind of joint revocable trust typically involves separate shares for each spouse, and the share of the first spouse to die becomes irrevocable upon their death.

in evaluating which type of revocable living trust is best suited to your needs and tailor an estate plan to achieve your goals.

Jerry Clinch

Clinch Law Firm, LLC (www.clinchlawfirm.com) focuses on preserving wealth by assisting clients with their estate, asset protection, and business planning needs.

29

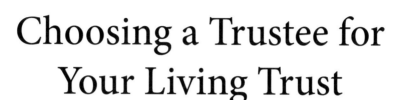

Choosing a Trustee for Your Living Trust

By Arthur Pauly (Roseville, California)

O ne of the most important questions I am asked by clients is whom they should name as their trustee. In most cases, the person who creates a living trust (or spouses who create a joint trust) acts as the initial trustee of the trust until that person dies or becomes mentally incompetent. It is crucial that the trust instrument name a successor trustee—and an alternate successor trustee—to step into the role when the original trustee is no longer able to fill it.

WHAT IS A TRUSTEE?

A trustee is the legal owner of the assets held by the trust. The following chart[1] provides an overview of a trustee's responsibilities, which vary depending upon whether the trustmaker is incapacitated or has died.

---

1   WealthCounsel, LLC, *Duties and Responsibilities of a Trustee*, Est. Plan. (Nov. 5, 2020), https://www.estateplanning.com/duties-and-responsibilities-of-a-trustee.

WHAT A TRUSTEE DOES

AT INCAPACITY

- Oversees care of ill person
- Understands insurance benefits and limitations
- Looks after care of any minors and dependents
- Applies for disability benefits
- Puts together team of advisors
- Notifies bank and others
- Transacts necessary business
- Keeps accurate records and accounting

AT DEATH

- Contacts attorney to review trust and process
- Keeps beneficiaries informed
- Puts together team of advisors
- Inventories assets, determines current values
- Makes partial distributions if needed
- Collects benefits, keeps records, files tax returns
- Pays bills, does final accounting
- Distributes assets to beneficiaries as trust directs

A trustee is exactly what the term implies: a trusted person, who is known by law as a fiduciary. It is someone you trust to follow the instructions you have provided in the trust document. A trustee has a legal obligation—that is, a fiduciary duty—to manage, invest, and distribute the trust assets in the best interests of the trust beneficiaries, so it is important to choose a trustee that is not only trustworthy but also has the knowledge and ability to perform their duties and the willingness to seek the help of an estate planning attorney or other advisor when necessary.

Trustees may be called upon to navigate special circumstances, such as when a trust beneficiary is a spendthrift or suffers from an addiction. For example, consider the situation of my clients from many years ago. They had an estate valued at $11 million. Their only child, a son, was ready to graduate from a prestigious college and had a high-paying job awaiting him. However, my clients believed that their son's fiancée spent too much money, and they wanted to be sure that the money that would go to their son would not be spent quickly. I suggested that the money be held in a trust and that the trust's income be distributed to their son each year. Then, when their son reached a certain age, all of the funds in the trust would be distributed to him. Consequently, their trustee needed to be capable of managing and investing the funds held in the trust in the best interests of the son and distributing them outright to the son when he reached the age specified in the trust document. I also had clients who had a son who was a drug addict. My clients did not want to disinherit their son, but they also did not want any money to go directly to him. The trust document instructed the trustee to buy their son what he needed but not give him cash. In this situation, the trustee needed to play a more active, hands-on role, had to strictly adhere to the instructions in the trust document, and had to resist any pressure from the son or other family members to provide him with cash.

CAN THERE BE MORE THAN ONE TRUSTEE?

Parents who create a trust may want all of their children to act as joint trustees. This is certainly permitted, but it is important to keep in mind that joint trustees typically act as a pure democracy. For example, if there are two trustees and they disagree about a particular action or they just do not get along with each other, then there may be a deadlock that prevents any action. In deciding whether to name your children as joint trustees, you should consider how well the children get along. If there is an even number of children, include another trustee who can act as a tiebreaker.

Another solution for parents who want all of their children to serve as trustees is to provide for a succession of trustees in the trust document. For example, the trust could name the oldest as the first trustee. If that child is not able to serve as the trustee, then the second or third child could serve as the trustee.

DOES THE TRUSTEE'S LOCATION MATTER?

Given modern methods of communication and document transfer, it is no longer as important for the trustee to be in the same location as the trustmaker, although it certainly can simplify administration. However, an out-of-town trustee will occasionally need to travel to deal with your trust's assets. For example, if your trustee is your son who lives on the east coast and you live on the west coast, it will be necessary for him to travel across the country when he needs to be physically present to sign documents. If there is more than one trustee, meeting logistics may be a challenge.

CAN A NONFAMILY MEMBER SERVE AS TRUSTEE?

You can name someone you trust outside of your immediate family to act as your successor trustee. A lawyer could also serve as your trustee; however, I do not act as the trustee in situations where I have created the trust for the clients, because I believe it presents a conflict of interest. In addition, a certified public accountant, banker, or financial planner could be named as the trustee. It is important to ask the person you want to serve as your trustee to ensure that they are willing to take on the responsibility.

There are also professional fiduciary companies that serve as trustees. Many banks have them, or you could hire an independent professional fiduciary. They will not become involved until you die or become mentally incompetent, at which point they will become the successor trustee. Some clients feel there are drawbacks to using professional fiduciaries. For example, professional fiduciaries charge a fee, which may be substantial. They may also be fairly impersonal and may not be concerned about family dynamics.

Selecting a successor trustee is not a decision that should be taken lightly. In fact, when I meet with clients to create a trust, I do not ask them to select a trustee right away. The estate planning process must not be rushed. You should take time to carefully consider whom you would want to name as a trustee. Many families, mine included, have a meeting with the children to ask who they think would be a good trustee. My brothers and sisters thought that I, as the only lawyer in the family, should serve as the trustee for my parents' trust.

CAN THE SUCCESSOR TRUSTEE SERVE AS A GUARDIAN FOR MINOR CHILDREN?

The trustee can serve as a guardian for minor children, but the two jobs are very different. The chosen guardian must be someone you would be comfortable with stepping into your shoes as a parent. They will need to shelter, care for, educate, and love your children as a parent. In contrast, the trustee manages the assets. You carry out both roles as a parent, but that is a big burden to place on someone else. Many of my clients like the idea of having different people fill the two roles as a way of providing checks and balances.

IS THE TRUSTEE ENTITLED TO COMPENSATION?

The law allows the trustee to charge a "reasonable fee." In my experience, the reasonableness of the fee is typically based on what banks and other professional fiduciaries charge. The trustee is also entitled to be reimbursed for any expenses they may incur.

WHAT IS A TRUST PROTECTOR?

If you do not want to exclude a family member but are not entirely confident in their ability to serve as a trustee, you can consider appointing a trust protector. A trust protector has powers over the trustee, and if the trustee does not administer the trust as required by the trust document or does so in a way that harms the interests of the trust beneficiaries, the trust protector can remove the trustee and appoint another one.

CONTACT YOUR QUALIFIED ESTATE PLANNING ATTORNEY

The attorney sitting across the table from you during your estate planning meeting is the most valuable source of information you will find. Most can share stories based on their previous experiences with clients, the decisions they made, and the results of those decisions—good and bad. Take advantage of their knowledge and experience.

RECAP

1. Identify your wishes for your estate before selecting a successor trustee.

2. The successor trustee should be a person or persons you trust to carry out your wishes.

3. If you select more than one trustee, make sure they get along.

4. Seek advice from your estate planning attorney. An experienced estate planning attorney can share a wealth of knowledge with you.

With thirty years' experience as an estate planning attorney, Arthur Pauly brings his knowledge, expertise, resources, and philosophy to every client he serves. He provides personal and professional estate planning in your own home or business.

Arthur Pauly

30

Funding Your Trust

By Becky Cholewka (Gilbert, Arizona)

A safe can be fireproof. It can be waterproof. It can be burglarproof. But if there is nothing in the safe, it is merely an expensive box that does not protect anything.

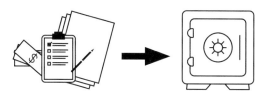

A trust is like a safe. A trust is a legal document that provides many protections. But if assets are not titled in the name of the trust, it does not protect anything.

Trust funding is the process of transferring or retitling your assets from your individual name (or joint names if you are married) to the name of your trust. To do this, you must physically change the titles of assets such as property deeds and bank accounts. You may also change beneficiary designations on assets such as life insurance policies to name your trust, which means these assets will be transferred to your trust at your death. Unless you take this very important step, your trust will not enable your family or loved ones to avoid court proceedings if you become incapacitated or avoid probate when you die.

WHO IS RESPONSIBLE FOR FUNDING MY TRUST?

You are ultimately responsible for making sure all of the appropriate assets are transferred to your trust. Your attorney may assist you with transferring all or some of these assets and should provide guidance on how to fund your trust.

WHAT SHOULD I DO FIRST?

You should discuss funding your trust with your attorney. Depending on your specific estate planning goals, how your trust is structured, and the types of assets you have, your attorney can tell you which assets should be titled in the name of your trust now and which assets should be transferred to your trust when you die. Making the wrong decision could have adverse tax or probate consequences.

HOW DIFFICULT IS THE FUNDING PROCESS?

Funding is not difficult, but it can be cumbersome and time-consuming. Many people get sidetracked or procrastinate, which is why their trust remains "empty." To be successful, prioritize funding your trust and keep going until you are finished. Make a list of your assets, their values, and their locations. Start with the most valuable assets and work your way down the list. Each time you buy a new asset or open a new account, consult with your attorney to determine whether it should be titled in the name of your trust.

WHAT HAPPENS IF I FORGET TO TRANSFER AN ASSET TO MY TRUST?

If you have a trust, you should also have a pour-over will that acts like a safety net. When you die, the will "catches" any forgotten asset and "pours" it into your trust. The asset will likely be included in your state's probate court proceeding first, but eventually, it will be distributed according to the instructions in your trust.

HOW DO I TITLE ASSETS IN THE NAME OF MY TRUST?

You should request paperwork from institutions such as banks and brokerage companies to change your accounts from your individual or joint name to the name of your trust. A common format for retitling assets to your trust is as follows:

> Tony Stark, Trustee of the Avengers Trust dated May 4, 2012, and any amendments thereto.

WHICH ASSETS SHOULD BE TITLED IN MY TRUST NOW?

Do you remember the candy called Now and Later®? Just like the candy, some of your assets should be titled in the name of your trust now, and some of your assets should be titled in the name of your trust later. Most of your liquid assets and personal belongings should be retitled in the name of your trust now. Here is a general list, though as mentioned above you should discuss with your own attorney before proceeding.

- **Personal belongings** such as household items, pictures, electronics, clothes, jewelry, and tools can be titled in the name of your trust in the trust document or by an Assignment of Tangible Assets to your trust. Your attorney can help with this.

- **Checking and savings accounts** should be retitled in the name of your trust. Some banks may not allow trust accounts, and some banks may insist that you open a new account instead of transferring your existing account into the trust's name.

- **Brokerage accounts** should be retitled in the name of your trust, similar to a checking or savings account.

- **Paper stocks** can be retitled by opening a brokerage or investment account in the name of your trust and depositing your original certificates in this account.

- **Paper bonds** can be mailed to the US Treasury after you open a new account at http://www.treasurydirect.gov. You should consider purchasing insurance when you mail the paper bonds.

- **Business interests** should be discussed with your business attorney. Partnership and limited liability company interests can be retitled in an assignment document. Corporate interests can be retitled by canceling shares held in your name and reissuing shares in the name of your trust.

- **Vehicles** can be retitled in the name of your trust through the motor vehicle department of your state if your state does not have a vehicle beneficiary form.

- **Boats** can be retitled in the name of your trust. In some states this is done through the game and fish department, and in other states it is through the motor vehicle department.

- **Real property** should be retitled in the name of your trust unless your state allows a beneficiary deed that can transfer your interests to your trust at your death. Some states tax the transfer of real property between an individual and a trust.

WHICH ASSETS SHOULD BE TITLED IN MY TRUST LATER?

Some assets cannot be funded into your trust without adverse consequences until you die, such as individual retirement accounts and 401(k) plans. Some assets can be titled in the name of your trust effective upon your death under your state's laws. Here is a general list.

- **Real property** can be transferred to your trust when you die through a beneficiary deed, but fewer than twenty states currently recognize these types of deeds. This type of deed may be preferred if you still have a mortgage on the property.

- **Retirement accounts** must be titled in the name of an individual but can be transferred to a trust at death by naming the trust as a beneficiary on a beneficiary form. These assets are subject to complex Internal Revenue Service rules and titling formats. You should consult your attorney before naming your trust as the beneficiary of your retirement accounts.

- **Insurance and annuity policies** are transferred to a trust by naming the trust as a primary or secondary beneficiary on the beneficiary form.

- **Vehicles** can be transferred to a trust using a beneficiary form available from your state's motor vehicle department. About fifteen states currently offer these forms.

- **529 accounts** are typically held by an individual rather than a trust, but you can name a successor custodian on these accounts.

- **Cryptocurrency** that cannot be held in an account owned by a trust should be listed on your trust schedules so that your trustee is aware of these assets. In a separate document, you should detail how the trustee can find and access your wallet, keys, and coins.

HOW OFTEN DO I NEED TO FUND MY TRUST?

You should review your current assets with your attorney every two years to ensure that all are properly titled. Determining which assets to title to your trust now, later, or never will depend on current tax laws, goals such as Medicaid planning, and how your trust is structured to leave money to your beneficiaries.

Becky Cholewka realized the importance of estate planning when her dad unexpectedly died when she was only nineteen years old. She specializes in estate planning and probate in Gilbert, Arizona.

Becky Cholewka

31

Operation and Merger of Trusts for the Next Generation

By Roger McClure (Fairfax, Virginia)

P aul and Mary have set up two living trusts: one for Paul, who is a medical doctor at high risk for a malpractice lawsuit, and one for Mary, who buys, sells, and rents out rental homes. Although they have a solid lifetime marriage and hold almost everything in joint accounts, they use separate trusts to limit liabilities for the other spouse and discourage lenders from requiring joint guarantees. They have an estate of $3 million that is growing as Paul makes contributions to his retirement account and as the value of Mary's real estate portfolio increases. They have three children: Paul Jr., Sarah, and Martha. Martha and Sarah are medical doctors. Paul Jr. was a race car driver, but had a bad accident in an Indianapolis 500 race and has never fully recovered. He has mental and physical disabilities and cannot support himself.

Paul purchased life insurance that he has placed into an irrevocable life insurance trust (ILIT), with Mary and the three children as beneficiaries. The ILIT has two major advantages: it allows the life insurance policy benefits to avoid being subject to estate taxes and protects the cash value in the policy against the personal creditors of Paul and Mary.

Mary has a limited liability holding company that owns her buy-and-hold real estate. Her children are silent partners in this limited liability company (LLC). She has separate LLCs for properties that she renovates and sells for an immediate profit. The LLC documents specify that, upon her death, her membership interests will pass to her living trust, and Sarah and Martha will take over the management of the LLC.

Under their ILIT, the LLC, and their living trusts, all of the inheritances allocated to the children will go to three separate trusts for the children created in each trust document. The trust documents for the living trusts and the ILIT create separate trusts for Paul Jr., Sarah, and Martha. These trusts will go into effect upon the deaths of Mary and Paul and the completion of administration. The separate share trust provisions for each child created in the ILIT and the Paul and Mary living trusts contain identical language, identical trustees, and Paul Jr., Martha, and Sarah as beneficiaries.

Because they were created in Paul's and Mary's trust documents, the separate share trusts provide the following benefits: (1) asset protection for the daughters (who, as doctors, are in a profession with high liability risk); (2) estate tax-exempt status for most of the assets in the children's estates; (3) the establishment of the trust assets as distinct from marital assets subject to division upon a child's divorce; and (4) trust assets shielded from limiting the government assistance provided to Paul Jr.

Mary and Paul die, leaving a total estate of $6 million, including the death benefit of the life insurance policy held in the ILIT. Each child will receive $2 million because Mary and Paul divided their estate equally among their three children.

The assets in the three trusts will be liquidated into cash and securities during estate administration. As trustees, Sarah and Martha must then follow the language of the living trusts and the ILIT that require the merger of trusts when the trustees and the beneficiaries are the same and such a merger does not interfere with the rights of the trust beneficiaries. Mergers are also usually permitted under state law. The trustees order the mergers to go into effect by signing the merger agreement. The beneficiaries consent to the mergers after appropriate notice. Now, there is just one Paul Jr. trust, one Martha trust, and one Sarah trust. The Paul living trust is chosen to be the recipient of the other trusts to enable the use of its retirement plan provisions.

It will be difficult to administer the three separate share trusts using the provisions of the Paul living trust because it includes many provisions applicable to Paul and Mary while they were alive and few about the trusts created for the children. Banks, brokerage houses, and title companies do not have sufficient staff to search through the trust document to determine which provisions apply, for example, only to Paul Jr.

The solution to this problem is to name a trust protector who can decant and restate the merged trusts into separate new trust documents. Then, there will be a trust document for the Paul Jr. trust that can be given to a financial institution or trust company that will apply only to Paul Jr.

At this point, the trust protector must determine whether there must be a subtrust or a separate trust to hold any retirement accounts from Paul Sr. The trust protector will also determine whether the trust for Paul Jr. will be a special needs trust that allows Paul Jr. to receive trust distributions only for his special needs, without losing his access to government disability benefits.

To establish the separate standalone trust documents, the trust protector decants these trusts into three separate new standalone trusts for Sarah, Martha, and Paul Jr. The trust protector orders the creation of the standalone trusts with the consent of all of the beneficiaries to the new trust documents. If there is no trust protector, the decanting may be done by the trustees. Once the trusts are created, the trustees, Sarah and Martha, distribute all of the assets from the Paul and Mary living trusts and the ILIT to the new standalone separate share trusts of Martha, Sarah, and Paul Jr. The trustees named in each standalone trust instrument consent to serve as trustees.

Sarah is now the trustee of her standalone trust and appoints her certified public accountant (CPA) as a co-trustee. Sarah and the CPA can determine which investments are proper for her trust. She has the discretion to take out funds for her health, education, and maintenance. Since the trust is in a higher tax bracket than Sarah is, she distributes the net taxable income out of her trust every year to herself. Because the assets in her trust are highly protected against lawsuits and marital claims, she invests in growth stocks to provide for a very good retirement income and as part of her plan to leave a lot of the assets in protected trusts to her children.

Martha decides to retire early and, with her funds and the income from her trust, she pursues a Ph.D. in art history and becomes a low-paid museum curator in late Renaissance Italian art.

Paul Jr. is receiving government assistance and cannot be a trustee. Sarah and Martha serve as his primary trustees, but delegate investments and tax reporting to trusted professionals. The trust for Paul Jr. pays for his special needs for the rest of his life. Since Paul Jr. did not marry, if there are funds left in his trust at the end of his life, then those funds go to Sarah and Martha and their children.

By creating their trust-based estate plan, including the provisions allowing the merger of trusts and the appointment of trust protectors, Paul and Mary have created efficient multigenerational safety nets and launching pads for their children and grandchildren.

Roger McClure has over forty years of experience in business and estate planning, has published many articles in national publications, and is a sought-after national speaker. He provides very practical and useful advice to family-owned businesses, from basic to very advanced planning.

Roger McClure

32

Trust Decanting and Modification

By Gregory Herman-Giddens
(Naples, Florida and Chapel Hill, North Carolina)

Irrevocable trusts have been popular estate planning tools for many decades. Tax savings, asset protection, Medicaid planning, and management of the property of minors and disabled persons are all reasons to use an irrevocable trust. The trouble with irrevocable trusts, however, has been that they cannot be revoked or changed. In the past, if a trust became outdated or no longer fit the needs of the grantor or beneficiary, there was little that could be done in most situations.

However, with the adoption of the Uniform Trust Code (UTC) by many states in the early 2000s, it has become much easier to change an irrevocable trust. As of August 2021, thirty-five states have adopted the UTC. Although the UTC includes the word "Uniform" in its name, this does not mean that all states have the same laws. Each state has made its own adaptations to the UTC. That being said, in general, each state's version of the UTC has similar features that now allow an irrevocable trust to be modified in certain circumstances.

WHY MIGHT YOU WANT TO CHANGE A TRUST?

A trust would need to be modified in order to take the following actions:

- Move the trust to another state to avoid state income taxes or take advantage of more favorable trust laws

- Correct errors or omissions in the trust

- Remove and replace a recalcitrant trustee

- Add family members as beneficiaries

- Provide the beneficiaries with greater protection from possible lawsuits, divorce, substance abuse, etc.

- Qualify a beneficiary for needs-based governmental benefits, such as Medicaid

- Obtain a step-up in the tax basis of appreciated assets at the death of the trust beneficiary

Many older trusts are not designed to allow a step-up in basis. When there is a step-up in basis, the cost basis of an owner's appreciated asset is adjusted up to its fair market value when it passes from an owner to the heir on the owner's death. The new "stepped-up" basis at the time of inheritance becomes the heir's cost basis for tax purposes. The benefit to a beneficiary of a step-up in basis is that the beneficiary's capital gains tax (i.e., the tax on the difference between an asset's cost basis and its market value at the time it is sold) is minimized. If the appreciation is significant, the tax savings can amount to hundreds of thousands of dollars.

There are two primary mechanisms for modifying a trust: trust modification and decanting. Trust modification can be further subdivided into nonjudicial modification and judicial modification.

NONJUDICIAL MODIFICATION

When the person who set up a trust (the grantor or settlor) is still alive and competent, a trust can be changed by agreement between the grantor and the beneficiaries without court approval. In some states, a trust can be modified by agreement and without court approval even if the grantor is not alive or not competent, if certain other conditions are met. If the beneficiaries are minors, a parent can generally act on their behalf. The trust is then modified by written agreement among the parties. Sometimes, just one or two clauses are changed, but the trust can also be entirely redone.

Most nonjudicial modifications are done in accordance with the law of the state that controls the trust. Virtually all trusts contain provisions that establish the trust's situs (where the trust is located) and governing law (the law that must be followed in the administration of the trust). The requirements of this law must be followed to implement the modification.

Nonjudicial modification can also be accomplished by including language in a trust that allows an independent trustee (i.e., a trustee who is not a beneficiary or a family member of the beneficiary) or an independent trust protector to change a trust. The advantage of these provisions is that they avoid the stricter requirements of state law and the need to have all beneficiaries agree. However, these provisions must be included at the time the trust is drafted, so they are rarely seen in older trusts.

JUDICIAL MODIFICATION

If the grantor is not alive or able to consent, the grantor is alive but the parties cannot agree on a change, or a nonjudicial modification is otherwise not feasible, a beneficiary (or a trustee, at least in some states) can petition the court to modify the trust. If the grantor is deceased, the court will generally approve the change only if all parties agree and the material purposes of the trust are not violated. If the beneficiaries do not unanimously agree to the change, the court will often not approve it without a significant reason. An example of a significant reason would be to allow the trustee to have more control to ultimately protect and benefit a beneficiary who has become addicted to drugs.

TRUST DECANTING

Trust decanting occurs when the trustee of one trust pours some or all of the assets of that trust into another trust. A trustee can decant into an existing trust or create a new trust to receive the assets. Like trust modification, decanting is usually done in accordance with the law of the state governing the trust, though some states' decanting laws also apply to trusts administered in the state. The beneficiaries must be notified and given the opportunity to object in court. In at least some states, when the grantor of a trust is deceased, decanting is usually easier to accomplish than trust modification.

A trustee's ability to decant can be built into a trust document, in which case the trustee must simply follow the decanting instructions in the trust. Compliance with state law is not required. While such a provision is rarely seen in trusts that are more than a few years old, it can be very useful should circumstances change in the future.

Finally, in some states, a trustee can decant under common law—that is, general principles of law that are not written into statute. In some cases, common law decanting can be easier than following statutory law.

EXAMPLE OF STATUTORY DECANTING

Suppose a husband's late mother created a Florida trust with the husband as trustee and beneficiary. At the husband's death, the trust was to pay out all of the trust assets to the husband's wife and children. Since the trust provided substantial income for the couple, the husband did not want to leave his wife without support should he be the first to die.

The trust did not include a provision allowing an independent trustee or trust protector to change the trust, nor did it have a decanting provision. Nonjudicial modification was not available since the grantor was deceased, and judicial modification would have been expensive, with an uncertain outcome. So, the husband was left with statutory decanting as the best option.

Based on the wording of the distribution standard in the trust, decanting under Florida law would not achieve the desired result of providing lifetime income to the wife. Luckily, the trust included a provision to allow the trustee to change the trust situs to another state. North Carolina, where the couple lived, has somewhat more liberal decanting laws, so the situs and governing law were changed to that state. The trustee then resigned and appointed an independent trustee, as decanting cannot be done by a trustee who is also a beneficiary.

The new trustee gave the required notice to the husband and his children as beneficiaries, with a copy of the proposed new trust. The beneficiaries waived the sixty-day waiting requirement. The trustee was then able to immediately execute the new trust with the husband as trustee and beneficiary, with a provision granting the husband a testamentary general power of appointment.

The effect of including the power of appointment was twofold. First, it allowed the husband to exercise it in favor of his wife at the time of his death, by directing that the trust assets be held in trust for her benefit for her life, with the remainder to their children. Second, it made the trust assets includible in his estate for federal estate tax purposes, so that all appreciated assets in the trust would get a step-up in tax basis at his death, potentially saving tens of thousands of dollars or more for the benefit of the family.

As you can see, there are multiple ways to fix a broken trust. If you or someone you know is the grantor or beneficiary of a trust that is in need of a change, consult with an experienced trust attorney. Chances are that there is at least a partial fix available.

Based in Naples, Florida, with an office in Chapel Hill, North Carolina, and a second home in Manhattan, Greg Herman-Giddens, JD, LLM, TEP, CFP® works with clients throughout Florida, North Carolina, and New York. A board-certified specialist in estate planning and probate law, Greg also serves as an expert witness in trust and estate litigation.

Greg Herman-Giddens

33

The Importance of Keeping Your Estate Plan Updated

By Michael Monteforte Jr. (Woburn, Massachusetts)

IMAGINE THIS . . .

You have done your research and have found an estate planning attorney that is a perfect fit. The attorney has glowing reviews and has published work in the field of trusts and estates. After the consultation, you know that your estate plan will be done right. You pay a good-sized fee, but the peace of mind is worth it because the estate plan addresses all of your concerns. You now have a last will to direct where your property will go when you pass, a durable power of attorney (POA) naming someone to make financial decisions for you if you cannot do it yourself, a healthcare proxy (HCP) naming someone to make healthcare decisions for you if you cannot do it yourself, and a family trust to ensure the inheritance you leave for your children is used for their benefit, no one else's, and is distributed over time at specified intervals.

You feel smart, accomplished, and relieved—the planning you had been putting off is finally done. You put your documents in a lockbox and never pull them out again.

Time ticks by. You never go back and review the plan, and you never have any further contact with your lawyer. Years later, you are not even sure of their name. But that is okay, because you did it, right? And once it is done, it is done. Isn't it?

No, it is not. Not by a long shot.

Imagine that twenty years have gone by and you have not thought about your estate plan again. During those twenty years, you got married, had three children, got divorced, remarried, had a fourth child with your second spouse, found a great job with a great salary, bought a home, and are now planning for retirement. Those are common life events. However, you never bothered to change your estate plan; you thought they would all be covered by your decades-old plan.

Ten more years go by. Now you are in your late sixties and showing some signs of early onset dementia. You have some money set aside for retirement, and it is a nice nest egg. Long-term care seems like it is still down the road, but it is a lot closer than you think. Although you are not aware of it, there have been substantial changes in the law. You suffer a stroke. You do not have the legal ability to make your own financial and healthcare decisions or determine where your assets should go. Now what?

AN OUTDATED ESTATE PLAN MAY HAVE HORRIBLE CONSEQUENCES

Some states automatically revoke provisions for or appointing your former spouse (and possibly your former spouse's relatives) in your existing plan if you divorce after you created it. If you die with a will that only names your spouse as a beneficiary, you will be intestate, which is when someone dies without a will. If you die intestate, the law of the state in which you live determines where your assets go. The shares for your family, including your children from the first marriage and your younger child from your second marriage, would be determined under those state laws.

If your home state *does not* revoke your estate plan because of the divorce and your old documents are still fully valid, you are stuck with the *wrong* plan. The estate planning needs of a sixty-year-old are vastly different from those of a thirty-year-old.

First, your old plan does not include all of the right people. Your ex-spouse is still your named POA and HCP. Obviously, that is inappropriate. The backup agent is your brother, because you made these documents before your second marriage. Your ex-spouse is concerned about her children receiving their share, and she does not care if any inheritance goes to your current spouse and youngest child. Likewise, your old will does not even mention your youngest child, and your ex-spouse insists that you would have added your youngest if you had wanted her in the will. Your spouse and youngest child may be entitled to shares of your estate under your state's omitted spouse and omitted child statutes, but those shares might not be the amounts you actually want your spouse and youngest child to receive. An updated will, POA, and HCP completed after your second marriage would have prevented these problems. Instead, your ex-wife and current wife are preparing for war, your kids are in the middle of it, and the estate funds will be squandered on tens of thousands of dollars (at least!) in attorney's fees.

Your old family trust does not provide any estate tax protection. At the time you created the plan, you did not have enough money to be affected by estate taxes. Now, if you die with a substantial enough estate, the government is going to take a huge bite before *any* family members get a share. With a revised trust, hundreds of thousands of dollars in estate taxes could have been saved.

Your old plan does not provide any protection for your home against long-term care costs, and you will need long-term care because of the stroke. An updated plan could have included a Medicaid irrevocable income-only trust for your home to protect it from a Medicaid lien for long-term care costs. Instead, a lien may attach to your home for every single penny that Medicaid pays to your nursing home, and Medicaid would be entitled to all of that money if the home is sold. There goes your home equity.

Sadly, this happens all the time when estate plans are not updated after life events. Regular updates to your plan will save you time and money, reduce taxes, protect your assets, and keep your family from killing each other and blowing money on lawyer fees.

If you already have a plan, it does not end there. A good estate plan should be updated regularly, and you should review it with your estate planning attorney at least once per year. Let your lawyer know about changes in your life, and your lawyer can talk with you about changes in the law. If you do not, you risk making this story come true. Do not let this happen to you and your family.

A WORD ABOUT LONGEVITY OR LEGACY PLANS

More estate planning attorneys are offering legacy plans that make it easier for you to stay in touch and make changes to your plan over time. The process never really ends. How can it? Your family and finances are constantly changing. The law is constantly changing as well. What good is an estate plan that does not change with you?

Firms that offer legacy plans stay in touch regarding changes in your life and in the law. A legacy plan helps ensure that your plan never gets stale. Think of it as a mechanic who checks your car regularly, so that no matter what happens, the engine will always start.

WONDERING WHAT TO DO NEXT?

Take some action. If you do not already have an estate plan, get started ASAP. If you have one, review it with your lawyer. Whatever it costs, it is a lot cheaper than the nightmare scenario above.

Michael Monteforte Jr. is an estate planning and elder law attorney in Woburn, Massachusetts. He is the CEO and managing attorney of Monteforte Law P.C. and has published three books on estate planning and elder law.

Michael Monteforte

34

Six Reasons Your Estate Plan May Need Revising

By Kevin Pillion and Jada Terreros (Sarasota, Florida)

A common myth is that once you have completed your estate plan, you will not have to revise it later. In reality, your estate plan may require updating to reflect major events in your life or the lives of your loved ones. Otherwise, your estate plan may fail or not work as you intended, resulting in family disputes, unintended beneficiaries, avoidable inheritance or income taxes, probate, guardianship, or conservatorship.

Some examples of major life events include death, marriage, divorce, disability, incapacity, having a child, moving, winning the lottery or receiving a significant inheritance, starting a business, changes in the law, or changing your mind as to the persons you want to inherit your property (called *beneficiaries*) or to serve in trusted roles (called *fiduciaries*), such as your financial or healthcare agent.

This chapter looks at six questions that will help you identify when to revise your estate plan documents. For the purposes of this article, estate plan documents include (1) a durable power of attorney (POA) for property; (2) a last will or trust; (3) healthcare directives, such as a living will, designation of healthcare surrogate, durable power of attorney for healthcare, and a Health Insurance Portability and Accountability Act (HIPAA) authorization; (4) a declaration designating a preneed guardian or conservator;(5) a deed for real property (e.g., beneficiary or transfer-on-death deeds); and (6) beneficiary designation forms for your financial accounts.

To ensure that your estate plan does not produce unintended consequences, consider having a qualified attorney periodically (at least every five years) review your estate plan documents, beneficiary designation forms, and the titling of your assets.

1. DO YOUR ESTATE PLAN DOCUMENTS CONTAIN FATAL ERRORS?

Fatal errors are mistakes in your estate plan documents that cause your documents to be ineffective. A qualified attorney can discover these mistakes during a periodic review of your documents.

There are two types of fatal errors. The first stems from failing to follow all required legal formalities when signing your documents, such as notarizing, initialing necessary provisions, or signing in the presence of witnesses. Such mistakes will likely cause your documents to be invalid.

The second type involves having poorly tailored estate plan documents. Here, the content of your documents is deficient, causing them to be less effective than they could be or to have undesirable effects. This commonly occurs with do-it-yourself, online, and even some attorney-prepared documents.

For example, documents that conflict with homestead property laws may not work as intended and are a common source of this second type of fatal error. If your state of residency has homestead property laws, check in with your attorney to ensure that your last will, trust, and deed comply with your state's homestead laws.

2. ARE YOUR ESTATE PLAN DOCUMENTS OUTDATED?

Your documents may be out of date for several reasons, four of which are listed below along with expanded questions and commentary.

- **You or someone important to you has experienced a major life event.** What if you are going through a divorce but you die before the divorce is final? Your assets will likely transfer to your soon-to-have-been ex-spouse. What if more grandchildren are born after you have signed your existing documents and you want to include them in your estate plan? What if your daughter gets married and you are concerned about protecting her inheritance if she and her spouse divorce? Perhaps children or grandchildren who were underage at the time you signed your documents are now adults and you believe they will be better fiduciaries than other persons you originally named in your documents. What if your named fiduciary becomes disabled, passes away, or declines to serve (because you have a falling out, for example)? You could end up in a guardianship or conservatorship proceeding, with the judge appointing someone you would never have wanted to act on your behalf as your fiduciary.

- **You have moved to a new state.** Although your estate plan documents are likely to be valid in your new state of residency, references to the state laws in your old documents may conflict with the laws in your new state. A myriad of other issues could also arise: (1) your estate may be subject to avoidable state estate or inheritance taxes; (2) out-of-state executors or personal representatives may not be eligible to serve in your new state under your last will; (3) your POA and health-care directives may not be consistent with the laws in your new state; (4) valuation and titling issues may arise when moving into or out of a community property state; and (5) the transfer of your primary residence may not work as intended upon your death if your new state has a constitutional law restricting whom you may transfer it to, as is the case in Florida.

- **Significant changes in the law have made your last will or trust outdated.** Some important issues to monitor are changes to the favorable federal estate, gift, and generation-skipping transfer tax exemption levels (currently $12.06 million in 2022). Your estate may become subject to one or more of these taxes in 2026, when the levels revert to $5 million as indexed for inflation or approximately $6.4 million—or sooner, if legislation altering the exemption amount is passed before 2026. (Keep an eye out for legislative changes resulting in higher federal and state income taxes too.)

- **Your documents are old or suboptimal.** If your estate plan documents are more than five years old, there is a good chance that one or more of your documents may be outdated. Does your last will or trust contain special provisions to protect your beneficiaries from creditors or predators? Does it protect a special needs beneficiary from losing public benefits? What if you named only one fiduciary in your POA or healthcare directives and that person is unavailable to serve due to incapacity or death?

3. HAVE YOU UPDATED THE BENEFICIARY DESIGNATION FORMS ON YOUR FINANCIAL ACCOUNTS?

If you update your last will or trust, you should review the beneficiary designation forms on your financial accounts to ensure that they are correct. Check in with your financial advisor and confirm that your bank, investment, retirement, life insurance, and annuity accounts are properly titled, especially if you have experienced a recent divorce, disability, or death in the family.

4. HAVE YOU FOLLOWED THROUGH AFTER SIGNING YOUR ESTATE PLAN DOCUMENTS?

Be sure to follow up with your fiduciaries and inform them that you named them in your estate plan documents and where your documents are located. Better yet, consider giving your primary fiduciaries a copy of any documents that name them as your fiduciary. You should also consider contacting your beneficiaries and informing them that you included them in your estate plan. This may help avoid surprises and family disputes.

If your estate plan includes a trust, it is critical that you fund it; otherwise, it may not work as you intended. Funding your trust refers to the process of transferring ownership of your assets into the name of your trust. If you fail to complete the funding process, your estate will likely go through probate upon your death, resulting in possible delay, added expenses, and unintended beneficiaries. Check in with your attorney or financial advisor and confirm that your trust has been properly funded.

5. DOES YOUR ESTATE PLAN ADDRESS YOUR ONLINE ACCOUNTS AND DIGITAL ASSETS?

Do your estate plan documents specifically authorize your fiduciaries to access your online accounts and digital assets (e.g., cryptocurrency, nonfungible tokens (NFTs))? Without written authority in your estate plan documents, your fiduciaries may face additional difficulty accessing your online accounts, digital assets, and digital devices, especially if you become incapacitated or pass away.

6. DOES YOUR ESTATE PLAN INCLUDE PLANNING FOR YOUR PETS?

Do not forget to plan for your beloved pets; otherwise, they may be sent to a shelter and euthanized. Consider including a special provision in your POA, last will, and trust.

Kevin Pillion   *Jada Terreros*

Kevin Pillion is a Certified Elder Law Attorney (CELA), Florida licensed attorney, and graduate of Georgetown University Law Center. Jada Terreros is a Florida licensed attorney and graduate of the William S. Boyd School of Law at the University of Nevada, Las Vegas. Their email addresses are kevin@lifelawfirm.com and jada@lifelawfirm.com, respectively.

Providing for Your Beneficiaries

35

Considerations for Choosing a Guardian

By Megan Bray (Overland Park, Kansas)

A desire to ensure that their children are taken care of is often a primary reason parents begin the estate planning process. Many parents feel that nominating a guardian in preparation for a situation in which they cannot care for their children is the most important and difficult decision they will make. In this chapter, a guardian is defined as a child's caretaker who ensures that the child's needs, including shelter, education, clothing, food, and healthcare, are met, although some states also refer to a financial custodian as a "guardian." In estate planning, a potential guardian is frequently referred to as a "nominated" or "designated" guardian. Reviewing the following issues is helpful when deciding whom to nominate as your child's guardian. The considerations presented are intended to focus and narrow your options and determine situations for which you may need guidance, not to find the person who perfectly checks all the boxes.

THE GUARDIAN'S ABILITIES

A guardian's abilities can include several things. You should consider someone's physical and mental capabilities, other obligations, and teamwork mentality. Would a seventy-two-year-old grandparent be able to keep up with a very young child over the long term? Could a single sister with a high-stress job, living in a small apartment in the city, manage the significant life change required by a guardianship? Can your brother work well with other members of your family to provide well-rounded emotional care? You may consider writing conditions into your plan to provide for changes in circumstances over time.

Keep in mind that financial abilities may not be a consideration. A guardian is appointed separately from the person who manages the financial resources available for your child's care (typically a trustee). Do you want the guardian and trustee to be the same individual? Depending on their wishes and the personalities and strengths of the people they designate, some parents prefer that the same person act as both the guardian and trustee for the sake of simplicity. Other parents prefer checks and balances on care and finances and would rather split those responsibilities.

CHANGES TO RELATIONSHIPS

If you nominate a married couple as guardians, do you want them both to continue to co-parent your child if they divorce? Or if one of them passes away, do you want the other to continue to be the sole guardian or do you want an alternate guardian to step in?

GUARDIAN'S LOCATION

Is the guardian's location important to you? Would a long-distance move be problematic for your child? Would you be happy with the school system or community where the nominated guardian currently lives? What if your child is a high school student? Would you want a teen to have to transfer during their last years of school? What about a child who receives specific services or is in clubs, athletics, or community activities that may not be available in other schools or communities? If you do want your kids to go to a school in a different location, would the guardian's children go to the same school? Consider whether you might want to allow the guardian to live in your house with your child for a designated period.

SIMILAR BELIEFS

The guardian will step into your shoes regarding decisions for your children. Does the nominated guardian have a similar parenting style and similar religious, education, financial, and moral beliefs? If not, would they be willing to share your beliefs or provide time with others who share your beliefs? You may want to provide guidance and instructions about beliefs and principles that are important to you.

LONG-TERM OR SHORT-TERM GUARDIANS

Once you have determined whom to nominate as a long-term guardian and a few alternates, consider whether that person can also be named as temporary guardian (or first responder). The first responder should be a person who can immediately take care of your child in an emergency. Therefore, they should live nearby so they can get to your child within a short time (typically less than an hour). This person should be someone your child feels comfortable with and who can provide care during a potentially difficult time. The temporary guardian will care for your child only until you are again available or able or until a permanent guardian has been appointed. A family member or friend who lives close by or even a trusted neighbor is a good choice. (It is prudent to name a few alternates.) State laws vary regarding the nomination of a temporary guardian, so it is important to talk to your attorney about your options.

ACTION STEPS

All of these considerations and options can be overwhelming. You do not have to figure it out on your own. An attorney who specializes in estate planning will be extremely helpful in explaining the options and conditions that you can include in your plan and will help you consider different scenarios. You can also include guidance and intentions that are not legally binding but that will help your named guardian make decisions and follow through on your wishes. Also, talk to your attorney about excluding any people you do not want to be appointed as a guardian.

Do not let indecision or disagreement with your spouse delay your planning. If circumstances change or you reconsider your choices, you can usually amend your written documents quickly and inexpensively. Any decision you make and put in writing regarding a person who can step in to care for your child if you cannot is better than no decision at all.

Bray Law Office is a boutique law firm that focuses on providing exceptional planning services in Kansas, Nebraska, and Missouri to families with minor and young adult children as well as families who have members with special needs.

Megan Bray

36

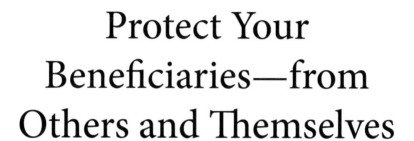

Protect Your Beneficiaries—from Others and Themselves

By Linda Sommers (Lakewood, Colorado)

Ask yourself the following questions about the people you are naming as beneficiaries in your estate plan:

- Are they knowledgeable and mature enough to handle a lump-sum inheritance?
- Are they too young (under eighteen) to legally receive an inheritance?
- Do you want to protect the inheritance from their divorcing spouse or creditors?
- Are they receiving government benefits?
- Are you concerned that their spouse may take or spend the inheritance?
- Do they have drug, alcohol, gambling, or spending problems?
- Do they have a job that has a high risk for lawsuits?
- Do you want to ensure that your assets are protected from actions by the government to recover benefits and taxes for future generations?

- Do you want to ensure that when they die, even if it is years or decades after your death, the remainder of the inheritance goes where you want it to go (for example, to your grandchildren rather than to a son- or daughter-in-law)?

Let's define a few terms. Please refer to other chapters in this book that explain what a *trust* is and what it does. For purposes of this chapter, a *beneficiary* is the person who has the use of the assets left by someone who has died. Generally, beneficiaries receive money or other assets from the trust when the trustmaker dies. A *trustee* is an individual or a legal entity responsible for administering the property and assets held within the trust pursuant to the terms of the trust and for the benefit of another individual (the beneficiary).

If your estate plan distributes the inheritance outright, the beneficiary will typically receive the inheritance and commingle the inheritance with their own personal and marital assets. Once that happens, the assets are vulnerable to claims by the beneficiary's divorcing spouse and creditors. When the beneficiary dies, the remaining inheritance will be transferred according to their estate plan, if they have one, or to their default beneficiaries under state law (which may include their spouse).

There ARE ways to protect your beneficiary's inheritance long after you are gone. Some call it "controlling from the grave," but others call it "protecting from the grave." It is all a matter of your goals and perspective.

The protections are built into the provisions that your attorney includes in your revocable living trust. You can include any provisions, requirements, or constraints in the trust that you want (so long as they do not go against public policy; for example, you cannot require that a beneficiary take up smoking). Regardless of whether the beneficiary is a mature adult, in a solid marriage, or single, there are benefits to leaving their inheritance in trust.

Protective trusts can be flexible or restrictive, though many fall somewhere in the middle. These types of trusts vary based on your goals, so please seek the advice of a competent estate planning attorney for direction about which type will best achieve your objectives and needs. These types of trusts are commonly referred to as beneficiary protection trusts, beneficiary-controlled trusts, dynasty trusts, spendthrift trusts, inheritor's trusts, perpetual trusts, or special needs trusts.

Trusts with a high degree of flexibility can allow the beneficiary to have very broad access to the income and principal of the protective trust during their lifetime. In this scenario, the beneficiary may be named as the trustee of the protective trust and may control the assets. Essentially, with a few restrictions, the beneficiary has nearly all the rights, benefits, and control over the inheritance that they would have with an outright distribution—*and* they have the added benefit of tax, creditor, and divorce protection, which are not obtainable with outright ownership.

If you wish to include more restrictive provisions to protect the beneficiary from themselves and others, the beneficiary may receive benefits from the trust distributed by an independent trustee (chosen by you) instead of having direct access to the trust assets. The independent trustee could have complete discretion over the distributions and use of the trust assets. Often, the restrictive provisions allow the independent trustee to pay bills or make purchases on behalf of the beneficiary. For example, someone with drug or alcohol problems may need support with rent or a residence. The independent trustee may pay the monthly rent or purchase a residence with the inherited assets held by the protective trust. A residence owned by the protective trust would be safeguarded from the beneficiary and possible creditors, divorcing spouses, and the like. Additionally, the beneficiary would not have access to use the inherited assets to finance their addictions and less-than-desirable lifestyle.

In both the flexible and restrictive scenarios, upon the beneficiary's death, the remaining inheritance can go to whomever *you* have named in your original revocable living trust, such as your grandchildren. When properly designed, your trust can then direct that the inheritance yet again be held in trust for the person's benefit and protection.

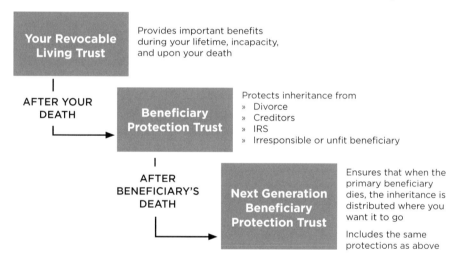

Here is an example: Michelle was divorced, had no boyfriend, was good with money, had a great job, and retired early. Her dad was not concerned about providing her with asset protection because she was the ideal child. She was the most responsible child of three. When he passed, she was in charge of taking care of his affairs and distributing the sizable estate among his three children.

After her dad had passed, she found herself in a romantic relationship with someone she met online. Unfortunately, she was naive and never realized that the person she had met was actually a predator. He had convinced her to spend most of her money, sign contracts for business "deals" that were either fake or going nowhere, and then disappeared from her life. She was left with several lawsuits and a bankruptcy.

When it came time to distribute the assets from her dad's estate, instead of receiving her one-third share of the estate, most of her inheritance was used to settle the lawsuits and satisfy the bankruptcy claims. She had to reenter the workforce and start all over. Had her dad provided her with a trust to hold the inheritance, the money would have been out of the creditors' reach. She would have had the resources to get back on her feet, preventing the need to reenter the workforce at an advanced age.

LEAVING AN INHERITANCE IN THE RIGHT KIND OF TRUST FOR YOUR BENEFICIARY

- protects the inheritance from beneficiaries who are not knowledgeable or mature at the time of the inheritance;

- provides a smooth transition of benefits and protections to a beneficiary who is a minor;

- protects the inheritance from divorce, creditors (current or future), or actions by the government to recover benefits;

- protects the continuation of government benefits for a special-needs beneficiary;

- protects the inheritance from "unintended beneficiaries" (such as a son- or daughter-in-law or step-grandchildren);

- protects the inheritance when drug, alcohol, gambling, or spending issues are a concern;

- protects the inheritance for beneficiaries who are at a high risk of being sued (such as doctors, business owners, and the like);

- provides for future estate tax protection for beneficiaries with a high net worth; and

- gives you control over how the balance of your estate is distributed for generations to come.

Sommers Law Group's mission is to be a client-centric business. We strive to be our clients' indispensable advisors, helping them make smart estate planning decisions through uncompromising integrity, value, commitment to excellence, and gratitude.

Linda Sommers

37

Custodial Accounts for Minors

By Rodney Gregory (Jacksonville, Florida)

A custodial account is an account maintained by one party on behalf of another. The custodian of the account acts in the interests of the account's eventual beneficiary. Although the term applies to any account with a custodian, such as a company-managed retirement account, this chapter addresses the most common use in an estate planning context: a savings account controlled by an adult on behalf of a minor.

Custodial accounts have certain benefits not provided by other types of wealth transfer devices. They can be savings accounts, mutual funds, or even brokerage accounts. Unlike some types of accounts, such as individual retirement accounts (IRAs), there are no income limits, contribution limits, or withdrawal penalties.

The beneficiary of the custodial account is a minor, but the minor does not gain effective control of the account until they reach the age of majority (typically eighteen or twenty-one depending on the state and account terms). The custodian of the account makes investment decisions until the account transfers into the minor's control.

TYPES OF CUSTODIAL ACCOUNTS FOR MINORS

There are two types of custodial accounts for minors, Uniform Gift to Minors Act (UGMA) and Uniform Transfers to Minors Act (UTMA) accounts. Both types of accounts are allowed in most states. Because neither of these types of accounts require the creation of a trust, they are simpler asset transfer tools. Unlike education -specific accounts, these accounts can hold multiple types of assets and be used for any purpose. The main difference between the two types of custodial accounts lies in the assets that each can hold.

UGMA accounts have been used since 1956. Today, every state allows UGMA accounts, with some variation, to be opened on behalf of minors. UGMA accounts are generally limited to cash and securities and do not allow highly speculative instruments such as options.

UTMA accounts, the offspring of the UGMA, were birthed in 1986 and are permitted in most states. They allow the transfer of almost any kind of asset, including cash, securities, and intellectual property. Many states have amended their versions of the UTMA to allow the age of majority to be as high as twenty-five—at the request of the custodian or the creator of the account, depending on the state—potentially extending the life of the account. In Florida, the beneficiary has the option to terminate at age twenty-one, the age of majority, or defer receipt of the funds until a later age.

ADVANTAGES AND DISADVANTAGES OF CUSTODIAL ACCOUNTS

ADVANTAGES

Custodial accounts are a relatively simple wealth transfer tool that allows the transfer of assets from the donee to the donor without the creation of a trust. They can be established and maintained at financial institutions such as FDIC-insured banks or brokerage companies.

Contributions are not subject to gift tax up to a certain amount (for 2022, $16,000 for individuals and $32,000 for married couples electing to split gifts) because of the annual gift tax exclusion. Additional contributions may qualify for the lifetime gift exclusion. Any earned income on assets held by the account, such as stock dividends or the sale of appreciated property, is taxed as income to the minor. This generally means a lower tax rate unless the minor makes more than the donor. If certain conditions are met, parents or guardians of the beneficiary can elect to report earnings on custodial accounts on their own tax returns to claim the Tax on a Child's Investment and Other Earned Income deduction.

There are no yearly contribution limits. Distributions can be made for the benefit of the child, typically for education purposes (but any expense can be allowed).

DISADVANTAGES

Only one beneficiary can be selected per account, and the beneficiary cannot be changed once the account is created. Until the beneficiary reaches the age of majority, becomes emancipated, or is otherwise self-supporting, the account is includable in the donor-custodian's taxable estate, although the account is includable in the beneficiary's estate if the beneficiary dies before reaching the age of majority. The assets in the account are considered owned by the child even before they reach the age of majority, so the account may negatively affect the minor's financial aid applications based on need. Finally, contributions are irrevocable.

SHOULD YOU CREATE A CUSTODIAL ACCOUNT?

Custodial accounts are a simple way to transfer assets to a minor without having to establish a trust or give up control. Ultimately, the decision to use a custodial account, or a more complex device such as a trust, Coverdell, IRA, or 529, depends on the amount and types of assets to be transferred, as well as the age and interest of the donor and donee. Seek advice and counsel from a competent lawyer experienced in custodial accounts for minors to determine how best to transfer wealth and assets to beneficiaries.[1]

Rodney G. Gregory, the American Barrister, has an LLM in Advanced Civil Litigation from Nottingham Trent University and a JD from Washington and Lee and represents individuals and families in wealth planning.

Rodney Gregory

---

1   Arya Salehi, my esteemed senior law clerk and a 3L at Washington and Lee School of Law, provided invaluable assistance in the preparation of this chapter.

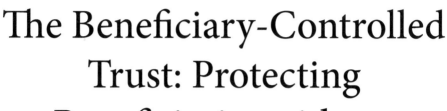

38

The Beneficiary-Controlled Trust: Protecting Beneficiaries without Controlling Them

By Benjamin J. Sowards (San Jose, California)

Most trust-based estate plans call for an outright or staggered distribution (e.g., one-third at ages twenty-five, thirty, and thirty-five) upon the death of the settlor (the individual who created the trust). An outright distribution upon the death of the client is common for older clients who believe their beneficiaries are responsible adults capable of managing their own affairs. Staggered distributions are commonly chosen by parents of minor children or young adults who prefer the inheritance to be available for the beneficiaries' health, education, maintenance, and support (the HEMS standard), but want the assets to be managed by a trustee until the beneficiaries reach certain ages (e.g., twenty-five, thirty, or thirty-five) or milestones (e.g., graduation from college with a four-year degree). Many estate planning attorneys advise that it is better to protect the kids from themselves by staggering the distributions over time than to give a young adult full access to their entire inheritance all at once. This protection only lasts while the assets are held in trust: all protection is lost once they are distributed to your beneficiaries. But there is a better way to leave a legacy for your beneficiaries that can protect them from losing their inheritance to lawsuits, divorce, or bankruptcy.

BENEFICIARY-CONTROLLED TRUSTS

In many states, a beneficiary-controlled trust is the seasoned estate planner's preferred way to help you leave a legacy for your beneficiaries. In the states where this type of trust works, it allows the beneficiary a significant degree of control over the trust assets while providing the assets some protection from divorce, creditors, and lawsuits. These types of trusts can be established under revocable or irrevocable trusts. They protect the trust funds by limiting who can be paid from the trust—only the beneficiaries. When creditors and plaintiffs' attorneys find out they cannot gain access to the beneficiary's trust assets or cannot do so easily, they are much more likely to settle or dismiss lawsuits against that beneficiary. Beneficiary-controlled trusts can hold assets in trust for the life of the beneficiary (or until the trust funds run out) to potentially protect a beneficiary from the following threats:

- losing their inheritance in a divorce
- losing assets in bankruptcy
- subjecting trust assets to lawsuits filed against the beneficiary
- subjecting the trust assets to the ever-changing estate tax

TRUSTEE CONTROL

One key to a beneficiary-controlled trust is allowing your beneficiary to maintain control while there are no issues with creditors, divorce, or lawsuits, but to consider engaging other trustees to hold some or all of the trustee powers when there is a potential threat against the beneficiary. Initially, or at least while the beneficiary is young, the beneficiary-controlled trust can be set up to be managed by a family member, friend, or professional fiduciary. As the beneficiary matures and becomes more responsible, it is common to allow the beneficiary to become a co-trustee of the trust so that they can learn how to properly manage their trust and prepare themselves if they eventually become the trustee. A common practice is to allow beneficiaries to become co-trustees at age thirty and then sole trustee a few years later, for example, at age thirty-five. At that point, the beneficiary will have broad control of the trust. However, the beneficiary can always appoint another trustee if a lawsuit or divorce is on the horizon.

If the beneficiary prefers to remain the trustee in the face of any of the threats noted above, the role of trustee can be bifurcated into a management trustee and a distribution trustee. The management trustee handles the day-to-day operations of the trust while the distribution trustee determines when to make distributions to the beneficiary. A trust can allow the beneficiary to serve in both roles until a potential problem arises. At that point, the beneficiary can appoint a distribution trustee to provide a shield against lawsuits and creditor claims. Although the beneficiary cannot control the distribution trustee, the beneficiary can have the right to remove and replace a distribution trustee under circumstances specified in the trust document, for example, if the beneficiary believes that the trustee is not acting in the beneficiary's best interest.

For a beneficiary serving as trustee, it is usually wise to limit or eliminate fully discretionary distributions and allow only distributions according to an ascertainable standard, such as the HEMS standard. However, an independent trustee or a distribution trustee can be allowed to make fully discretionary distributions, and the trust will still provide asset protection. You should never give the beneficiary the right to make discretionary distributions if they are involved in a lawsuit, bankruptcy, or divorce.

DEAD-HAND CONTROL

Settlors of beneficiary-controlled trusts can tell the trustees how distributions should be made to the beneficiaries. Some clients prefer to put few restrictions on the discretionary distributions to the beneficiaries. Others worry that their children will become lazy or fail to become a productive member of society. Settlors can consider the following types of language as guidance:

- **Liberal discretionary distributions**
  In making discretionary distributions to the beneficiary, it is my desire to provide for the well-being and happiness of the beneficiary. Although I request that my trustee consider the other known resources available to the beneficiary before making distributions, I also request that my trustee be liberal in making any distributions to the beneficiary. I acknowledge that the principal of the trust established for the beneficiary may be exhausted in making such distributions.

- **Conservative discretionary distributions**
  In making discretionary distributions to the beneficiary, it is my desire that the beneficiary develop a strong work ethic, be a productive and contributing member of society, and provide for those who are dependent on the beneficiary for care and support. Accordingly, my trustee shall be mindful of and always consider the other known resources available to the beneficiary before making discretionary distributions. It is my desire that preservation of principal be a priority for purposes of this trust and that genuine need be shown by the beneficiary before my trustee makes any discretionary distribution.

BUILDING A LEGACY

Your control over the beneficiary-controlled trust does not have to end when your beneficiary dies. Properly structured beneficiary-controlled trusts can last ninety or more years after your beneficiary's death in most states—up to four or more generations! A few states allow the trusts to remain in place indefinitely, but most states prohibit perpetual trusts. When the trust ends, the remaining funds can be distributed to persons you choose, for example, all of the lineal descendants of your chosen beneficiaries. While the property remains in trust, the cascading trusts created from the original trust instrument will give each subsequent beneficiary the same protection enjoyed by their ancestors. If you do not care if your assets continue to be passed down your bloodline and want to allow your beneficiaries to redirect the inheritance to their spouse, charities, or descendants upon the beneficiary's death, you can give your beneficiary a lifetime or testamentary power of appointment. The power of appointment allows your beneficiary to redirect trust funds to their chosen beneficiaries rather than to those you chose.

CONCLUSION

A beneficiary-controlled trust should be considered for any beneficiary for whom you would consider an outright or staged distribution, but this type of trust is particularly valuable for the following high-risk beneficiaries:

- any beneficiary who is in a troubled marriage that seems headed to divorce
- any beneficiary who is unskilled at managing money
- any beneficiary who is in a career with a high probability of lawsuits (physicians, entrepreneurs, and builders)

There is always a balance to be struck between control and protection. Usually, the lesser the beneficiary's control, the greater the protection. In states where such trusts work as intended, a beneficiary-controlled trust is the best way to allow your beneficiaries some control while also protecting them from themselves and others.

The Sowards Law Firm is a boutique Silicon Valley law firm focused on estate planning, wills, trusts, asset protection, estate administration, and business law. The members of our firm have been helping California families for over twenty-five years. Benjamin Sowards is certified by the State Bar of California Board of Legal Specialization as a specialist in estate planning, probate, and trust law.

Benjamin Sowards

39

Beneficiary-Controlled Descendants' Trusts

By James N. Voeller (San Antonio, Texas)

Most people who set up wills and revocable trusts leave their assets outright in equal shares to their children when they die. If this describes your estate plan, you may not realize that by leaving your child's inheritance to them outright, you may be unintentionally disinheriting your grandchildren! Suppose you die leaving assets to your son, and shortly after your death, he passes away too. It is likely that his will, if he has one, leaves everything to his spouse—who may very well spend the inheritance on herself, or worse yet, give it to a new spouse in *her* will—leaving your grandchildren with no part of the inheritance.

Instead of leaving your assets outright to your children, consider the potential advantages of leaving your assets in irrevocable trusts for the benefit of your children, which you can design and create during your lifetime.

A descendant's trust is an irrevocable trust created by you within your will or revocable trust that names your child as trustee and beneficiary when you die. For example, if your daughter is named Mary Smith, the trust would read "Mary Smith, as Trustee of the Mary Smith Trust."

There are many good reasons to leave assets in a descendant's trust for each of your children, created as part of your overall estate plan:

- The assets may be protected from your child's spouse in the event of divorce.

- The assets can be protected from your child's creditors in the event of financial hardship or bankruptcy.

- The assets may be sheltered from lawsuits to which your child may become a party.

- The assets will not be part of your child's probate estate in the event of the child's incapacity or upon their death.

- The assets can be removed from your child's estate so that no further estate taxes will be due when the property passes to the next generation.

- Upon your child's death, the unused assets will go to your blood relatives (such as grandchildren) instead of in-laws or others who are not a part of your plan.

A descendant's trust makes it much easier for your child to keep assets separate from a spouse when the assets have been left to the child in trust. At the time of your death, all of your assets are retitled directly from either your estate via your will or from your revocable trust to your child's trust. There is a world of difference between enabling an adult child to tell a spouse "my parents left this money to me in a trust" and having the child receive the inheritance "in hand," which would require the child to take active steps to keep those assets separate from the spouse or shelter the assets from an unexpected lawsuit.

A descendant's trust may be drafted to provide that, during your child's lifetime, the child has access to the income and the principal of the trust, so that you are not necessarily giving a "gift with strings attached" or "ruling from the grave." (If circumstances are warranted, however, you may elect to impose tighter control over the assets.) But you can ensure that, when your child dies, the unused portion of that inheritance goes to your grandchildren or to a charity you would like to support. The trust can provide that until your grandchild reaches an age when the grandchild will likely be more responsible—say age thirty—someone else will manage the assets, distributing as much of the assets as may be needed for the grandchild's health, education, maintenance, and support. Once the grandchild reaches age thirty, you may want the grandchild to be the trustee of their own trust. If a child dies without leaving children behind, the assets of that child's trust could go to the trusts created for your other children.

The time to design these trusts for your children is now—when you are preparing your own estate plan. Upon your death, your plan will provide this important protection for your children. In the overwhelming number of states, once your children have inherited assets from you, it is too late for them to create their own protective trusts.

If you are going to leave it all to them anyway, consider leaving your children's inheritance to them in a protected trust by doing some additional planning for them today. Your children will greatly appreciate what you have done to put them on the right track to plan for themselves and their families. Talk to your estate planning attorney about how to incorporate these ideas into your trust.

James N. Voeller focuses his practice on helping families structure their affairs to protect their assets from lawsuits and government intervention and save millions of dollars in estate taxes and probate costs.

James Voeller

40

The Power of the Power of Appointment

By Jennifer Elliott (San Clemente, California)

T he power of appointment is an often misunderstood strategy that can be a helpful tool to create flexibility in your estate plan and provide significant tax savings. It is sometimes confused with a power of attorney because both can be general or limited, but it is important to understand the distinctions. A power of attorney is a document that names an agent authorized to act for the principal. This power granted to an agent may be general or limited, but it expires on the principal's death. In contrast, a power of appointment confers the ability to assign assets owned or controlled by one person, the donor, to another person, the powerholder. A power of appointment may be created during the donor's lifetime or at the donor's death.

A power of appointment has both benefits and drawbacks, so it should be used with the guidance of an experienced estate planner knowledgeable about its potential tax benefits and burdens.

GENERAL VERSUS LIMITED POWERS

A *general power of appointment* is defined in § 2041 of the Internal Revenue Code (I.R.C.) as a power "exercisable in favor of the powerholder, the powerholder's estate, the powerholder's creditors, or creditors of the powerholder's estate," meaning that at least one of those people or entities can be selected by the powerholder to receive the asset. In fact, the person or entity named as the powerholder might not be subject to any restrictions on selecting a new owner for the donor's assets. For example, the powerholder could be free to name themselves or their favorite charity as the beneficiary of the donor's assets.

In contrast, a *limited* or *special power of appointment* restricts who can be named as the beneficiary so that the assets cannot be appointed to the powerholder, the powerholder's estate, the powerholder's creditors, or creditors of the powerholder's estate. This special or limited power typically requires the powerholder to name beneficiaries from among a class of people, such as the children or grandchildren of the donor. This special power can give another person (the powerholder) the ability to make choices for the donor that would be in-line with the donor's wishes if the donor were still living. A limited power of appointment will not cause the assets subject to the power to be included in the estate of the powerholder for estate tax purposes because the powerholder does not have the right to nominate themselves as an appointee and thus will not be considered the owner of the assets. A power can also be limited if it is restricted to an ascertainable standard, for example, to be used for the beneficiary's health, education, maintenance, or support.

LIFETIME AND TESTAMENTARY POWERS

In addition to general versus special powers, there is also a distinction between testamentary powers of appointment and powers that can be exercised while the powerholder is living.

A *testamentary general power of appointment* may only be exercised at the powerholder's death or, in other words, the beneficiary can be changed only at the death of the powerholder. The donor may require that the power be exercised by a will, and typically, the powerholder will specifically state in their will that they are exercising the power and identify the beneficiary.

In contrast, some powers of appointment can be exercised while the powerholder is living. For example, a *lifetime general power of appointment* allows the powerholder to take a gift for themselves right away or to designate an appointee at any time during the powerholder's lifetime. In addition, it does not impose any other conditions.

ADVANTAGES OF POWERS OF APPOINTMENT

The biggest advantage of a power of appointment is that it provides flexibility in an estate plan. For example, if the donor intends to leave assets to a grandchild, the grandchild's parent, who could be named as the powerholder, will likely live longer than the donor and can determine the amount and timing of assets that would be in the grandchild's best interest. For example, a donor who makes an outright gift of $100,000 to a grandchild immediately upon the donor's death may not know at the time they drafted their will or trust that the grandchild would later have a drug problem or a gambling addiction, or that the grandchild was a spendthrift, resulting in the money not being used as intended. The power of appointment can be exercised decades after the death of the donor, allowing the powerholder to act in the best interest of the beneficiaries to address unforeseen circumstances.

A second reason for using a power of appointment is to reduce capital gains tax. Granting a general power of appointment over appreciating assets means that the assets will receive a stepped-up cost basis at the powerholder's death. In other words, a general power of appointment, regardless of whether it is exercised, results in a cost basis based on the asset's fair market value at the time of the powerholder's death for federal estate tax purposes. If the property is sold later, this strategy can result in huge savings in capital gains tax because the property is included in the deceased powerholder's estate before it is passed on to the beneficiary.

DRAWBACKS OF POWERS OF APPOINTMENT

Powers of appointment should be used with caution because, as mentioned, a general power of appointment causes inclusion in the powerholder's taxable estate. If the powerholder has a sizable estate, the power of appointment may cause the powerholder's estate to owe estate tax. I.R.C. § 2041 states that the value of the gross estate shall include the value of the following property:

> *To the extent of any property with respect to which the decedent has at the time of his death a general power of appointment created after October 21, 1942, or with respect to which the decedent has at any time exercised or released such a power of appointment by a disposition which is of such nature that if it were a transfer of property owned by the decedent, such property would be includible in the decedent's gross estate under sections 2035 to 2038, inclusive.*

Powers of appointment should be used only with the help of an attorney who has a thorough understanding of the tax implications. The uninformed use of general powers of appointment can cause the value of all or part of the donor's estate (the assets subject to the power) to be treated as part of the powerholder's estate for estate tax purposes, potentially resulting in or increasing estate tax liability for the powerholder. Consider providing a limited power for a nonspouse to avoid inclusion in the powerholder's estate and reserving the general power of appointment for a spouse, for example, when trying to take advantage of the unlimited marital deduction.

Granting a power of appointment allows the powerholder to change the donor's beneficiaries. This power should not be included in estate plans where the donor does not intend to grant this ability to alter the donor's wishes. The donor should consider whether the powerholder might use the power in a manner contrary to the donor's wishes. For example, if the donor's intent was to encourage their grandchildren to be drug-free when they received the inheritance, a spiteful powerholder could appoint the addicted child as a beneficiary, and the inheritance could be wasted or used in a way that would be harmful to the beneficiary—the opposite of the donor's intent.

Naming a trust protector in your trust instrument may help you balance the advantages of flexibility and tax savings against the disadvantage of causing a taxable estate. Since a trust protector is not the grantor, testator, principal, or powerholder, the Internal Revenue Service allows trust protectors to have considerable power to make changes to trust instruments without the need for court involvement. Trust protectors can ensure the proper use of powers of appointment so that wealth is passed to the donor's loved ones in accordance with their intent while minimizing the tax due.

Jennifer Elliott owns San Clemente Estate Law, P.C. in South Orange County, California. She devotes her practice to estate planning, probate, trust administration, and asset protection.

Jennifer Elliott

41

Do You Have a Contingency Plan If Your Beneficiary Dies Before You?

By Shawn Garner and Adam Hansen (Yuma, Arizona)

Nobody wants to think about their child or someone they love dying before them, but it happens. Therefore, when you are creating an estate plan, it is important to consider how your property will be distributed if one of your beneficiaries dies before you.

Once you have made your decision, it is the attorney's job to use the correct terms to ensure that your wishes are carried out and legally binding. A single word can make a big difference.

To illustrate, we will use John as our hypothetical client. John is a widower with four children and six grandchildren. The following chart illustrates his family tree.

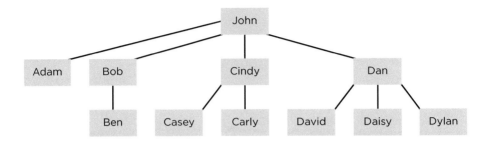

Assume that the value of John's estate upon his death will be $400,000. He has a valid will, and he has elected to distribute his estate disproportionately among his children as set forth below.

	Share	Amount
Adam	45%	$180,000
Bob	30%	$120,000
Cindy	15%	$60,000
Dan	10%	$40,000
Total	**100%**	**$400,000**

EQUAL VERSUS PROPORTIONATE

John decides that if a child predeceases him, that child's share will be divided equally among the others. The attorney explains that an equal distribution will produce a much different outcome than a proportionate distribution. To help John appreciate the difference, the attorney compares the outcomes under both equal and proportionate distribution contingency plans.

First, assume Adam predeceases John, and Adam's 45 percent share is divided equally among John's surviving children. The result is shown below.

	Original Shares	Original Amount	Additional Share	Additional Amount	Modified Share	Modified Amount
~~Adam~~	45%	$180,000	—	—	—	—
Bob	30%	$120,000	15.00%	$60,000	45.00%	$180,000
Cindy	15%	$60,000	15.00%	$60,000	30.00%	$120,000
Dan	10%	$40,000	15.00%	$60,000	25.00%	$100,000
Total	**100%**	**$400,000**	**45.00%**	**$180,000**	**100.00%**	**$400,000**

Each of the surviving children will receive one-third of Adam's 45 percent share (15 percent). This formula treats those of John's children with a larger share the same as those with a smaller share. When seen in this light, the distribution may not achieve John's wishes for the division of the property.

Now assume Adam's share is distributed proportionately among John's surviving children.

	Original Shares	Original Amount	Modified Share (Orig. % ÷ 55% = Mod. %)	Modified Amount
Adam	45%	$180,000	—	—
Bob	30%	$120,000	54.55%	$218,182
Cindy	15%	$60,000	27.27%	$109,091
Dan	10%	$40,000	18.18%	$72,727
Total	**100%**	**$400,000**	**100%**	**$400,000**

Subtract Adam's share (45 percent) from the total (100 percent) to find the difference (55 percent). Divide each beneficiary's original share by 55 percent to determine the modified percentage of the estate each of the surviving beneficiaries will receive. The modified percentage multiplied by the total ($400,000) is the modified share each beneficiary will receive.

This option allows each of John's surviving children to inherit in proportion to their original inheritance. It is John's decision to determine what is fair, but it is the attorney's job to explain his options and how they may play out.

Of course, John has infinite options for selecting contingent beneficiaries. This is just one example of how one word (equal versus proportionate) can make a big difference in how the estate is distributed in the event that a beneficiary predeceases you.

INTESTATE SUCCESSION

If John does not choose a specific option as a contingency plan and dies without a will, the deceased beneficiary's share will be distributed as specified under the applicable state law. There are two main approaches: per stirpes and per capita.

Per stirpes is Latin for "by the branch." Another way to describe this approach is "through the blood line" or "directly to the descendants of the deceased beneficiary."

Per capita is a Latin phrase that translates literally as "by the head." In a per capita distribution to a person's children, a deceased child's share is redistributed to the surviving children at that generation rather than being passed down to the deceased beneficiary's descendants.

Which approach is fair? Most states do not believe that either approach in its pure application is fair. Accordingly, each state uses a combination of these approaches to create its own set of laws. Certain states call their particular combination of these approaches "by right of representation." In other words, the phrase "by right of representation" can mean something very different depending on the state.

The individual states apply the different approaches in a variety of ways. We will focus on explaining the traditional concepts of each approach and their outcomes using John's family to illustrate our scenarios.

TRADITIONAL PER STIRPES

Assume that John did not specify in his will who would receive the share of a child who predeceased him, and he lived in a state that applied the traditional per stirpes approach.

If Bob and Dan die before John, Bob's share will go to his child, Ben, and Dan's share will be divided into three equal shares among his three children, Daisy, Dylan, and David. John's grandchildren stand in for their parents, or represent their respective parents' branches. About one-third of US states use this seemingly commonsense approach.

TRADITIONAL PER CAPITA

Under the traditional per capita approach, if for example, John's will leaves his estate to his children, per capita, the estate is divided among only the surviving beneficiaries, unless specifically stated otherwise (e.g, among his issue or descendants, per capita). In our scenario, if Bob and Dan die before John, only the two surviving children, Adam and Cindy, will receive distributions from Bob's estate, each receiving half. John's grandchildren from Bob and Dan do not inherit their deceased parent's share under this approach.

This is not commonly selected by individuals who understand the concept and it is not a common default approach used by many states.

PER CAPITA AT EACH GENERATION

Many states use a variation of per capita and per stirpes. For example, Arizona uses this blend of the per stirpes and per capita approaches, which ensures that the surviving children will receive their designated shares and pools the deceased children's shares together to be distributed equally among their combined children.

Returning to the original example, if Bob and Dan predecease John, the estate will be divided four ways. Adam and Cindy will each receive their designated shares. The shares of Bob and Dan will be combined and then divided equally among their collective children. In other words, one-half of John's estate will be divided equally among Ben, Daisy, Dylan, and David. Each will receive one-eighth of John's estate.

If you are like most people, you do not want state law to dictate the distribution of your estate. That is why creating an estate plan is so important. It allows you to make your own rules for designating who will receive your estate upon your death. Just as importantly, it defines a contingency plan for distributing the share of any beneficiary who happens to die before you.

Shawn Garner

Adam Hansen

Attorneys Shawn Garner and Adam Hansen have drafted over ten thousand trusts. They have given hundreds of lectures in public forums and to professional groups about the benefits of proper estate planning. They are frequent contributors to newspaper editorials and host a weekly radio show, Life, Death, and the Law.

42

Protecting Your Trust with a Trust Protector

by Anthony Fantini (Pittsburgh, Pennsylvania)

Naming a trust protector in a trust is a relatively recent innovation in trust law, at least in the United States. The acceptance and use of trust protectors have become increasingly popular. This is especially true for trusts that are designed and expected to last for longer terms or hold and control legacy assets of significant value (e.g., family business interests).

Despite the intriguing title of this chapter, a trust protector does not actually "protect" the trust in the normal understanding of the word. Rather, you can provide your trust protector with the power and ability to modify select provisions of your trust in the event that changes are needed. As facts and circumstances change, it may be warranted and advantageous for your trust protector to make occasional changes or modifications. Do you intend to hold and control significant assets in your trust? If your answer is yes, or perhaps even maybe, then without a doubt, you should consider adding a trust protector to your trust. It is universally accepted that the only constant is change, so this could be one of the most important provisions you incorporate into your trust and the most important step you take to ensure that your estate planning achieves your intended result.

IF NOT NOW, WHEN?

You may not think that your trust requires a trust protector. Although not all trusts need one, you should critically review your plan. Consider the real possibility that the future may not unfold in quite the way you envision. It is better to have a trust protector and not need one than to need a trust protector and not have one.

SIMPLY PUT . . .

Mistakes happen. Circumstances change. Laws change. People change. Any of these situations may prevent your trust from accomplishing its intended purpose. Can you be sure that your trust is equipped to weather every storm? Have you really been able to plan for every possible contingency? If you already have a living trust and your trust does not provide for a trust protector, you should revisit it. Your purpose is to ensure that your trust will be flexible, so the assistance of a trust protector will offer a better chance of accomplishing your intended results.

SELECTING YOUR TRUST PROTECTOR

Your trust protector is a person you name who is not a trustee but who holds certain predefined powers over your trust. Your trust protector should be a person who can address future changes in state laws affecting trusts, state and federal tax laws, the identity of the trustee, trust assets, and the beneficiaries' personal circumstances such as substance abuse, gambling problems, debt, or disability.

Your trust protector should be a third party who is respected, perceptive, intelligent, financially aware, mature, wise, and most importantly, trustworthy. The trust protector will be granted specific powers within your trust to assist with its management and distributions. Since the position is likely to have a long duration, it is prudent to select a trust protector who is younger than the grantor. You want to ensure that your trustee acts within the intent and guidelines laid out in your plan as expressed by your trust documents, and that the trust protector will be around long enough to ensure that the trustee does so.

WHAT POWERS SHOULD YOU CONSIDER GRANTING TO YOUR TRUST PROTECTOR?

Depending on the grantor's needs and goals, the trust instrument might empower the trust protector to do any of the following:

1. review or approve accountings prepared by the trustee

2. review and approve (or disallow) the trustee's proposed investments

3. in certain circumstances, veto an investment decision made by the trustee

4. remove or replace the trustee for good cause or for any reason

5. appoint a successor trustee or add a co-trustee

6. change the situs or governing law of the trust

7. in special circumstances, amend the trust (narrowly or broadly) to comply with tax or other law changes, obtain more favorable tax status, make technical corrections, or correct scrivener's errors

8. authorize and approve litigation by the trustee against third parties

9. settle disputes between trustees, beneficiaries, or trustee and beneficiary

10. determine whether an event has occurred that may require termination of the trust

The trust instrument might grant the following distribution powers to a trust protector, including the power to do the following:

1. require the trustee to consult with the trust protector regarding distribution decisions

2. direct the trustee about how and when to make distributions

3. veto a distribution decision

4. amend the trust's distribution provisions

5. change the beneficiary or act as a beneficiary's advocate with the trustee

6. consent to or veto an exercise of a power of appointment and modify the terms of a power of appointment

CONCLUSION

If the person you select to act as your fiduciary trust protector is not an attorney or another professional who carries professional liability insurance, that person may be required to post a bond. Trust protectors who are fiduciaries are required to act in good faith. This simply means that they must act as a prudent person would act regarding the trust's purpose and they must act in the best interests of all of the trust's beneficiaries. While the inclusion of a trust protector is not required, it is comforting to be assured that your intentions in establishing your trust can be followed without any further action on your part. Your trust protector could become the most valuable part of your trust plan.

In working closely with clients, Anthony Fantini employs a variety of advanced legal strategies and techniques focused on minimizing taxes while preserving and protecting clients' legacies for their beneficiaries and providing them with comfort and peace of mind. Fantini Law Firm provides the superior level of service expected from a boutique law firm.

Anthony Fantini

43

Blended Family Traps

By Riley Kern (Tulsa, Oklahoma)

Estate planning for a blended family introduces some complications that may not exist when planning for an individual or a couple in their first marriage. In a successive marriage, each spouse often brings their own assets and liabilities, children, and unique values, hopes, and anxieties. Your attorney's first job is to learn about your network of relationships, assets, and priorities and help you understand the legal *and* relational obstacles and opportunities you need to address.

In this chapter, we will discuss a strategy commonly used to protect separate property and reduce the strain on the surviving family's relationships. This strategy, called a bypass trust or a family trust, is just one of several planning options you should discuss with your attorney.

BLENDED FAMILY CONSIDERATIONS

Many blended families anticipate two issues—one financial and the other relational—if one spouse dies before the other.

Financially, spouses want to ensure that their assets are transferred to the right people at their death. This usually involves the desire to have certain assets remain with the surviving spouse while other assets are immediately transferred to their children. In other cases, you may want all of the assets to be available to the surviving spouse while making certain you can accomplish four additional priorities:

1. Assets cannot be commingled with a new spouse if the survivor remarries.

2. Assets are not exposed to the survivor's creditors.

3. Assets are not depleted if the survivor requires long-term care or has other major medical needs.

4. Assets will eventually flow to your children and grandchildren, rather than to other unintended beneficiaries.

Client scenario: It is a second marriage for Casey and Jesse. They each have children from a previous marriage, and they each come into the marriage with their own assets. Casey, an entrepreneur, has an existing business, and Jesse has inherited a family farm. If Casey dies before Jesse, Casey wants to ensure that Casey's financial interest in the business, but not the management rights, remains with Jesse during Jesse's lifetime. Similarly, if Jesse dies before Casey, Jesse wants to ensure that the income produced by the farm continues to benefit Casey. Casey and Jesse also want to be certain that their separate interests eventually flow to their own descendants, rather than their stepchildren, a future spouse of the survivor, creditors, or other unintended beneficiaries.

Relationally, spouses recognize that after they pass, there could be tension or suspicion between their children and the surviving spouse, especially when the use and benefit of assets are concerned. They want to decrease these relational complications as much as possible.

Consider Casey and Jesse again. If Jesse dies before Casey, Jesse's children may be worried about losing the family farm to Casey and Casey's children. Or, if Casey has a chronic illness, Jesse's children may become concerned that the farm interest will be lost to long-term care costs. If Casey remarries, Jesse's children may be anxious about how the new spouse and their family will impact the ongoing interest and future inheritance of the farm. These are all valid legal concerns, and each concern is rife with the potential to destroy the relationship between Jesse's children and Casey.

WHAT IS THE SOLUTION?

One simple solution for blended families is to create an estate plan that includes a bypass trust. Bypass trusts were originally created to reduce or eliminate estate taxes, but with the estate tax exemption continuing to climb (at least as of the time of this writing), very few families need to use a bypass trust for this purpose. So, what else can a bypass trust accomplish?

We recommend a bypass trust that is created only when one spouse dies before the other. It (usually) is not active during the spouses' joint lifetimes, and it is never created in the event of a simultaneous death. The assets held by the bypass trust do not *belong to* the survivor, but the survivor is the beneficiary (or one of the beneficiaries) of the bypass trust for the rest of their life (see illustration below).

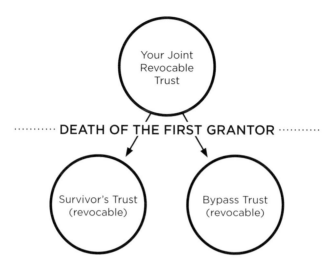

As illustrated, while you and your spouse are both alive, all of your assets—whether joint or separate—are owned by your joint revocable trust. When the first spouse dies, the bypass trust provisions become effective, and the trustee, who is most often the surviving spouse, is responsible for dividing assets in a predetermined way between two new trust shares—the survivor's trust and the family trust. The survivor's trust, which remains revocable by the surviving spouse, owns the survivor's separate assets and possibly a portion of joint assets. The family trust, which is irrevocable by the survivor, owns all or a portion of the deceased spouse's separate property and possibly a portion of the joint assets.

HOW DOES A BYPASS TRUST HELP BLENDED FAMILIES?

Whether or not the value of Casey and Jesse's assets raises estate tax concerns, the best tool to address their priorities is to integrate a bypass trust into their estate plan. The business or farm interest of the first spouse to die can be used to fund the irrevocable bypass trust. The bypass trust may be structured in a variety of ways, but it essentially holds the assets in trust for the continued benefit of the survivor. Because the bypass trust is irrevocable (and typically includes a few additional safeguards), each spouse can rest assured that the assets will eventually flow to their descendants and be protected from any future financial misfortune or exposure the survivor may experience.

By funding the bypass trust with the business or the farm, each of these concerns may be addressed and alleviated. You cannot guarantee that your children and your surviving spouse will have a wonderful relationship, but you can reduce the possibility that the use and benefit of assets will be the root of any problems.

A BRIEF ASIDE ABOUT RETIREMENT PLANS

Most clients have retirement plans, such as an individual retirement account, 401(k), 403(b), or 457. During your lifetime, these accounts are owned by you, rather than your trust, and are transferred by designating beneficiaries with the plan administrator. There are often tax consequences and asset protection issues related to whom you designate as your retirement plan beneficiary. If you have significant savings in a retirement plan, you should carefully discuss these issues with your attorney, financial planner, and tax advisor.

For instance, it may or may not be advisable to name a trust with bypass trust provisions as a primary beneficiary of your retirement plan, either for the benefit of your surviving spouse, children, or other beneficiary. If you name a trust as the beneficiary, it may be advisable to structure that trust as a conduit trust or an accumulation trust. The purpose of this chapter is not to describe these options or to explain the opportunities and problems associated with each, but it would be negligent not to underscore that retirement plans have special characteristics that require scrutiny outside the scope of this chapter.

WHAT SHOULD YOU DO NEXT?

1. If you have a blended family, meet with an estate planning attorney to have a frank discussion about your financial and relational priorities and concerns.

2. If you have an existing trust, review it with an estate planning attorney to see what provisions, if any, your trust contains for a bypass trust.

3. If provisions for a bypass trust already exist, or if you amend your trust to include a bypass trust, make sure it will be funded with the assets you are most worried about and that it is not simply created based on a boilerplate estate-tax formula. For example, Jesse and Casey would want language like the following: *Upon the death of Jesse, if Casey is still alive, our trustee shall allocate all of Jesse's interest in the farm to the nonmarital share. Our trustee shall administer the nonmarital share as provided in Article X. The nonmarital share shall be known as the Family Trust.*

In Jesse's and Casey's example, Article X of the trust should contain clear provisions identifying the beneficiary of the family trust, its irrevocability and other safeguards, how the trustee should allocate and distribute income and principal, guidelines for discretionary distributions, and effects on the family trust of future events, such as a survivor's remarriage.

4. Finally—and this is a critical but often ignored step—discuss your estate plan with your children, letting them know you have anticipated this potential problem and made provisions to protect your assets and keep the peace among those who mean the most to you.

Riley Kern and family

Tallgrass Estate Planning, LLP is owned by wife-and-husband team Laurel and Riley Carbone Kern. Tallgrass Estate Planning, LLP is a home-based estate planning law firm with attorneys in Oklahoma and Washington.

44

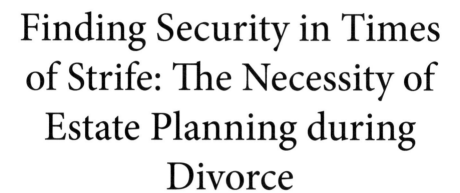

Finding Security in Times of Strife: The Necessity of Estate Planning during Divorce

By Patricia De Fonte (San Francisco, California)

D ivorce can be chaotic and destabilizing. From acrimony between soon-to-be former spouses to confusion about the future, divorce is a legal process that leaves many in a vulnerable state of unease. Clients sometimes hope that their attorney can just make their problems vanish.

Terrific divorce lawyers can be a wonderful resource, but they cannot provide a client with the security for the future that is available through estate planning. Although estate planning might be the last thing on a client's mind during such a challenging time, an empathetic and experienced estate planning lawyer with a broad network can provide an oasis of calm and productivity.

CASE STUDY: CHRIS LEARNS THE VALUE OF A SOLID ESTATE PLAN

Chris was married to Jordan for fifteen years before filing for divorce. They have two minor children, but Jordan's increasingly erratic behavior, substance abuse, and money problems drove them apart. Jordan put the final proverbial nail in the marriage coffin by announcing a relationship with a much younger person from the office.

Chris hired divorce counsel hoping the lawyer would handle all of the problems associated with the marital dissolution, including protecting Chris's and the children's financial interests. The divorce lawyer quickly dispelled that notion, however, by explaining to Chris that a divorce lawyer's focus is on custody issues, asset division, temporary restraining orders, and court filing requirements and deadlines.

The divorce lawyer did give Chris a long list of "chores" but could not help Chris complete these tasks. Naturally, this left Chris feeling tremendously stressed, which was compounded by the fact that Jordan had always handled their finances, insurance, and estate planning. How could Chris possibly ensure that Chris and the children would be taken care of moving forward?

As Chris discovered, in the absence of an estate plan, state law provides default guidelines with little regard to personal wishes. For example, if Chris were to die before the divorce finalized, Jordan might inherit everything. The court could even assign custody of the children to Jordan despite proof of drug abuse in the home. Alternatively, should Chris become incapacitated, Chris's extended family would have to ask a judge for permission to make healthcare decisions, conclude the divorce, or even pay hospital bills. These types of concerns left Chris frozen with anxiety.

Luckily, a close friend knew exactly what Chris should do: **talk to an estate planning attorney.** Experienced estate planning attorneys have the technical skills, emotional intelligence, and breadth of knowledge to prepare a personalized estate plan. They can also spot issues in related fields and should have the network needed to help their client build a new team of advisors the client can rely on.

THE DIVORCEE PROTECTION PLAN

Divorcing clients cannot simply fill out forms and sign documents. They need a partner to help them transition to independence. A great estate planning attorney provides this partnership through empathy, taking the time to gain an understanding of the client's fears about divorce, and knowledge of family finances. Moreover, an estate planning attorney who devotes much of their practice to divorcing clients has the expertise to help each client navigate the path to financial independence by focusing on three key areas:

- Documents
- Insurance
- Advisors

Documents. Estate planning documents answer three questions: "Who is in charge when I cannot be?," "Who gets my stuff when I die, and how?," and "Who will care for my children?" The centerpiece of the estate plan is the revocable trust (also referred to as a living trust). A revocable trust is a complex document, but boiled down, it is a description of what happens to assets upon incapacity and death.

Incapacity planning is a potent tool that enables the divorcing client to prevent their ex-spouse from making any decisions about their healthcare and having any control over their finances moving forward. Advance healthcare directives and powers of attorney can allow divorce proceedings to move forward—even in the event of incapacity. Chris found this protection quite empowering, especially the prospect of not having to worry that Jordan would call the shots in a hospital setting or that the divorce would settle in Jordan's favor by default.

Many divorcing clients worry that their ex-spouse could get their hands on the children's money. A revocable trust that excludes Jordan from serving as a successor trustee and specifically precludes Jordan from seeking funds from the trust to meet Jordan's parental obligations addressed Chris's concerns by ensuring that Jordan could not abuse any position of power or deplete their children's inheritance.

A trust can also affirmatively provide for therapy and other important mental healthcare measures for the children. Chris's trust ensured that concerns about money would never prevent the kids from spending time with Chris's family. (Note: Whether a revocable trust can be signed, and the extent to which it can be funded, *pending divorce,* is a matter of local family laws. No assets should be transferred to a revocable trust pending divorce proceedings without the advice of a family law attorney.)

In conjunction with a revocable trust, a strongly worded nomination of guardians can provide the court with a roadmap for individuals in the children's lives who are better suited to raise them than a neglectful parent like Jordan.

Insurance. Every divorcing client should conduct a full insurance audit with an independent broker. This audit examines all types of insurance (home, auto, renters, umbrella, life, health, disability, and long-term care) to identify where the client may be underinsured. Proper levels of insurance mitigate financial pitfalls. In some scenarios, a divorcing client may also be able to purchase a life insurance policy naming the trust as the beneficiary prior to the completion of the divorce, thereby safeguarding the children's financial futures.

Advisors. Successfully navigating the correct path through the divorce minefield is always a team effort. In addition to divorce and estate planning attorneys, a financial planner or money coach, a certified divorce financial analyst, insurance experts, mediators, realtors, organizers, tax professionals, therapists, and other professionals can help a client not only survive but thrive.

Chris Puts the Divorcee Protection Plan into Action

Chris was worried, vulnerable, and insecure. By implementing the divorcee protection plan, Chris gained a sense of empowerment, security, and strength, especially knowing that the interests of the children would be fully protected.

Chris's estate plan portfolio now contains a list of new advisors for casualty insurance, financial planning, tax preparation, disability and life insurance, and long-term care insurance.

Chris named trusted friends and family members as successors, agents, and guardians, putting people who are reliable, responsible, and trustworthy in charge should the unexpected occur.

Once Chris's divorce was finalized, the only task left to complete was transferring assets to the trust. Chris's team of advisors received a copy of Chris's certification of trust to ensure that the correct designations were made and to provide a second set of eyes for Chris as the years pass to ensure that the revocable trust remains properly funded. The estate plan was completed. Instead of more stress and hard work after the final divorce decree was issued, Chris was able to face the future with full confidence.

Patricia De Fonte, JD, LLM practices Estate Planning With Heart.™ At De Fonte Law PC, preserving family harmony and creating empowered savvy clients and heirs is at the core of what we do.

Patricia De Fonte

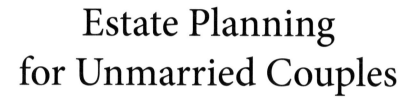

45

Estate Planning for Unmarried Couples

By Nicole Ramos Takemoto (Walnut Creek, California)

It has become increasingly common for committed couples to maintain long-term relationships without ever getting married. Unmarried couples often have children and acquire assets together, and their day-to-day lives are no different from the lives of other families. However, unmarried couples must be mindful about legal issues that may arise because they do not have the same legal rights and responsibilities as spouses. If you are in a committed relationship and intend to stay unmarried, proper planning can avoid unexpected legal challenges and ensure that your wishes are carried out.

ADVANCE HEALTHCARE DIRECTIVES

State statutes and case law support the concept of identifying the "closest available relative" as the person to make healthcare decisions on behalf of a patient who is incapacitated, has no written advance healthcare directive, and is not under a conservatorship of the person or guardianship. Some states have a default hierarchy of decision makers for such situations, while other states, such as California, do not. If a patient is married, the closest relative is generally the spouse. If you and your partner are not married, without proper planning you may encounter difficulty participating in each other's healthcare decisions or receiving confidential medical information from your partner's healthcare provider.

An advance healthcare directive (AHCD) is a document in which a person can designate an agent who will have the authority to make healthcare decisions for them if they are unable to make those decisions for themselves. It is important for unmarried partners to execute AHCDs so that it is clear to healthcare providers that a partner may visit a healthcare facility and speak with healthcare workers. The federal Health Insurance Portability and Accountability Act (HIPAA) includes rules relating to the privacy of health information. The HIPAA privacy rules specifically permit covered entities to share information with family members, friends, or other persons identified by a patient. The federal regulations relating to HIPAA include the terms *spouse* and *marriage* in the definition of the term *family member*. Since the law does not consider a patient's unmarried partner as family, the patient should execute an AHCD with a HIPAA authorization to expressly grant their partner access to protected health information.

POWERS OF ATTORNEY

A power of attorney is a document in which a person grants an agent the legal authority to take various financial and legal actions on their behalf, in contrast to AHCDs, which relate to healthcare matters only. Powers of attorney can allow one partner to manage the financial affairs of the other if they become incapacitated. This document is useful when partners maintain separate bank accounts. Partners who contribute jointly to living expenses may face difficulty if one partner becomes incapacitated and cannot personally cover the usual expenses. In addition, a power of attorney can authorize the agent to execute contracts such as lease agreements. The incapacity of one partner need not disrupt the family's lifestyle.

WILLS AND TRUSTS

If you die without a will or trust, state intestacy laws dictate who will inherit your property. Generally, only spouses and blood relatives inherit under intestate succession; unmarried partners get nothing. Thus, executing estate planning documents to provide an inheritance for your partner at your death is important. Also, in your estate planning documents, you can designate your partner as your personal representative. A personal representative is responsible for administering a decedent's estate. Many states give priority to the surviving spouse to act as the personal representative when a decedent has no estate plan. Other family members and interested persons may petition to be appointed personal representative, but the court gives weight to the nominee in the decedent's will.

PROPERTY CO-OWNERSHIP

The high cost of home ownership often causes unmarried partners to jointly purchase their family residence. The partners may take title to the property as joint tenants or as tenants in common. Joint tenancy includes a right of survivorship, meaning that a deceased joint tenant's property interest passes by operation of law to the surviving joint tenant without probate or trust administration. Therefore, joint tenancy is popular as a matter of convenience. The drawback of joint tenancy is that the co-owners have no flexibility in designating their beneficiaries. The surviving joint tenant becomes the sole owner of the property and can dispose of it as they wish. Furthermore, if the relationship ends, the partners must sever the joint tenancy if they do not want their former partner to inherit their property interest.

In contrast, tenants in common have no right of survivorship. The property interest of a deceased tenant in common passes to the decedent's legal heirs or the beneficiaries of the decedent's will or trust. When partners co-own property as tenants in common, each one can direct the disposition of their property interest in their respective estate plans. Sometimes this means that partners leave their property interests to the survivor of them, but a partner may instead give their property interest to other beneficiaries, such as their children. Tenants in common may transfer their interests to the trustees of their living trusts. Each partner controls the disposition of their share of the property, including the ability to designate beneficiaries and provide whether the beneficiaries receive their interests outright or in trust.

JOINT TENANCY AND TENANCY-IN-COMMON AGREEMENTS

It is good practice for co-owners of property to enter into written agreements that set forth each party's rights and responsibilities. Marriage imposes certain rights and obligations on the spouses. If a married couple jointly owns property and divorces, the court adjudicates the property's disposition as part of the dissolution process. Unmarried couples who end their relationship do not have a similar system to protect them. Instead, they must create their own agreement. A joint tenancy or tenancy-in-common agreement can include provisions relating to the management and disposition of the property, such as payment of expenses or what will happen if one owner wants to sell their share. Such agreements can outline a process for resolving disputes between the parties. If one co-owner wants to sell the property and the other does not want to sell, a written agreement will help the parties avoid the burden and expense of going to court. For example, a tenancy-in-common agreement can require the selling party to first offer their property interest to the other co-owner in a buyout. The agreement can set forth a timeline in which a buyout must happen and a method of valuing the property interest for sale. Creating a written plan in advance expedites separation and reduces conflict if the partners decide to end their relationship.

CONCLUSION

Unmarried couples lack the same legal protections and benefits that married couples have. An estate planning attorney who has experience working with unmarried couples can help you navigate the issues and plan for incapacity, death, or separation.

Nicole Ramos Takemoto leads Candelaria PC's trusts and estates practice. Candelaria PC is a full-service family law and estate planning firm with offices in Walnut Creek, California and Oakland, California.

Nicole Ramos Takemoto

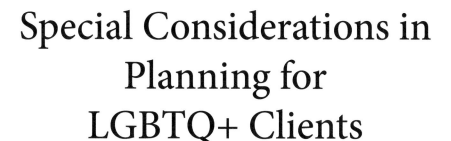

46

Special Considerations in Planning for LGBTQ+ Clients

By Kevin C. Martin (Washington, DC)

Everyone who engages an attorney for estate planning has a unique set of circumstances; this chapter focuses on the LGBTQ+ community and the special considerations that should be addressed for optimal planning. This chapter begins with a brief background of the community and recent trends. It then focuses on planning considerations. Throughout the chapter, approval of same-sex marriage is used as a rough proxy of acceptance of the LGBTQ+ community.

A BRIEF BACKGROUND AND RECENT TRENDS

The history of the LGBTQ+ community has, until very recently, been quite bleak. Individuals and same-sex couples have routinely encountered outright discrimination and (sometimes deadly) violence. This experience slowly changed beginning in the 1960s and 70s with the repeal of sodomy laws, the Stonewall riots, and the election of openly gay politicians. Progress slowed in the 1980s because of the HIV/AIDS epidemic, but it slowly resumed in the 1990s and 2000s with the end of the Don't Ask Don't Tell policy and the passage of the Matthew Shepard Act, which expanded the 1994 hate crime law.

The 2010s were an exciting time for the community, and gay marriage finally became legal in 2015. In *Obergefell v. Hodges,* the US Supreme Court legalized same-sex marriage, struck down state bans on same-sex marriage, and required states to honor out-of-state same-sex marriage licenses. Several counties in some states, including Alabama, Kentucky, and Texas, refused to issue same-sex marriage licenses; however, these issues were quickly resolved in favor of issuing the licenses.

It is striking to witness the change in public opinion toward same-sex marriage. Although prejudice toward same-sex marriage continues, according to Pew Research Center, public support for it rose from 37 percent to 62 percent from 2007 to 2017, including 74 percent of millennials and 65 percent of Gen Xers.

ESTATE PLANNING CONSIDERATIONS FOR THE LGBTQ+ COMMUNITY

As the old saying goes, when planning for your estate, you do not know when you will die, how much you will have, or what the estate tax will be. I add more for the LGBTQ+ community: you do not know where you will be living or what your relatives really think about your sexuality. If you are a member of the LGBTQ+ community, you should consider the following when planning your estate.

ENSURE YOU HAVE A PLAN

While estate planning is important for everyone, it is **critical** for members of the LGBTQ+ community. If you are in an unmarried partnership or live in a state that does not recognize domestic partnerships, without adequate estate planning, you are exposing yourself, your partner, and any children to potentially serious negative outcomes. For example, if you have assets such as a house or retirement account in your name alone and lack a will or trust, state law will dictate who receives your assets at your death. You should also consider what will happen to you or your family in case of a health emergency or incapacity. If there is no documentation in place prior to these events, there could be unintended consequences with respect to your medical care, the right to stay in your home as long as possible, or who has access to your bank and investment accounts to pay for your care.

UNDERSTAND THE BASICS OF YOUR STATE'S RELEVANT LAWS

Ideally, consult with an attorney to find out whether your state has a domestic partnership law and understand the rights it provides. Eight states have domestic partnership laws (or, in Hawaii, reciprocal beneficiaries) that generally function the same as marriage laws. These laws were passed in the 1990s to circumvent federal laws that did not recognize same-sex marriage.

CONSIDER A TRUST-BASED PLAN

A trust-based estate plan is often better than a will-based plan for several reasons:

- In general, it is harder to contest a trust-based plan than a will-based plan.

- Your attorney can help you keep the trust plan up to date, but you may not be likely to update your will, especially if you choose to create it by yourself.

- Assets are titled in the name of the trust, which may be evidence that you spent time, thought, and effort creating the trust, refuting an allegation of undue influence or fraud.

- Trust administration is generally a private affair, whereas a will-based plan will generally involve probate. Probate is a public process, and there will be additional costs involved (court costs, legal fees, accounting fees, etc.)

- Trusts often detail what occurs during incapacity, but because a will takes effect upon death, it does not address incapacity. A power of attorney, which can be part of either type of plan, can cover incapacity; however, powers of attorney can be more difficult than trusts to use during incapacity.

EFFECTS OF PLANNING ON CHILDREN

Beyond making end-of-life decisions, proper estate planning ensures that, in the case of your incapacity or death, your children will be cared for by someone you chose. For couples who are not married or do not live in a state that recognizes domestic partnerships, and one partner is the biological parent, it is especially important to designate temporary and permanent guardians before an issue arises. Otherwise, a court will decide who is the best person to raise the child, and that may not be someone you would have chosen.

CONCLUSION

I have been involved in situations where there has been little to no planning before someone passes away. Sometimes death is sudden and unexpected. Other times, planning occurs when there is a health crisis, which is never ideal. In almost every case, there is a complication that could have been avoided with proper planning. The LGBTQ+ community has special considerations that should be carefully contemplated.

Members should consult with an estate planning attorney to understand state law and discuss various scenarios.

Kevin C. Martin, Attorney at Law, PLLC, focuses on estate planning for working professionals in the Washington, D.C. area, as well as US citizens living overseas. As a proud member of the LGBTQ+ community with over a decade of experience working and living overseas, Kevin Martin has a great deal of experience understanding and navigating the unique needs of these communities.

Kevin Martin

SECTION 5

Tax Principles
and Planning

47

An Overview of the
Estate, Gift, and Income
Tax Rules Pertaining
to Estates

By Linda A. Burrows (Westlake Village, California)

It has been said that nothing in life is certain but death and taxes. Although there is no way to minimize death, there is at least a way to minimize taxes.

Here are two of the most important steps to minimize estate, gift, and income taxes, whether your estate is big or small:

- Be aware that there are tax rules that apply at your death and to your estate (but there may be exemptions and exclusions).

- Consult knowledgeable advisors who will consider your situation, including your relationships and your assets.

STEP 1 TO MINIMIZE TAXES: BE AWARE OF TAX RULES

Two of the most common types of taxes at death are transfer taxes and income taxes. Most people will transfer money and property after they die, and many have assets that will earn income after their date of death. This means that you are likely to have something that will be taxable when you pass away. However, there may be an exemption or exclusion that will reduce or eliminate the tax due.

The estate tax and the gift tax are examples of transfer taxes, which are taxes on property you transfer to another after you die or during your life. Since the law is subject to change—and often does—be aware that today's exemption amounts, exclusion amounts, and tax rates are not likely to be the amounts and tax rates in effect when you die or make a particular gift. Therefore, it is important not only to be aware of the current law but also to pay attention to changes in the law that may necessitate updates to your estate plan.

The income tax for estates is a tax on the income earned by your assets after your death but before the assets are distributed out of your estate. Your estate will have a new tax identification number under which the income will be reported to the Internal Revenue Service (IRS). The rate will not be your previous individual rates but rather the rates determined under the brackets for estates and trusts, which usually result in a higher overall rate. If income is distributed out of the estate to beneficiaries, then they, rather than the estate, can bear the tax—and they do so at their individual rates.

The following scenarios demonstrate transfers and income that could be subject to tax, although exemptions and exclusions may apply:

Scenario	Could this be subject to estate tax?	Could this be subject to gift tax?	Could this be subject to income tax?	Could an exemption or exclusion apply and reduce or eliminate tax?	What should you discuss with an advisor?
You die with a bank account that is earning interest, and your children will inherit the account.	✓		✓	✓	Ask about estate tax exemptions and options to hold cash accounts.
In December, you give your child $50,000 to help with a down payment on a house.		✓		✓	Ask how and when to make cash gifts to your children to qualify for annual exclusions.
You die, and your spouse gets everything you own.	✓			✓	Ask about the marital deduction and portability.

Scenario	Could this be subject to estate tax?	Could this be subject to gift tax?	Could this be subject to income tax?	Could an exemption or exclusion apply and reduce or eliminate tax?	What should you discuss with an advisor?
You allow your cousin to live rent-free in your cabin.		✓		✓	Ask about annual gift exclusion amounts.
You plan to have your executor sell all assets (including highly appreciated technology stocks) and then give the money to charity.	✓		✓	✓	Ask about best approaches for charitable giving that reduce estate taxes and capital gains taxes, leaving more to go to charity.
You give your child money for tuition, which is then paid from the child's account to the university.		✓			Ask how to pay for education expenses so the payment may qualify for an exclusion.
You pay for your child's apartment at college.		✓		✓	Ask how to keep track of any transfers to your child, either directly or indirectly, where full consideration (measured in money or money's worth) is not received in return such as paying for rent.
Your estate nets $100,000 in rent from the apartment building you owned at death.	✓		✓		Ask about options to transfer real property and rental income.

Scenario	Could this be subject to estate tax?	Could this be subject to gift tax?	Could this be subject to income tax?	Could an exemption or exclusion apply and reduce or eliminate tax?	What should you discuss with an advisor?
You add your child as a joint owner of your $500,000 account, and your child withdraws some funds.	✓	✓		✓	Ask about the types of transfers that constitute gifts even if you did not intend to make a gift.
You locate your dad's first car (now valuable) on the internet and buy it for him.		✓		✓	Ask about annual gifting amounts and reporting requirements.
The night before you die, you give your child a famous original painting by a French impressionist artist.	✓	✓		✓	Ask about basis rules, whether to transfer assets before you die, and gifts made before death.
You take your parents on a cruise around the world.		✓		✓	Ask about using a spouse's annual exclusion to double the amount.
You give your aunt money to help her pay for medical expenses.		✓		✓	Ask about the impact of direct payments for someone's medical care.
You die with a $1 million life insurance policy.	✓			✓	Ask about life insurance trusts.

STEP 2 TO MINIMIZE TAXES: CONSULT KNOWLEDGEABLE ADVISORS ABOUT YOUR SITUATION

Because almost all money and property is subject to a transfer tax or an income tax after your death, it is best to regularly consult knowledgeable advisors about the tax impact of transfers both after death and during life, as well as the income likely to be generated by assets after you die.

For information about the taxes that may be owed at your death, ask your advisor to help you create a list of what you own, how you own it, and how to calculate an estimation of the total value at your death. Ask advisors about exemption amounts, exclusions, and tax rates, and then follow up with them every year about tax law changes.

Lastly, consult the IRS website at irs.gov to learn more about estate, gift, and income taxes as well as the following documents:

- IRS Form 706, U.S. Estate (and Generation-Skipping Transfer) Tax Return
- IRS Form 709, U.S. Gift (and Generation-Skipping Transfer) Tax Return
- IRS Form 1041, U.S. Income Tax Return for Estates and Trusts
- IRS Publication 559, Survivors, Executors and Administrators

Linda A. Burrows is the founder of Claritas Law, APC. She is a certified specialist in Estate Planning, Trust and Probate Law by the State Bar of California Board of Legal Specialization.

Linda Burrows

48

Multijurisdictional Issues

By Jeanne Vatterott-Gale (Yuma, Arizona)

S nowbirds with residences in more than one state or retirees who are considering changing their residency to another state must plan carefully. The law of the state in which you reside generally guides the terms of your trust or will, but other factors should also be considered in your decision-making: your income tax liability, state estate tax or inheritance tax liability, and certain provisions affecting beneficiaries.

TRUSTS, RESIDENCY, AND TAXATION

Much of estate planning is driven by the desire to avoid federal estate tax, state estate or inheritance tax, and income taxes. States may impose estate, inheritance, income, sales, and property taxes.

Generally, the location of a trust's administration will determine which state tax rates apply to trust income. Often, there is no restriction on a trustee's ability to change the location of the trust's administration. However, a change in the trustee's residency or the trust's administration may affect the tax rates applicable to the trust. In the event of litigation, it could also affect the court's jurisdiction and even certain procedural matters, regardless of statements in the trust as to governing law. It is important to be aware of these issues and to build flexibility into your trust documents to enable you and your successor trustee to address them if they arise in the future.

Trusts can hold property located in more than one state. When you own real property, such as residences, in more than one state, a revocable trust is usually the preferred method of ownership because it avoids probate. This is especially important if you have homes or other real property in more than one state not held with rights of survivorship; holding them in a revocable trust will avoid probate proceedings in each state.

State laws vary considerably regarding the best practice for holding title to your personal residence. In Arizona, for instance, holding a primary residence in a trust may prevent the homeowner from qualifying for the state's long-term care program. Therefore, many Arizona estate planners advise clients to hold their residence in their own names and prepare a beneficiary deed that transfers it to their trust upon their death. Further, be aware that in certain jurisdictions, adverse property tax consequences may result when you change your primary residence. In California, for instance, if you cease using your California home as your primary residence, your family, which might otherwise be eligible to prevent increased property taxes upon your death, will lose that ability. Further, be sure to compare the relative tax liability on the sale of your residence if you change residences. The homeowner's exemption from capital gains taxes cannot be used against a home that is not your primary residence.

An inheritance tax is based on the value of a specific bequest (an inherited item). Although a decedent's estate is responsible for paying the estate tax, the beneficiary is liable for the inheritance tax. Among the states that impose inheritance taxes, most exempt immediate family members such as spouses and the deceased's children. Inheritance taxes are applicable in Iowa, Kentucky, Maryland, Nebraska, New Jersey, and Pennsylvania.

States with no income tax typically attract retirees. As of 2022, Alaska, Florida, Nevada, New Hampshire, South Dakota, Tennessee, Texas, Washington, and Wyoming do not impose income taxes. A lack of income tax does not mean that there are no investment taxes assessed on trust income for irrevocable trusts, inheritance taxes, or estate taxes.

An estate tax is based on the overall value of the deceased person's estate. The state of Washington, for instance, has an estate tax. The amount you can pass tax-free in Washington is $2.193 million per person in 2022. Thus, if you own a residence in Seattle, where home values have skyrocketed over the past few years, your estate may be liable to the state of Washington even though your primary residence is in Arizona.

Other states do not have sales tax, for instance, Oregon. However, Oregon has one of the highest income tax rates in the country.

There are certain taxation privileges that relate to a taxpayer's residency requirements, which may differ for purposes of voting, income taxes, or estate taxes. California has a very complex system of constitutional amendments that affect a homeowner's ability to pass on certain property tax savings to their heirs.

COMMUNITY PROPERTY STATES

Many western states are community property states. They provide couples with greater tax benefits upon the death of the first spouse than do separate property states. If a married couple purchases and holds rental real estate as joint tenants, upon the death of the first spouse, the surviving spouse will receive a step-up in basis (assuming the value of the property has increased) on the one-half of the property inherited. However, if the couple holds the property as community property with rights of survivorship or converts it by deed into community property before transferring it to their revocable trust, the surviving spouse will normally be entitled to a step-up in basis as to the entire community interest on the death of the first spouse. This may provide enormous tax savings for the surviving spouse.

DETERMINING YOUR RESIDENCY

If you are retiring and wish to sell your principal (primary) residence, you are entitled to avoid taxation of certain capital gains under the federal tax code up to certain levels ($250,000 or $500,000 if married filing jointly). You must meet certain eligibility tests relating to the number of years that you have held the residence. There are also partial exclusions of gain in certain situations.

The Internal Revenue Service (IRS) rules state, "An individual has only one main home at a time." If you own and live in just one home, then it is your main home. If you own or live in more than one home, then a facts and circumstances test is applied to determine which property is your main home. Although the most important factor is where you spend the most time, other factors listed below are relevant as well. The more of these factors that are true of a home, the more likely it is to be considered your main home. The IRS will consider the following factors:

The address listed on your

- U.S. Postal Service record,
- voter registration card,
- federal and state tax returns, and
- driver's license or car registration.

The home is near

- where you work,
- where you bank,
- the residence of one or more family members, and
- recreational clubs or religious organizations of which you are a member.

SPECIAL NEEDS BENEFICIARIES

In the context of special needs beneficiaries, the beneficiary's residency should ultimately be the determining factor of the appropriate trust terms. This is because, with the exception of Medicare and Supplemental Security Income, most public benefit programs are administered by the states. These programs vary significantly by state. Funds that flow from the federal government into the Medicaid program then flow through the states. Therefore, eligibility requirements for those benefits are set out in state law. Mechanisms should be built into a special needs trust to transfer the trust into another eligible trust if the location of a special needs beneficiary changes.

In view of these considerations, you should have your estate plan reviewed by a qualified attorney admitted to practice in the state of your residency and wherever you own property or administer a trust.

Jeanne Vatterott-Gale is an estate and trust law specialist certified by the Arizona Board of Legal Specialization and a partner in Hunt & Gale, whose attorneys are also admitted in Alaska, California, Colorado, Missouri, Oregon, Texas, Washington, and Wyoming.

Jeanne Vatterott-Gale

49

State Death Taxes: Potential Impact and Strategies

By Jeffrey Knapp (Basking Ridge, New Jersey)

Is your estate subject to one or more state death taxes? For a quick answer, refer to the chart included at the end of this chapter and check the Estate and Inheritance columns for each state in which you own property. At the time of publication, thirty-three states are essentially not collecting any death taxes. Nevertheless, you should be aware that state death taxes are in flux because some are coupled with the federal estate tax system, which may soon be substantially altered.[1] In addition, all or nearly all of the fifty-one U.S. jurisdictions are currently operating with budget deficits on a consistent basis. Keep this in mind, especially if you are considering relocating to or already own property in one or more states that have either an estate or an inheritance tax.

Estate taxes are based on the size of a decedent's estate. Historically, few states have had separate estate taxes. A larger number have had "pick-up taxes" tied to the federal credit for state death taxes, which has been phased out. Inheritance taxes are levied

---

1   The federal estate tax exemption, adjusted annually for inflation, is currently $12.06 million, and is scheduled to be cut in half on January 1, 2026. The federal annual gift tax exclusion is currently $16,000 per recipient.

on one's right to inherit property. An inheritor is classified by the degree of their relationship to the decedent, with different exemptions and tax rates applied to each class. Spouses and children are often exempt from inheritance taxes, but siblings, nieces, and nephews generally incur an applicable inheritance tax. Although Oregon's law, for example, refers only to an inheritance tax, it does not appear to distinguish among classes of beneficiaries, so its tax is categorized as an estate tax in the chart.

ESTATE AND INHERITANCE TAXES

You may recognize some of the figures in the Estate column in the chart. Although the federal basic estate tax exclusion amount was temporarily doubled to $10 million (indexed for inflation) as part of the 2017 tax reform legislation, in prior years, it was significantly lower. In 2001, Congress increased the prior federal estate tax exemption from $675,000 to $1 million, then to $2 million, then to $3.5 million, before moving to $5 million (indexed for inflation) for 2011.

Most of the states currently collecting an estate tax provide an exemption for either the first $1 million, $2 million, or $5 million (indexed) of the estate's value. While the states generally publish marginal rates of 5-16 percent on the taxable portions above the exempted amount, most of these states have effective rates of 37, 39, or even 41 percent on relatively small (approximately $50,000 to $100,000) slices of estates just over the respective exemptions of $1 million or $2 million. This hidden reality creates planning incentives for those with estates that are perhaps 5-25 percent over their state's applicable exemption. Could you, by gifting your assets down to the point of your state's exemption, avoid both the state tax and the need to file an estate tax return?

CONSULT LOCAL COUNSEL

This is where the concept of local rule and the absolute necessity of consulting local estate planning counsel come into play. For example, note that the chart does not capture the intricacies of exemptions under the various inheritance taxes. On the topic of gifting, several states (including Connecticut and North Carolina) have separate gift taxes, and several other states (including Iowa and New Jersey) have clawback provisions that bring gifts made within thirty-six months of death back into one's estate for state death tax calculations. Some state death taxes exempt life insurance (Pennsylvania), and some state death taxes apply to nonresident owners of local real estate (New Jersey).

If you have substantial assets, including property in two or more states, it is advisable to engage local counsel in each of those states in conversations about domicile and situs as well as the local rules applied to these terms. Generally, domicile is where you spend 183 or more days per year, and situs refers to place or location. Usually, tangible property has a tax situs where it is physically located, and intangible property has a tax

51 – JURISDICTION TAX TABLE
CURRENT AS OF JANUARY 1, 2022

© JEFFREY L. KNAPP, EPLS

State	Estate Tax[1]	Inheritance Tax	Individual Income Tax	Avg Sales Tax	Notes
Alabama			2%-5%	9.22%	
Alaska				1.76%	$1114/resident dividend for 2021
Arizona			2.59%-4.5%	8.4%	
Arkansas			2%-5.5%	9.48%	
California			1%-13.3%	8.82%	? + a new "wealth tax?"
Colorado			4.55% flat	7.72%	
Connecticut	^$9.1 mil; 11.6-12%		3%-6.99%	6.35%	Gift tax since 2005
Delaware			2.2%-6.6%	0	
Dist. of Columbia	^$4 mil*; 12-16%		4%-10.75%	6%	*for 2021. Indexing annually, beginning in 2022
Florida				7.01%+	
Georgia			1%-5.75%	7.33%	
Hawaii	^ $5.49 mil w/portability; 10-20%		1.4%-11%	4.44%	
Idaho			1.125%-6.925%	6.02%	
Illinois	^$4 mil; 0.8-16%		4.95% flat	8.83%	
Indiana			3.23% flat	7%	
Iowa		0-9%, phaseout 2025	0.33%-8.53%	6.94%	incl. gifts w/i 3 yrs of death
Kansas			3.1%-5.7%	8.7%	
Kentucky		0-16%	5% flat	6%	
Louisiana			2%-4.75%	9.55%	
Maine	^$6.01mil; 8-12%		5.8%-7.15%	5.5%	

---

1   The federal estate tax exemption amount for 2022 is $12.06 million.

State	Estate Tax[2]	Inheritance Tax	Individual Income Tax	Avg Sales Tax	Notes
Maryland	^$5 mil w/ port; 0-16%	0-10%	2%-5.75%	6%	
Massachusetts	^$1 mil; 0.8-16%		5% flat	6.25%	"Cliff" estate tax, incl. 709 $
Michigan			4.25% flat	6%	
Minnesota	^$3 mil; 13-16%		5.35%-9.85%	7.47%	
Mississippi			3%-5%	7.07%	
Missouri			1.5%-5.4%	8.25%	
Montana			1%-6.9%	0	
Nebraska		1-18%	2.46-6.84%	6.94%	
Nevada				8.23%	
New Hampshire			5% flat*	0%	*int. & divs. only; no wages
New Jersey	0, but Stay Tuned!	0-16%; gifts w/i 3 yrs of death included	1.4%-10.75%	6.625%	Inh. Tax on Non-Res. real estate
New Mexico		may be income?	1.7%-5.9%	7.84%	inheritance= income?
New York	^$6.11mil; 3.06-16%; 3-yr gifts included		4% to 8.82%	8.52%	"Cliff" tax from $1 up
North Carolina			4.99% flat	6.98%	
North Dakota			1.1%-2.9%	6.96%	
Ohio			2.85%-4.797%	7.22%	
Oklahoma			0.25%-4.75%	8.95%	
Oregon	^$1 mil; 10-16%	See "estate tax"	4.75%-9.9%	0	Called "IT"; no recent gifts included
Pennsylvania		0-15%	3.07% flat	6.34%	Adult children pay Inheritance Tax
Rhode Island	^$1,648,111* 0-16%		3.75%-5.99%	7%	*indexing annually

2   The federal estate tax exemption amount for 2022 is $12.06 million.

State	Estate Tax[3]	Inheritance Tax	Individual Income Tax	Avg Sales Tax	Notes
South Carolina			0%-7%	7.47%	
South Dakota				6.4%	
Tennessee				9.55%	
Texas				8.19%	
Utah			4.95% flat	7.19%	
Vermont	^$5 mil; 16% flat		3.35%-8.75%	6.24%	incl. gifts w/i 2 yrs of death
Virginia			2%-5.75%	5.75%	
Washington	^$2,193,000*; 10-20%			9.29%	*indexing annually
West Virginia			3-6.5%	6.51%	
Wisconsin			3.54-7.65%	5.43%	
Wyoming				5.39%	

situs at the domicile of the owner. As you can see in the chart, there may be reasons to either carefully document or change your domicile, or change the situs of property by utilizing certain trustees. If you have property in two or more states, you should minimize the possibility of being taxed both coming and going.

INCOME AND SALES TAXES

Lastly, if you are considering moving to another state or are choosing between two states where you already own property, note that the two left-hand columns in the chart are not the only pertinent tax factors. You likely have many healthy years ahead of you to pay income tax, sales tax, and property tax! Accordingly, the chart also summarizes state income taxes and general sales taxes. Counties and cities often add to the general sales tax and control property taxes to a degree that the chart cannot capture.

CONCLUSION

For more information on property taxes and the overall state-by-state tax burden, or to check changes in state taxes between future editions of this book, you may find www.retirementliving.com helpful. Another factor that may impact which state you choose to live in is how much of each federal tax dollar is returned to that state, so you may wish to track that amount at www.taxfoundation.org. Thorough research of dozens of

---

3   The federal estate tax exemption amount for 2022 is $12.06 million.

websites and publications did not yield one single source that was 100 percent accurate and current for all fifty-one U.S. jurisdictions. Thus, the caveat above bears repeating: consult local counsel in all pertinent states before taking any action.

Jeff Knapp, JD, AEP®, CFP®, is an Estate Planning Law Specialist, a Certified Legacy Advisor, a Fellow of the EPI, and the lead attorney at The Knapp Law Firm, LLC. He works with families throughout New Jersey and has helped transition client plans to twenty-eight other states. Jeff can be reached at 888-KNAPP-LAW or at jknapp@ knapplaw.net.

Jeffrey Knapp

50

Taxation of Trusts

By Brian Budman (Greenwood Village, Colorado)

> *Today, it takes more brains and effort to make out the income-tax form than it does to make the income.*
>
> —*Alfred E. Neuman*

Most Americans who embark upon the estate planning journey are presented with the option to use either a will or a revocable living trust as the foundation of their estate plan. If you choose the latter, you will be advised to fund the trust (i.e., transfer ownership of your assets from you to your trust). Further, your revocable living trust may be drafted in a way that provides for the establishment of additional trusts upon your death to hold part or all of your assets allocated to and for the benefit of some or all of your chosen beneficiaries. Determining the income tax treatment of these trusts can be challenging.

GRANTOR TRUSTS

A grantor is someone who conveys property or property interests to another person or entity, formally or informally and with or without consideration (money's worth). When you establish a trust and transfer money to that trust, you are a grantor. In a grantor trust, the grantor has the legal formality of a trust but does not give up all dominion and control over the property that the grantor conveys to the trust. The tax rules applicable to grantor trusts ask who has certain substantive powers over the trust property—that is, who should count as the owner of the trust assets for income tax purposes?

A revocable trust is, by its very nature, a grantor trust. To revoke means to withdraw, repeal, rescind, cancel, or annul. As such, the person who contributes property to a trust has the power to revoke the trust or their portion of it and is the income tax owner of the trust or that portion. Being treated as the income tax owner of a trust is significant. The grantor is liable for taxes on the income generated in the trust; the grantor cannot pass the income tax liability through to the beneficiaries. The effect is no different than not having established a trust in the first place. If the grantor is deceased, then the trust can no longer be considered a grantor trust for income tax purposes.

One intriguing aspect of tax planning and trusts is the opportunity to take advantage of the discrepancies between the income tax and estate tax provisions found in the Internal Revenue Code (I.R.C.). The grantor trust rules in the income tax provisions do not coincide with those in the estate tax provisions. It is therefore possible to create a trust that is treated as a grantor trust for income tax purposes so that any transaction between the grantor and the trust will be ignored under the income tax provisions of the I.R.C., but the trust assets will not be included in the grantor's estate for estate tax purposes!

NONGRANTOR TRUSTS

If the trust is a nongrantor trust, the adjusted total income will become the taxable income of the trust. The income tax rates applicable to trusts differ dramatically from those applicable to individuals because trusts have highly compressed tax brackets. For 2022, trusts reach the highest federal tax bracket of 37 percent at a taxable income of $13,450 (except capital gains, which are taxable at a lower rate). By comparison, the tax rate for single taxpayers on taxable income of $13,450 is only 12 percent. The highest federal tax bracket of 37 percent does not apply to most individual taxpayers until their taxable income reaches $539,900.

The term *deduction,* for our purposes, means a subtraction against the gross income of the trust. Of the various possible deductions permitted, the dominant one is the income distribution deduction (IDD). This is the computational deduction allowed for distributions of tax-accountable income to one or more beneficiaries of the trust.

The income derived from the trust assets is taxed either at the trust level, the beneficiary level, or allocated among the trust and the beneficiaries. Trusts are not to be used for tax avoidance. Whether the trust pays its own taxes depends on whether the trust is a nongrantor trust classified as a simple trust or a complex trust, or is a grantor trust.

A nongrantor trust is a simple trust for the tax year if

1.   all of its income is required to be distributed currently,

2. no charitable contributions are made or called for, and

3. no distributions from corpus are made.

If the trust does not meet the above definition, it is either a nongrantor trust that is a complex trust or a grantor trust.

In order to determine the IDD, you must first calculate the trust's *distributable net income* (DNI). DNI is defined in the I.R.C.: generally, it is an amount equal to total trust income (including tax-exempt interest but excluding capital gains and losses), less deductions such as state tax paid and trustee fees. The DNI is the income distributed and potentially taxable to all beneficiaries. It is computed on Form 1041, Schedule B: Income Distribution Deduction. Whatever evolves as the bottom line on Schedule B becomes an allowable distribution deduction against the taxable income of the trust. The exact same amount is mandatorily included in the gross income of the beneficiaries.

It is also important to note the sixty-five-day rule, which permits a trustee to make distributions to trust beneficiaries within sixty-five days after the year-end and treat those distributions as if they were made in the previous tax year.

CONCLUSION

Family members and the professionals assisting them often fail to discuss how certain choices can affect the taxation of a trust. Being aware of the income tax aspects of various estate planning tools can help lawyers and clients make choices that minimize the federal and state income taxes payable at different stages in a trust's existence. Trust taxation is complex but very important.

The Law Office of Brian Budman, P.C. is a full-service estate planning firm located in Greenwood Village, Colorado. Brian Budman, LLB, LLM, wishes to acknowledge the assistance of Skyler Budman on this chapter. Skyler attends Rutgers University Law School with an anticipated graduation date of May 2023.

Brian Budman

51

Using a Credit Shelter Trust and Marital Trusts to Reduce Taxes

By Christopher C. Papin (Edmond, Oklahoma)

This chapter addresses trust-based planning to foster effective estate administration and to help manage estate tax liability. However, it is important to recognize that these goals can be achieved with a myriad of planning tools.

HOW ESTATE AND GIFT TAXES WORK

The United States imposes a federal tax upon the transfer of assets from one generation to another. Many states impose a similar tax, but for the purposes of this chapter, I will focus on the federal taxes imposed by the Internal Revenue Code (I.R.C.). State law determines the existence and characterization of property rights, but federal law determines the taxation of assets by the I.R.S. These taxes are imposed upon the transfer of assets at a taxpayer's death or during a taxpayer's lifetime. The federal tax imposed on gratuitous transfers at death is the estate tax. The gift tax is imposed on gratuitous transfers during a taxpayer's lifetime.

The basic concept underlying these taxes is simple. Let's look at an example to illustrate it. A taxpayer passes away with an estate including assets valued at $15 million. A simple application of the estate tax would effectively tax those assets at the time of passing. Assuming a tax rate of 40 percent, the deceased taxpayer will owe an estate tax of $6 million ($15 million x 40 percent). Similarly, if a taxpayer gives their child $15 million during the taxpayer's lifetime, a gift tax of $6 million is imposed, assuming the same tax rate. There could also be some combination of transfers during life and at death. Suppose that the taxpayer gives their child $7 million during the taxpayer's lifetime and $8 million upon the taxpayer's passing. At the time of the $7 million lifetime gift, a tax would be imposed. At death, a tax would be imposed on the remaining $8 million. Although the I.R.C. combines the estate and gift tax to establish one lifetime exclusion amount, we will focus on the estate tax.

Chapter 11 of the I.R.C. addresses the federal estate tax, Chapter 12 addresses the federal gift tax, and Chapter 13 addresses the generation-skipping transfer tax. I.R.C. § 2631 establishes an exemption from tax on the first $12.06 million of assets (for 2022). This amount is known as the exclusion amount, and it changes from year to year to adjust for inflation. Application of the exclusion amount means that you will not pay any taxes on transfers at death or through lifetime gifts up to an aggregate of $12.06 million, but you will pay taxes on transfers of assets that exceed the exclusion amount. Continuing with our $15 million example, you will pay tax only on the $2.94 million that exceeds the exclusion amount. The tax would be $1.32 million ($15 million – $12.06 million = $2.94 million x 40 percent). Each spouse in a married couple has a $12.06 million exclusion (for 2022), so the exclusion amount is effectively doubled for married couples to $24.12 million.

The 2017 Tax Cuts and Jobs Act (TCJA) increased the exclusion amount through the end of 2025. Beginning January 1, 2026, the annual exclusion will revert to the pre-TCJA amount of $5.49 million, as adjusted for inflation. At that time, the exclusion amount is anticipated to be approximately $6 million per taxpayer if no changes in the law occur before 2026. The current large exclusion amount may create a false sense of security, as the lower federal estate tax exclusion amount will soon become a reality beginning in 2026.

Another important estate tax planning concept is portability. Portability became available to taxpayers after 2010. Portability allows the deceased spousal unused exclusion (DSUE) amount to be preserved and used by the surviving spouse. In short, if your entire exclusion amount is not used when you pass away, your surviving spouse can use it. There are requirements that must be met to preserve the DSUE: most notably, the executor of the estate must make a timely election by filing an estate tax return (Form 706) that both elects portability and calculates the portability amount.

ESTATE PLANNING STRATEGIES TO MINIMIZE TAXES

MARITAL DEDUCTIONS

I.R.C. § 2056 permits a marital deduction for qualifying transfers to reduce a taxable estate, and I.R.C. § 2523 permits a marital deduction for qualifying transfers to reduce the value of what may otherwise be a taxable gift. As a result, amounts given from one spouse to the other during the gifting spouse's lifetime, and amounts given by a deceased taxpayer to a spouse at death, may not be taxable.

One easy way to avoid estate taxes is to simply give all of your assets to your US citizen spouse at death. Many people want to do this in their estate plan. The marital deduction applies against the value of the estate and thus no tax is due. On the surface, this seems like a good option, but it can create a scenario in which the surviving spouse may have a taxable estate. Consider the following scenarios:

Scenario 1: Spouse A owns assets valued at $20 million. Spouse B owns assets valued at $5 million. If Spouse A passes away, Spouse A's estate would be valued at $20 million and would exceed the lifetime exclusion amount of $12.06 million, leaving $7.94 million subject to estate taxes. However, if the entire $20 million is left to Spouse B, the unlimited marital deduction reduces Spouse A's taxable estate to $0. Spouse B will then have an estate valued at $25 million.

Scenario 2: Same as above, but Spouse A only leaves $7.94 million to Spouse B and is allowed a marital deduction. This reduces Spouse A's estate to $12.06 million, the tax on which is offset by the lifetime exclusion. Now Spouse B has an estate of $12.94 million ($7.94 million from Spouse A + $5 million of Spouse B's assets). What about the $12.06 million exclusion amount? We will consider that situation in the expanded Scenario 2 below.

Leaving all of your assets to your spouse outright may not be the best option for reasons outside the scope of this chapter, and a trust or multiple trusts may be employed to address those issues. However, to reduce their tax burden, taxpayers can use a marital trust while ensuring that their needs are met.

CREDIT SHELTER TRUSTS

It is common for estate planners to use a marital trust and a credit shelter or family trust (CST) to achieve what is commonly known as A/B estate tax planning. The marital trust provides both administrative flexibility and a tax benefit because it qualifies for a marital deduction. The CST helps utilize the benefit of any lifetime exclusion amount that may be available.

The assets left to a CST are considered part of the decedent's taxable estate. However, the lifetime exclusion available to the decedent can offset the tax on the assets in the

CST. So, when a CST is coupled with a marital trust, it is very common for families to avoid any estate tax when the first spouse dies.

Consider Scenario 2 again. The $12.06 million that was not given to Spouse B could be left in a trust that qualifies as a CST. The CST can be for the benefit of Spouse B but must meet certain criteria so that it does not qualify for the marital deduction. Most frequently, this is achieved by giving the surviving spouse access to the trust assets for their health, education, maintenance, and support or allowing for possible distributions to the remaining beneficiaries while the surviving spouse is living. Upon the surviving spouse's death, the assets pass to the remaining beneficiaries, typically the couple's children.

Scenario 2 expanded: Spouse A passes, leaving $7.94 million to Spouse B in a marital trust and $12.06 million in a CST for the benefit of Spouse B until death, and then to their kids. A $20 million estate is reduced to $12.06 million using the marital deduction of $7.94 million. The remaining $12.06 million estate falls within the current exclusion amount of $12.06 million, resulting in a $0 estate. Zero x 40 percent equals **no taxes due** on Spouse A's death.

The CST holding $12.06 million in assets will not be subject to any estate taxes upon Spouse B's death because those assets are not owned by Spouse B (they are owned by the trust) and are therefore excluded from Spouse B's estate. However, the $7.94 million held in the marital trust will be added to Spouse B's assets at death.

There are some administrative requirements involved in creating the CST. The CST will need to obtain a tax identification number, file annual income tax returns, and be administered by a trustee. In some scenarios, the cost of administering a CST may be significant. It is important to recognize the complexities and maintenance that will be required after the first spouse's passing.

PORTABILITY

Using portability and the DSUE is a relatively new practice that many are not yet aware of. Frequently, clients are overcome with grief upon the death of a loved one and are overwhelmed by the administrative burdens of handling an estate. Similarly, attorneys who are not familiar with tax laws or do not practice in this area may be solely focused on helping families overcome their grief and the administrative burdens. However, it is important to consider whether portability can minimize taxes.

Suppose Spouse A passes away owning $8 million in assets. Surviving Spouse B has $15 million in assets. With a portability election, Spouse B can use $4.06 million of DSUE ($12.06 million – $8 million), increasing Spouse B's total exclusion amount (to $16.2 million, assuming Spouse B's exclusion amount is also $12.06 million). Filing an estate tax return and electing portability could save Spouse B approximately $1.176 million in estate taxes: because Spouse B's lifetime exclusion amount of $16.12 million (with DSUE) would exceed the value of Spouse B's $15 million in assets, no estate taxes would be due.

Ask your estate planner to assess portability and advise you about its potential benefits. You should consider several factors in connection with this tax planning strategy. In some instances, your estate planning attorney can partner with a tax attorney or certified public accountant to determine the potential benefit of portability, the value of the DSUE, and the costs of making that election. The DSUE does not require you to use a marital trust or credit shelter trust, and assets can pass outright to your spouse if desired. Clients without trust-based planning tools can utilize the DSUE after the fact. The executor can use the DSUE as a tool to minimize any damage resulting from the lack of proper planning in advance of death. Trustees can also be given discretion to utilize the DSUE, in the absence of or through an executor. One major benefit to using the portability election in trust-based planning is that you can avoid the administrative burden and costs associated with a CST and reap the benefits of the unused estate tax exemption of a deceased taxpayer.

BRINGING IT ALL TOGETHER

With the sunset of the TCJA in 2026 and the lifetime exclusion returning to an amount around $6 million, many more taxpayers will soon be exposed to estate taxes. Everyone has unique and important circumstances that deserve proper analysis and guidance. With your attorney's guidance, you can weigh your desired outcome against the legal landscape to achieve a tax-efficient and administratively convenient estate plan.

Christopher Papin

Papin Law, PLLC is a solo boutique law firm representing small businesses and small business owners that specializes in estate planning, businesses, and tax planning. Complementary accounting, tax, and advisory services are offered by Papin CPA, PLLC.

52

What Is Included in Your Estate?

By Linda A. Burrows (Westlake Village, California)

The term *estate* is often misunderstood to describe only a wealthy person's assets, which are assumed to be grander in scale than a modest home and a few savings, brokerage, and retirement accounts. However, these common assets are indeed part of an estate, perhaps even *your* estate.

Residences, rental properties, joint bank accounts, individual retirement accounts, and life insurance policies are just a few of the types of assets in estates that the Greatest Generation and also now baby boomers are transferring to the next generation and other beneficiaries. Some financial analysts have stated that the present marks the greatest transfer of wealth in the history of the world.

WHAT CONSTITUTES YOUR ESTATE

In brief, your estate, for federal estate tax purposes, includes most assets that you own or have an interest in at your death. If you think that is a very broad statement, you are correct. It is meant to be.

WHY YOU SHOULD KNOW AND CARE ABOUT WHAT IS IN YOUR ESTATE

There is both a *gross estate* and a *taxable estate*. The gross estate is the value of property, real or personal and tangible or intangible, that is includible in the gross estate according to the federal tax code. Unless there are specific exclusions, an asset will be part of your gross estate.

Your taxable estate is your gross estate minus allowable deductions, such as the marital deduction, charitable deduction, and casualty and theft loss deductions, as well as the deductions for state death taxes paid, expenses of administration, and claims against the estate.

Knowing what is included in your gross estate enables you to determine what your taxable estate is and whether it will be subject to an applicable federal estate tax. These are the key steps in the process:

1. Identify the assets that make up your estate.

2. Determine the value of the assets that will make up your gross estate.

3. Determine the deductions that can be applied, which will result in your taxable estate.

4. Compute the tentative estate tax against the taxable estate.

5. Apply any credits available against the tentative tax.

Your executor, trustee, or personal representative, in conjunction with the tax professional preparing your final tax return and the estate's or trust's tax returns, will determine your gross and taxable estates in accordance with applicable law. Certain credits, such as the unified credit, will also affect the amount of federal estate tax (if any) due by reason of your death.

SPECIFIC ASSETS THAT ARE INCLUDIBLE IN YOUR ESTATE

Broadly speaking, the federal tax code identifies the following types of assets that make up your gross estate:

Asset Group	Specific Asset	Included in Your Gross Estate
All property you have an interest in		
	Tangible personal property	✓
	Real property	✓
	Publicly traded securities	✓
	Closely held entities	✓
	Promissory notes	✓
	Shares in investment companies or mutual funds	✓
	Bonds	✓

Asset Group	Specific Asset	Included in Your Gross Estate
Certain transfers within three years of death		✓
Certain transfers with retained "strings"		
	Transfers with a retained right of income	✓
	Transfers with a retained right of use	✓
	Transfers with a retained right of reversion (of more than 5 percent)	✓
	Transfers with a retained right to alter, amend, revoke, or terminate	✓
Specific types of property transfers		
	IRAs	✓
	Annuities	✓
	Pensions	✓
	Joint interests (with rights of survivorship) such as with a spouse or another	✓
	Assets for which you had a general power of appointment	✓
	Life insurance that is received by your estate or that you owned at death	✓

VALUATION

The valuation of assets is an important component of determining your gross estate. Two key elements of valuation are ascertaining the time when the interest must be valued and using an accepted method of valuation to determine the fair market value. There is a presumptive date-of-death rule for the time of valuation, and there are a number of methods such as the market approach, the income approach, and an approach specified in an agreement, such as a buy-sell agreement.

ILLUSTRATIONS OF ASSETS INCLUDIBLE IN YOUR ESTATE

For illustrative purposes only, the following are a few scenarios that may shed light on what might be included in your estate:

- You open a joint account with $25,000, and your child later contributes $5,000 to the account. There have been no withdrawals up to the time you die. $25,000 will be included in your estate.

- Your employer owes you $25,000 in salary when you die. That amount will be included in your estate.

- You own real property in joint tenancy with your child. You purchased the property for $50,000. The property is worth $75,000 when you die. $75,000 will be included in your estate.

- You die owning a sole proprietorship business. The business assets (tangible and intangible) will be included in your estate.

- You die owning shares of an incorporated business. The value of the stock will be included in your estate. If the stock is publicly traded, the value will generally be based on the mean between the highest and lowest selling price on the valuation date.

- You created an irrevocable trust a number of years ago that provides you income for life. The trust document states that when you die, your children will get the assets of the trust. Two years before you die, you relinquish the income interest in the trust. The value of the assets in the trust will be included in your estate.

LEARNING ABOUT WHAT IS INCLUDED IN YOUR ESTATE

Personal consultation with experienced advisors regarding your specific circumstances is critical to making informed decisions about your estate. Here are some suggestions:

1. Make a list of what you own. You should include how much of an asset you own and what it is worth.

2. Schedule an appointment with an experienced estate planning attorney to review your list and discuss considerations for each type of asset.

3. Connect your estate planning attorney, your accountant, and your financial advisor and have them review the list and offer input about what is likely to be included in your gross estate and what is likely to be the resulting taxable estate.

4. With the benefit of your advisors' input, consider whether you want to take certain actions or make changes to your existing estate plan.

With the appropriate guidance, you will have a working knowledge of what is included in your estate and will be able to make sound decisions regarding it while you have the opportunity and desire to do so.

Linda A. Burrows is the founder of Claritas Law, APC. She is a certified specialist in Estate Planning, Trust and Probate Law by the State Bar of California Board of Legal Specialization.

Linda Burrows

53

Are Life Insurance Proceeds Taxable?

By Douglas G. Goldberg (Colorado Springs, Colorado)

Whether life insurance proceeds are taxable is an important question, and I have heard and answered it a million or so times during my law career. It is right up there with the questions "What is all of this going to cost?," "Should I do a will or a living trust?," and "What is better, an LLC or an S corporation?" It is definitely among my clients' top ten most frequently asked questions.

You would think that such a simple question would have a simple answer. However, as with most things in the legal and tax worlds, it does not, particularly when you understand who makes the rules (Congress and the Internal Revenue Service), who interprets the rules (the courts), and who helps families plan in light of the rules (lawyers and CPAs). So frankly, it is clearly not a simple topic. Most of the confusion surrounding the taxability of life insurance proceeds arises from the interplay between two different taxes—income tax and estate tax. Let's start our analysis by defining some terms:

Insured: the person whose life the policy insures

Beneficiary: the person who receives the life insurance proceeds upon the insured person's death

Decedent: a person who has died

Executor: a person or institution appointed by an individual to carry out the terms of the individual's will

Life insurance proceeds: the amount paid to the beneficiary when the insured dies (also called a death benefit)

Gross income: income from whatever source derived (Internal Revenue Code (I.R.C.) § 61(a))

Income taxable: the amount of life insurance proceeds included in the beneficiary's gross income for income tax purposes and on which the beneficiary pays income tax

Gross estate: the value of all property, real or personal, tangible or intangible, wherever situated at the time of death (I.R.C. § 2031)

Estate taxable: the amount of life insurance proceeds included in the insured's gross estate for estate tax purposes and on which the insured's estate may have to pay estate tax.

THE INCOME TAX RULES

Generally, life insurance proceeds are not included in the beneficiary's gross income, and the beneficiary does not have to report them. But as you might imagine, there are exceptions to this general rule.

First, suppose the policy's original owner transferred it to the beneficiary for cash or other consideration. In that case, only a portion of the life insurance proceeds is not income taxable to the beneficiary. To determine the taxable amount, subtract the amount paid for the policy, plus the additional premiums paid by the beneficiary until the insured's death, from the total life insurance proceeds. This is called the *transfer-for-value rule.*

Second, interest on life insurance proceeds is taxable and included in the beneficiary's gross income.

Third, income generated after the beneficiary has received the life insurance proceeds is taxable and included in the beneficiary's gross income.

THE ESTATE TAX RULES

I.R.C. § 2042 governs whether a decedent's gross estate includes life insurance proceeds on the decedent's life. It provides that the decedent's gross estate includes the total amount of the death benefit on two occasions: (1) if the life insurance policy is payable to the insured's estate, e.g., if the estate is the beneficiary of the life insurance policy or (2) if the decedent had any *incidents of ownership* in the life insurance policy on the date of death.

An incident of ownership includes the power to take any of the following actions:

- change the beneficiary of the policy

- surrender or cancel the policy

- assign the policy

- revoke an assignment of the policy

- pledge the policy for a loan

- obtain from the insurance company a loan against the surrender value of the policy

The current (2022) estate tax exemption is $12.06 million, meaning that the first $12.06 million of assets is not subject to estate tax. However, anything over $12.06 million is taxed at 40 percent. Additionally, existing law provides that on January 1, 2026, the exemption returns to $5.49 million, adjusted for inflation, unless Congress acts to change the amount before that date.

EXAMPLE

Jim, a successful business owner, owns a $5 million life insurance policy on his life. Jim names his wife, Jill, as the policy's primary beneficiary. Jim also owns other assets worth $10 million in the aggregate: his business, home, 401(k), Roth IRA, investment accounts, and rental property.

When Jim dies, the value of his gross estate is $15 million because he owned the life insurance policy in his individual name and had incidents of ownership in the policy. However, Jim's estate tax exemption is $11.7 million, leaving $3.3 million as Jim's taxable estate.

Assuming that Jim and Jill have done no estate planning, Jim's estate may owe federal estate tax of $1.32 million (40 percent of $3.3 million) even though Jill receives the entire $5 million in life insurance proceeds income tax-free. If Jim dies on or after January 1, 2026, after the exemption amount has reverted to $5.49 million, Jim's estate would owe about $3.8 million in estate taxes.

Because of the size of Jim's life insurance policy, Jill may need to either sell some of Jim's other assets, including their home, Jim's business, or investments, or use a portion of the life insurance proceeds to pay estate taxes.

SOLUTIONS

1. **Basic estate planning and proper retitling and funding of their assets to take advantage of the unlimited marital deduction and the federal estate tax exemption**

The unlimited marital deduction is a powerful estate tax planning tool that eliminates the federal estate and gift taxes on transfers of assets between spouses. It allows spouses to transfer as much property as they wish, during lifetime or at death, without incurring any federal estate or gift tax, thereby allowing married couples to delay payment of estate taxes upon the first spouse's death. However, the survivor's taxable estate will include all assets valued over the estate tax exemption.

Basic estate planning, potentially including a revocable living trust, will allow Jim and Jill to take full advantage of the unlimited marital deduction and, by correctly retitling their assets and naming proper beneficiaries to balance the ownership of their assets, also take advantage of both of their federal estate tax exemptions. Other benefits of a living trust-based estate plan include avoiding probate on both deaths and maximum privacy.

2. Remove the life insurance proceeds from Jim's gross estate, reducing it from $15 million to $10 million

Removing Jim's incidents of ownership in the life insurance policy will effectively remove the life insurance proceeds from his gross estate for estate tax purposes, saving between $1.3 million and $3.8 million depending on the law in effect at Jim's death. However, removing the incidents of ownership requires Jim to transfer the policy's ownership to someone else.

While that sounds simple enough, the choice of transferee of the policy is critical. Proper selection will ensure that the death benefit is not estate taxable when Jim dies and that Jill receives the death benefit when and how Jim wants. The choice of transferee is also essential to ensuring that the insurance policy is managed correctly and that premiums are paid on time during Jim's life. Transferee options include individuals, trusts, and business entities. Each has its own merits, disadvantages, and chances of success, but the correct choice will ultimately depend on Jim and Jill's planning goals.

SUMMARY

Are life insurance proceeds taxable? As you can see, it depends. Consult a qualified estate planning attorney and your CPA to discuss and work through the various options to determine your best course of action.

Douglas Goldberg

Goldberg Law Center, P.C. provides legal counsel and leadership in estate design, business representation, and asset protection. We help individuals, families, and entrepreneurs protect their loved ones, preserve their wealth, save taxes, and perpetuate philanthropy.

54

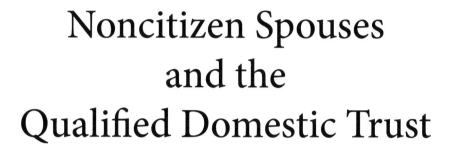

Noncitizen Spouses and the Qualified Domestic Trust

By Brett J. Barthelmeh and Heather B. Reid (Boston, Massachusetts)

I f you are married and your spouse is not a US citizen, it is important to be aware of the qualified domestic trust (QDOT). Although the QDOT is a technical planning tool, this discussion endeavors to make the strategy understandable for families whose planning could benefit from it.

If you are a citizen or resident of the United States, the Internal Revenue Code imposes a tax on the transfer of your taxable estate. While transfers to your surviving spouse typically qualify for an unlimited marital deduction, the deduction is available (except in certain limited circumstances) only if your surviving spouse is a US citizen. Therefore, without proper planning, assets you leave to your noncitizen surviving spouse do not qualify for the unlimited marital deduction and are taxed at your death as if they had been left to any other nonspouse beneficiary. The QDOT allows you to leave assets to your noncitizen surviving spouse so that the transfer qualifies for the unlimited marital deduction. Qualifying for the unlimited marital deduction is critical if the value of your estate exceeds the federal estate tax exemption amount ($12.06 million per person in 2022) or any applicable state estate tax exemption amount.

An explanation of the rationale behind these intricate rules is helpful for understanding them. Assuming that the value of your estate is taxable, Uncle Sam wants to ensure collection. However, married couples often depend on their combined assets for financial security and expect to consume them throughout their joint lifetime. Given this public policy consideration, the unlimited marital deduction delays collection of the estate tax until the death of the surviving spouse. This policy is often conceptualized as estate taxes delayed but not avoided, because US citizens ultimately pay taxes on their worldwide income and assets. But if your surviving spouse is not a US citizen, Uncle Sam is concerned that if collection of the estate tax is delayed for public policy reasons, your noncitizen surviving spouse might leave the country, making collecting the estate tax at their passing impractical or impossible. The QDOT structure imposes certain restrictions on the assets transferred to your noncitizen surviving spouse, which allows them to delay the estate tax while also giving Uncle Sam confidence that those assets will remain in the United States and ultimately be taxed.

For example, if Harry Husband (a US citizen) is married to Wendy Wife (also a US citizen) and Harry cooperates with actuarial tables by predeceasing Wendy, no estate tax is due on the value of the assets Harry leaves to Wendy (even if Harry's estate is otherwise taxable) because of the unlimited marital deduction. Instead, Uncle Sam will wait patiently until Wendy's death to collect any estate tax that might ultimately be due. However, if Wendy is not a US citizen, the unlimited marital deduction does not apply, and unless the assets Wendy receives qualify for an exception, estate tax will be due on the value of Harry's taxable estate at his death.

Though the current federal exemption amount of $12.06 million per person makes QDOT planning less of a consideration for many families, the technique is also useful for smaller estates subject to state estate tax. Assume that Harry was domiciled in Massachusetts and married to Wendy, a noncitizen, when he died in 2022 with an estate valued at $5 million. Although Harry's estate is below the 2022 federal exemption amount, it may incur a Massachusetts estate tax. With proper planning, the couple can use the Massachusetts applicable exclusion amount of $1 million and potentially shelter additional assets from Massachusetts estate taxes. Without the availability of the unlimited marital deduction, the balance of Harry's estate ($4 million of value) will generate a Massachusetts estate tax of approximately $300,000. Depending on the surviving spouse's needs, the composition of the estate's assets, and the liquidity to pay taxes, this result will almost certainly be burdensome. If Harry instead leaves assets to Wendy in a QDOT, thus qualifying for the unlimited marital deduction, no estate tax will be payable on the transfer at his death.

While this effective strategy produces an immediately better result for your surviving spouse, it is important to remember the guiding principle that estate taxes are delayed but not avoided. During Wendy's lifetime, she will receive income from the QDOT that will be subject to income taxes (but not estate taxes). If she needs a distribution from the trust's principal, ratable estate tax will become payable at the time of the distribution based on the estate tax in effect at Harry's death. The QDOT's trustee is responsible for withholding the estate tax payable at the time of distribution during Wendy's lifetime and paying the estate tax due on the assets remaining in the QDOT at Wendy's death.

A QDOT is therefore an irrevocable trust created for the purpose of allowing your noncitizen surviving spouse to receive assets from your taxable estate and qualify for the unlimited marital deduction (to the extent such assets exceed your federal or state estate tax exemption amounts). Property must be transferred to the QDOT prior to the deadline for filing your estate tax return, which is generally nine months from the date of death plus an available six-month extension if timely requested. A QDOT must have at least one trustee that is an individual US citizen or a domestic corporation. In addition, distributions of principal from the QDOT to your noncitizen surviving spouse, as well as the balance of the QDOT trust property remaining at their death, are subject to estate taxes. This enables QDOT administration to both mirror the estate tax rules and adhere to the principle of permitting estate taxes to be delayed but not avoided. If the QDOT property's value exceeds $2 million, its administration is subject to additional restrictions.

If your surviving spouse desires to become a US citizen, achieves citizenship before your estate tax return is due, and was always a US resident following your death, a QDOT is unnecessary, and your estate will be eligible for the unlimited marital deduction. Similarly, if your surviving spouse achieves citizenship after a QDOT has been created, it may be terminated, and the balance of the property will still be eligible for the unlimited marital deduction as long as your spouse was always a US resident following your death and either received no distributions of principal from the QDOT during that period or elected to treat any such distributions as taxable gifts. If such solutions are practicable, people often pursue them because QDOT administration is technical and often cumbersome.

To ensure compliance with all procedural requirements, it is important that you work with an experienced estate planning attorney when establishing and administering a QDOT. Although QDOTs are complex and a bit burdensome to administer, they are an invaluable planning tool if your spouse is a noncitizen, particularly if your estate is subject to federal or state estate taxes.

Squillace & Associates, P.C. provides estate planning, probate, and trust administration for individuals, families, and business owners, counseling private clients on creating and maintaining estate plans that are both values-based and tax-efficient.

Brett Barthelmeh   Heather Reid

55

Spousal Lifetime Access Trust

by Rodney J. Hatley (San Diego, California)

A spousal lifetime access trust (SLAT) may be the most used advanced estate planning strategy for married individuals who have significant wealth or are concerned about asset protection.

Why? A SLAT protects assets from both estate taxes and creditors while simultaneously preserving the grantor's potential access, through the beneficiary-spouse, to the assets placed in the trust.

The transfer of assets to a SLAT is usually structured as a completed gift (though in some cases, it may be appropriate to structure a transfer as an incomplete gift). A gift is generally completed if the grantor no longer has dominion and control over the assets transferred. Structuring a transfer as a completed gift often uses either a portion or all of the donor's lifetime gift tax exemption (and possibly also generation-skipping transfer (GST) tax exemption) to fund the trust. Using the exemption now actually preserves it, in a sense: if the exemption is reduced or eliminated while it remains unused, it could be lost in part or entirely.

Though any assets withdrawn by the beneficiary-spouse will be included in that spouse's gross estate, assets that are not distributed to the beneficiary-spouse remain in the trust and continue to grow free of estate and GST taxes (assuming GST tax exemption is allocated to the trust) for future generations.

Married individuals who have significant wealth or are concerned about asset protection but are leery of transferring assets to an irrevocable trust should consider a SLAT. With a traditional irrevocable trust, the grantor must give up access to the assets transferred to the trust. With a SLAT, however, access to the trust assets is preserved for the beneficiary-spouse, so the grantor still has potential access to the assets through the spouse.

HOW A SLAT WORKS

1. One spouse creates an irrevocable trust for the other spouse's lifetime benefit, or each spouse creates a nonreciprocal trust for the other. The trust will own the assets that are transferred to or acquired by the trust, which could include life insurance policies with cash value. Qualified retirement plan assets, however, generally should not be used to fund a SLAT because the transfer will result in a deemed distribution of the assets and be immediately taxable.

2. The grantor-spouse should not be the trustee of the SLAT created for the beneficiary-spouse, but the beneficiary-spouse may act as trustee as long as the power to make distributions is limited by an ascertainable standard, such as for a beneficiary's health, education, maintenance, or support, and assuming legal obligations of support do not cause inclusion in the beneficiary-spouse's estate. In addition, both spouses and a trust protector can be given the right to change the trustee and appoint an independent trustee to make discretionary distributions not limited to an ascertainable standard.

3. The SLAT must be funded with separate property of the grantor-spouse rather than from jointly held property. If there is insufficient separate property, then jointly held property can be given to the grantor-spouse, and held as separate property for a period of time before being transferred to the trust. For example, in California, which is a community property state, the attorney would prepare a transmutation agreement that the spouses would sign, rendering one-half of the assets the husband's separate property and the balance the wife's separate property. Either spouse could subsequently contribute his or her share of that property to a SLAT.

4. If the transfer of assets to a SLAT is a completed gift for federal gift tax purposes, a gift tax return will need to be filed for the year or years in which assets are gifted to the trust. No gift tax will be due on the transfers, however, unless the grantor has used up their lifetime gift tax exemption and the transfers do not qualify for other exemptions or exclusions (such as the annual exclusion).

5. During the grantor's lifetime, assets in the SLAT can be accessed by the trustee for the benefit of the beneficiary-spouse and any other beneficiaries of the trust. Because the beneficiary-spouse will have access to the SLAT assets, the grantor-spouse retains a sort of indirect access to the assets through that relationship.

6. When the grantor dies, the assets in the beneficiary-spouse's SLAT will not be included in the grantor's gross estate for federal estate tax purposes. The SLAT can then continue for the benefit of the surviving spouse (and any other beneficiaries) for their lifetime. Upon the surviving spouse's death, the assets will then pass to children, grandchildren, or other beneficiaries without being subject to estate tax in the beneficiary-spouse's estate.

7. When both spouses have established SLATs for each other, the death of a beneficiary-spouse cuts off access to the assets in the grantor's SLAT. The grantor will continue to have access to the deceased spouse's SLAT.

EXAMPLE

Bill and Mary are married and have a net worth of $20 million. The value of their estate is under the combined exemption amount of $24.12 million (for 2022), so they do not have a taxable estate, but when the exemption amount is reduced in 2026 (if not legislatively altered sooner), their estate will be taxable. By establishing SLATs now to take advantage of their combined exemptions, they can move part of their $20 million out of their estates using their lifetime gift exemptions and still have access to what they gave away. Plus, the assets left to their beneficiaries can be protected from any future lawsuits (creditors) and divorcing spouses (predators).

IMPORTANT CONSIDERATIONS

1. If both spouses are establishing SLATs, the documents should be carefully drafted to avoid the reciprocal trust doctrine. The reciprocal trust doctrine is a judicial rule that applies when trusts are so interrelated that the taxpayers are left in approximately the same economic position as they would have been if they had not created the trusts. Careful drafting by an experienced estate planning attorney is necessary to avoid application of the reciprocal trust doctrine.

2. SLATs must be carefully drafted and funded to avoid inadvertent inclusion in the estate of either the grantor or the beneficiary-spouse.

3. Distributions from a SLAT to the beneficiary-spouse or others should be maintained in a separate account that is not accessible by the grantor. However, the funds can be used by the beneficiary-spouse for expenses attributable to jointly owned property, joint spousal vacations, gifting, and any other anticipated future needs.

4. Divorce from or death of the beneficiary-spouse will impact the benefits of this technique for the grantor. Accordingly, the estate planning attorney should consider including a "floating spouse" provision in the SLAT, which would ensure that the trust assets would be available to the grantor's current spouse.

WHY ARE SLATS WORTH CONSIDERING?

As of this writing, federal estate tax laws are in a state of flux. Per the 2017 Tax Cuts and Jobs Act (TCJA), the estate and gift tax exemption for 2022, $12.06 million, will be reduced to an inflation-adjusted $5 million in 2026 and could be altered by Congress before then.

Up to the entire amount of this exemption can be used during a person's lifetime. Under current law, even if the exemption is later decreased or eliminated, any assets given away during life that exceed the exemption amount in effect upon that individual's death cannot be pulled back into the individual's estate. Consequently, this provides the opportunity to give away significant wealth completely tax-free if done before the laws change.

CONCLUSION

Including a SLAT in your estate plan provides the flexibility to adapt throughout your lifetime, the potential to maximize gifting opportunities, and the ability to be transformed in future financial and tax climates. Using your exemptions prudently while retaining indirect access to the funds transferred out of your estate in case you need them in the future is wise planning. By using SLATs as part of your overall estate plan, you can eat your cake and have it too.

Rodney J. Hatley, JD, LLM (Taxation), advises successful individuals and families on estate planning strategies that eliminate taxes and protect assets so they may leave legacies. Hatley Law Group, APC, views estate planning through the lens of asset protection.

Rodney Hatley

56

Sales to IDGTs

By Wayne M. Zell (Reston, Virginia)

For decades, tax practitioners have used a popular technique—the sale-to-IDGT—involving a transfer by installment sale to an intentionally defective grantor trust (IDGT) in exchange for a promissory note to minimize exposure to estate, gift, and generation-skipping transfer (GST) taxes. The technique usually requires the creator of the trust (grantor) to make a seed gift to a new trust of at least 10 percent of the value of the assets being transferred to the trust. The grantor then sells assets to the IDGT in exchange for the note and certain security interests. If done properly, this technique allows the grantor to shift future appreciation of the assets to younger generations without incurring transfer taxes. The use of valuation discounts for the transferred assets may enhance this technique. However, potential legislation may curtail this strategy.

WHAT IS AN IDGT AND HOW DOES IT WORK?

First, the grantor creates an irrevocable trust that is treated as a grantor trust for federal income tax purposes. As a grantor trust, the trust is ignored (i.e., it is "intentionally defective") for federal income tax purposes, but it is effective for transferring appreciation out of the grantor's estate. Even though the trust income is taxable to the grantor, the payment of income tax on behalf of the trust is not treated as a gift by the grantor to the trust (per Internal Revenue Service (IRS) Revenue Ruling 2004-64). The grantor's payment of income tax allows assets to grow inside the trust income tax free. Including of any of the following provisions in a trust allows the trust to qualify as a grantor trust:

- Grantor has the power to reacquire trust assets by substituting other property of an equivalent value

- Grantor has the power to control trust investments

- Grantor has a reversionary interest in the trust greater than 5 percent of the trust's value

- Grantor or grantor's spouse can receive trust income at the discretion of a nonadverse party

- Grantor can borrow from the trust without adequate interest or adequate security

INSTALLMENT SALE TO AN IDGT

The grantor first establishes the irrevocable trust and typically contributes cash or other assets worth at least 10 percent of the value of the assets to be sold to the trust. The initial transfer is treated as a gift to the trust. The gift typically utilizes the grantor's lifetime gift tax exemption ($12.06 million per person in 2022) and may qualify for gift-splitting with the grantor's spouse.

Next, the grantor and the IDGT's trustee enter into an agreement to sell the assets to the trust, and the trustee executes a promissory note payable to the grantor on behalf of the trust. The note may range in maturity from three to twenty years. In some cases, the note may only accrue interest currently and require a balloon payment at the end of the term. The note bears interest at the applicable federal rate (AFR) in effect for the month in which the sale occurs. To further bolster the efficacy of the arrangement, the trust typically grants a security interest to the grantor in the trust assets, and the beneficiaries may need to guarantee the note.

The installment sale is not taxable to the grantor for federal income tax purposes, because the grantor is effectively treated as selling the assets to themselves. In some states (e.g., Pennsylvania), the trust must file tax returns and pay taxes on its income, which could create major problems if the assets transferred include S corporation stock. Since no gain or loss is recognized on the grantor's sale of the assets to the IDGT, the grantor is not required to report the sale on the grantor's federal income tax return. Also, the grantor is not taxed separately on the interest payments that the grantor receives from the IDGT, and the grantor will continue to be taxed individually on all income generated by the IDGT as if it did not exist.

If the sale involves an interest in a closely-held entity such as a limited liability company (LLC), or a partial interest in property such as a tenancy-in-common interest in real estate, the value of the interest being sold may be subject to valuation discounts. In that case, the grantor should hire a qualified appraiser to value the interest being sold. The purchase agreement might describe the quantity of an asset being sold through the use of a formula expressing that quantity as a dollar amount rather than as a number or percentage of units, e.g., as $X worth of Newco, LLC membership interests rather than as XX percent of Newco, LLC. Recent cases indicate that the courts might recognize the effectiveness of such a formula to eliminate any gift if the IRS successfully challenges the valuation and argues that the assets being sold to the trust have a greater value than reported in the sale transaction. In the Newco, LLC example, the formula would reduce the membership interest percentage transferred so that the dollar amount transferred remains constant. If the formula is effective, the reduction in the percentage interest transferred avoids a gift.

COMPLIANCE

Both the gift and sale portions of the transaction should be reported on a timely-filed federal gift and GST tax return (Form 709), and the grantor can allocate the GST exemption to the seed gift to permit the IDGT to qualify for exemption from both the estate and GST tax. This return would include attachments, such as copies of the executed trust, the gift and sale documentation, the appraisal, and other support for the transaction. By filing the Form 709, the grantor starts the running of the statute of limitations, which limits the IRS's ability to challenge the transaction or the valuation discount after three years from the date the return was filed (or the due date, if later), absent fraud.

In subsequent years, the trustee must file Form 1041 for the trust and must allocate all trust income and deductions to the grantor. The grantor must report the trust's income on the grantor's income tax return. In certain cases, the trustee may reimburse the grantor for income tax paid on behalf of the trust, although any such reimbursement would reduce the transfer tax benefits of the arrangement. The trust agreement can give the trustee or another non-adverse party the right to turn off grantor trust status, but great care should be taken to avoid inadvertently accelerating income if the trust converts to a nongrantor trust.

Importantly, the grantor and the trustee must observe the formalities of the arrangement in the future to avoid IRS challenges.

ADVANTAGES AND RISKS

Advantages of the sale-to-IDGT transaction include the following:

- The strategy freezes the value of the transferred assets in the year of transfer, thereby shifting appreciation out of the grantor's estate in a low-interest-rate environment (i.e., any appreciation above the AFR is outside of the estate).

- The note's value is the only value included in the grantor's estate if the grantor dies while the note remains unpaid.

- The valuation discount on the trust assets and any income tax paid by the grantor on trust income reduces additional transfer taxes.

Disadvantages and risks include the following:

- The sale-to-IDGT technique has not been officially approved by Congress, the IRS, or the courts, although it is based upon tax practitioners' reasoned interpretations of various provisions of the Internal Revenue Code, reported cases, and rulings.

- If the grantor dies during the term of the note, the grantor trust status of the IDGT terminates and the grantor or the grantor's estate may have to recognize the deferred gain attributable to the unpaid portion of the principal of the note.

Example: Jed contributes assets worth $10 million to an LLC in exchange for an LLC interest.

Then, Jed creates an irrevocable grantor trust (IDGT) by contributing/gifting $500,000 in cash or other assets to the IDGT.

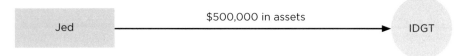

Next, Jed sells $5 million in LLC interests to the IDGT in exchange for a $500,000 down payment plus a $4.5 million promissory note payable in 20 years at an annual interest rate of 1.9 percent (August 2021 long-term AFR). Jed gets an appraisal for a 1 percent noncontrolling, nonmanagerial interest in the LLC equal to $65,000 (assuming a 35 percent combined discount for lack of marketability and lack of control). Based upon the appraisal, Jed sells 76.923 percent ($5,000,000 ÷ $65,000 × 1%) of the LLC to the IDGT. The IDGT grants a security interest in the LLC interest to Jed, and the IDGT beneficiaries guarantee the IDGT's obligations.

Assuming the appraisal withstands IRS scrutiny, Jed will have transferred $1.5 million in value [($10,000,000 × (1 − 35%)) − $5,000,000, worth $600,000 at a transfer tax rate of 40%] as a result of the valuation discount, plus 40 percent of the appreciation in the LLC interest going forward. Jed's estate may also be able to claim a discount on the interest retained at Jed's passing.

Several bills have been introduced in Congress over the past twenty years that would curtail or effectively eliminate the sale-to-IDGT technique. As of the date of this writing, no such legislation has been enacted. Nonetheless, high net worth taxpayers may want to discuss this strategy with their estate planning attorney before any legislation is enacted.

Zell Law provides niche estate, business, tax, and fiduciary services and serves as the lifetime lawyers for entrepreneurs, executives, business owners, and individuals undergoing life-changing events.

Wayne Zell

SECTION 6

Special Assets

57

Estate Planning after the SECURE Act

By Maribeth Berlin and Jeffrey Kabbe (Naperville, Illinois)

You may have heard about the Setting Every Community Up for Retirement Enhancement Act (the SECURE Act), a law that went into effect at the beginning of 2020. What you may not realize is that the SECURE Act affects everyone who has a qualified retirement account such as a 401(k), individual retirement account (IRA), 403(b), Roth 401(k) or IRA, or qualified annuity. The bottom line for estate planning purposes is that the SECURE Act impacts the longevity of your qualified retirement accounts after your death.

Most people who have qualified retirement accounts know that they must start withdrawing minimum amounts from these accounts at a certain age set by law. Similarly, beneficiaries who inherit retirement accounts are bound by specific rules that dictate how long they can hold onto the accounts before cashing them out.

Why does this matter? These deadlines matter because the assets in your qualified accounts are growing tax free or tax deferred until they are withdrawn. When you make withdrawals, this favorable treatment ends, so most account owners (including beneficiaries) want to leave the accounts intact for as long as possible.

The SECURE Act changed the deadlines for beneficiaries and requires most beneficiaries to cash out inherited retirement accounts much sooner than required under the prior rules.

THE OLD RULES

Prior to the SECURE Act, most beneficiaries of qualified retirement accounts were allowed to "stretch" the account over a period of time. Each year, the beneficiary was required to withdraw a portion of the retirement account and pay any income taxes due on that withdrawal. The length of the stretch was usually based on the beneficiary's life expectancy. Unless the beneficiary made additional withdrawals, the remainder of the account would remain invested and income taxes would be deferred. The annual required distributions would continue in this manner until the account was fully withdrawn. For many beneficiaries, the stretch was a good thing because it minimized their income taxes.

Prior to the SECURE Act, the stretch was available to all "designated beneficiaries," meaning individuals or certain trusts that met specific requirements set by law. A beneficiary that did not qualify as a designated beneficiary was required to withdraw the full amount held in the qualified retirement account within five years. In most cases, the five-year rule accelerated the rate at which the beneficiary had to cash out the account and pay any income taxes.

When a grantor named their trust as the beneficiary of a qualified retirement account under the old rules, there were two main outcomes. Either the trust did not meet the requirements of a designated beneficiary (no stretch was allowed and the five-year rule applied) or the trust did meet the requirements and the trust beneficiary was allowed to stretch the inherited account.

THE NEW RULES

The SECURE Act eliminated the stretch for most inherited retirement accounts and replaced it with a ten-year payout rule. Now, designated beneficiaries have ten years to cash out an inherited account and pay any income taxes due on the withdrawn amounts. If a trust does not qualify as a designated beneficiary, the inherited account must be cashed out under the five-year payout rule as before.

Although the SECURE Act largely limits beneficiaries to the ten-year payout, there are some situations in which the stretch is still available. For example, if a beneficiary qualifies as an *"eligible designated beneficiary,"* then the beneficiary can still take advantage of the stretch and cash out inherited retirement accounts based on their life expectancy. The following beneficiaries may still qualify for the life expectancy payout:

- The account owner's spouse
- The account owner's minor children, until they reach the age of majority (this does not apply to grandchildren or other minor beneficiaries who are not children of the account owner)
- Disabled or chronically ill beneficiaries
- Beneficiaries who are not more than ten years younger than the account owner

INDIVIDUAL BENEFICIARIES AND TRUST BENEFICIARIES

When an *individual* is named as the beneficiary of a qualified retirement account, they will either be subject to the ten-year payout (most typical for nonspouses) or the life expectancy payout (spouses and other eligible designated beneficiaries).

When a *trust* is named as beneficiary on a qualified retirement account, the beneficiaries of the trust are typically subject to the five-year payout rule, unless the trust includes special language to extend the payout period, which would become either the ten-year rule or the life expectancy rule. When it comes to paying out qualified retirement accounts, trusts fall into two main categories—conduit trusts and accumulation trusts.

A conduit trust requires that all amounts withdrawn from the retirement account be paid directly to, or for the benefit of, the beneficiary at the time they are withdrawn. The trust is merely a conduit or pipeline for these funds; none of the funds that are withdrawn from the retirement account are retained in the trust. With the conduit structure, the trust's beneficiaries can qualify for the ten-year rule or the stretch, depending on whether they are a designated beneficiary or an eligible designated beneficiary.

An accumulation trust does not require the trust to give the cashed-out portions of the retirement account directly to the beneficiary. Instead, the cashed-out funds can remain in the trust. The trustee then uses its discretion, or follows the rules the trustmaker has set in the trust, in deciding when and whether to distribute any funds to the beneficiary.

An accumulation trust does *not* automatically qualify the beneficiary for a longer payout period. Many accumulation trusts fall under the five-year rule. To qualify a designated beneficiary for the ten-year rule or an eligible designated beneficiary for the life expectancy rule, an accumulation trust must be drafted to comply with a complex set of Internal Revenue Service rules. Sometimes, this is accomplished with a stand-alone retirement trust, which is specifically designed to obtain a longer payout period for the beneficiaries.

Although the SECURE Act limits your beneficiary's ability to stretch a retirement account that they inherit from you, there are strategies you can use in drafting your trust to make sure that your beneficiaries at least have the ten years allowed under the SECURE Act.

The attorneys at Kabbe Law Group focus their practice on helping families transfer wealth and protect their loved ones, giving clients the peace of mind that comes with comprehensive and personalized planning.

Maribeth Berlin   *Jeffrey Kabbe*

58

Should You Name Your Trust as Beneficiary of Qualified Retirement Accounts?

By Maribeth Berlin and Jeffrey Kabbe (Naperville, Illinois)

Your retirement account may be one of your largest assets, and the reality is that it may outlive you. Perhaps you have planned for this by naming your children or grandchildren as beneficiaries on your retirement accounts. But what you might not realize is that you can protect the assets that you leave your beneficiaries—including your retirement accounts—by naming *your trust* as the beneficiary and leaving the assets in ongoing trusts for your children and grandchildren.

A trust can safeguard your beneficiary's inheritance from their potential liabilities (such as divorce, bankruptcy, creditors, and lawsuits) or lack of financial maturity if they inherit at a young age. A trust also can ensure that your assets pass from your children to your grandchildren someday, rather than to a child's spouse or someone outside of your family.

Creating a living trust is the first step, and you should make sure your living trust is drafted to include ongoing beneficiary trusts. Then, you will fund your trust by making your trust the owner or beneficiary of your accounts and property. For retirement accounts, you will remain the account owner during your lifetime, but you will make the important decision of whether to name *your trust* as beneficiary, taking into consideration the unique nature of these accounts.[1]

WHY QUALIFIED RETIREMENT ACCOUNTS ARE DIFFERENT

Qualified retirement accounts, such as 401(k)s, individual retirement accounts (IRAs), 403(b)s, Roth 401(k)s and IRAs, and qualified annuities, are desirable for their tax advantages. Depending on the type of account, the assets can grow either tax-free or tax-deferred until they are withdrawn. There are limits on when funds can be taken out of these accounts during your lifetime, as well as rules that tell you when you must start withdrawing from the accounts later in life.

Qualified retirement accounts also come with strict rules for the beneficiaries who inherit these accounts at your death. The rules require your beneficiary to withdraw the funds held in the accounts within a certain amount of time. Because the assets in the accounts have been growing tax-free or tax-deferred, there are income tax implications for your beneficiaries when they cash out the accounts.

The payout deadline for beneficiaries can be as short as five years and partly depends on whether they receive the account in trust. The decision of whether to name your trust as the beneficiary of your qualified retirement accounts comes down to balancing the goals of protecting your beneficiaries' inheritances for them and giving them the best tax treatment available under the law.

THE BENEFITS OF ONGOING BENEFICIARY TRUSTS

If you have a trust as part of your estate plan, it likely is a revocable living trust. You completely control a revocable living trust, and the assets within it are available to you at any time, making it the most flexible (and most common) type of trust. When you pass away, your trust becomes irrevocable: the trust cannot be changed and is now for the benefit of others.

If drafted properly, an irrevocable trust has great potential to provide asset protection to its beneficiaries—your children and grandchildren. To do so, your trust must be designed to give each beneficiary their share in an *ongoing trust* rather than *outright*.

---

1   This chapter focuses on nonspouse beneficiaries, such as children and grandchildren. The rules and outcomes for spouses who inherit retirement accounts are different and not included in this discussion.

When a beneficiary receives their share of a trust outright, the trust assets, whether cash, stock, or real estate, are transferred into the beneficiary's name and into their personal accounts. These assets are now entirely owned by the beneficiary and exposed to the beneficiary's personal liabilities.

When a beneficiary instead receives their share from an ongoing beneficiary trust, the assets are transferred into the name of their trust. The beneficiary can be in charge of their separate trust and gain access when needed. The trust acts as a vault for the funds that remain. The trust can protect the inherited assets from the claims of third parties. In the case of a minor or young adult beneficiary who does not have the experience necessary to manage assets, the trust can be managed by a trusted adult and then handed over to the beneficiary at a certain age. Finally, the trust can instruct that any funds remaining in the trust at the end of the beneficiary's life will go to their children or your other descendants, staying in your bloodline. Once you establish a living trust, you must decide whether to use that trust to receive your qualified retirement accounts upon your death to protect those assets for your beneficiaries.

NAMING YOUR TRUST AS BENEFICIARY OF QUALIFIED RETIREMENT ACCOUNTS

If your trust includes ongoing beneficiary trusts, then it is safe to assume that asset protection and bloodline protection are important to you. The next step is to make sure you designate your trust as the beneficiary on your qualified retirement accounts. If you fail to do so, then the assets in your retirement accounts will bypass the ongoing beneficiary trusts and your beneficiaries will receive the accounts outright. If your beneficiaries inherit outright, it is too late for them to redirect the assets back into your trust and receive the benefits of the ongoing trusts.

When your trust is named as the beneficiary of your qualified accounts, each beneficiary receives their share in a separate ongoing trust. The trustee will manage the inherited retirement account along with the other assets you have left to your beneficiary in trust. The beneficiary can be the trustee, or you can name someone else as trustee if you feel that your beneficiary is too young or does not have the skills or experience to be their own trustee.

Retirement accounts that are inherited in trust typically must be cashed out by the end of the five-year period that starts at the account holder's date of death. The cashed-out portions of the account, after income taxes are paid, can stay in the trust. The funds can then be invested and continue to receive asset protection. The cashed-out portions are also available to be distributed to the beneficiary under the trustee's discretion.

Some trusts and beneficiaries can qualify for a longer payout period on qualified retirement accounts, which can minimize the income tax implications. If you are interested in a longer payout period for your beneficiary, without sacrificing the protections of the ongoing beneficiary trust, there are various trust strategies to consider. One of these strategies is a standalone retirement trust that is drafted to meet the requirements for a ten-year payout period. In certain circumstances, a beneficiary may be eligible to stretch the account and withdraw the funds over their life expectancy.

Another option to be considered under the guidance of your financial and tax advisers is to convert qualified retirement accounts to Roth accounts, paying the income taxes now and eliminating income tax implications for your beneficiary.

The attorneys at Kabbe Law Group focus their practice on helping families transfer wealth and protect their loved ones, giving clients the peace of mind that comes with comprehensive and personalized planning.

Maribeth Berlin   *Jeffrey Kabbe*

59

Using Standalone Retirement Distribution Trusts

By Rebecca Mackie (Monona, Wisconsin)

When you decide who will receive funds after your death through your estate plan, you may feel uneasy about having money distributed directly to those people. It is common to want to provide protection for beneficiaries—perhaps from themselves, or from divorce, lawsuits, or creditors, now or later in life. This interest in providing a protective structure for your beneficiaries suggests that you should discuss a revocable living trust with your attorney. If you have large retirement accounts, however, you should also consider creating a standalone retirement distribution trust to specifically protect those accounts.

A standalone retirement distribution trust allows you to separate your retirement accounts from your other assets and manage how and when beneficiaries receive the distributions from retirement accounts after your death.

An account with deferred income tax, such as an individual retirement account (IRA), a 401(k), or a 403(b), presents a unique planning problem. When you withdraw money from a deferred income tax account, also known as a tax-deferred account, you must pay income tax on the amount withdrawn. After your death, your beneficiaries must also pay income tax when they withdraw money from the tax-deferred account.

Your beneficiaries must follow strict rules about how and when to withdraw money from inherited tax-deferred accounts, similar to the required minimum distributions you are required to take after a certain age during your lifetime.

In most cases, if you name a trust as the beneficiary of a tax-deferred account, the Internal Revenue Service (IRS) currently requires all money in the account to be withdrawn within five years after your death. However, a carefully crafted standalone retirement distribution trust is not subject to a five-year withdrawal requirement. The withdrawal requirements are based on the beneficiaries of the trust.

In addition to withdrawal rates, it is important to factor in possible income tax consequences. If money is withdrawn from a retirement account but held in a trust for the entire year, the income is taxed at trust income tax brackets. Since trusts reach their highest tax bracket significantly faster than individuals do, a trustee will sometimes distribute income to the beneficiary so that taxes can be paid using the beneficiary's tax bracket.

This necessitates a balancing act for every standalone retirement distribution trust: providing a supportive, protective structure for each beneficiary that matches the beneficiary's unique circumstances while also providing the trustee with the flexibility to minimize taxes whenever it seems reasonable and practical.

To accomplish this balancing act, there are two different types of distribution methods for standalone retirement distribution trusts: the conduit distribution method and the accumulation distribution method. You can apply different distribution methods to different beneficiaries, designing a uniquely tailored standalone retirement distribution trust to accomplish your goals.

CONDUIT TRUST

Every time the trustee withdraws money from a retirement account, the trustee has to distribute all of that money to, or for the benefit of, the beneficiary. This allows for the best income tax treatment but eliminates protections when the money is distributed directly to the beneficiary.

Conduit Retirement Trust

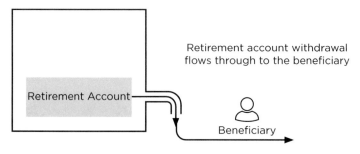

ACCUMULATION TRUST

When the trustee withdraws money from a retirement account, the trust holds and accumulates that money. The trustee only makes distributions to the beneficiary when the trustee determines that those distributions are appropriate, using instructions you have provided in the trust document to help make that determination. For example, you could direct the trustee to pay education expenses for the beneficiary, but only if the beneficiary is enrolled full-time.

Accumulation Retirement Trust

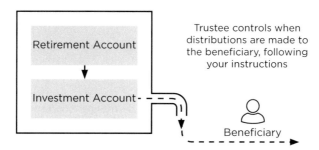

Retirement account withdrawal flows
into an investment account in the trust

Use of these two distribution methods changed dramatically after the enactment of the Setting Every Community Up for Retirement Enhancement (SECURE) Act. Before the SECURE Act was signed into law on December 20, 2019, your retirement account beneficiaries could gain the financial security of a steady stream of income by withdrawing a percentage of the IRA each year over their entire lifetime. We called this withdrawal method the lifetime stretch.

In most cases, the SECURE Act now requires withdrawal of all money in an inherited retirement account within ten years of the account owner's death rather than over the remaining lifetime of the beneficiary.

If you created a standalone retirement distribution trust before the SECURE Act was passed, this change in distribution rules will likely significantly impact how your trust works. You should discuss the potential impact with your estate planning attorney.

If you are considering a standalone retirement distribution trust for the first time, you can choose your distribution method to fit both your beneficiaries' circumstances and the new IRS rules.

WHEN MIGHT A CONDUIT DISTRIBUTION METHOD MAKE SENSE?

A conduit distribution works well when you want to control the timing of payments to the beneficiary, and you do not mind having money paid directly to the beneficiary as it comes out of the retirement account. The following are examples of the benefits of conduit distributions:

- **Enforcement of the maximum payout period.** If you want your beneficiary to withdraw money from your retirement accounts in smaller amounts over the maximum payout period but question whether your beneficiary has the self-control to do so, you can use a conduit trust and appoint a third-party trustee to enforce the maximum payout period.

- **Minimization of income taxes.** With a conduit arrangement, the trustee can team up with the beneficiary and the beneficiary's accountant to plan larger withdrawals and distributions in years that the beneficiary will have more deductions, keeping the income in lower tax brackets. Using this arrangement for a standalone retirement distribution trust unburdens your beneficiary and allows you to choose a third-party trustee to help create the best withdrawal plan.

WHEN MIGHT AN ACCUMULATION DISTRIBUTION METHOD MAKE SENSE?

An accumulation distribution is useful when you do not want all the money paid directly to the beneficiary as it comes out of the retirement account, likely because you want increased protection of that money. The following are examples of beneficiaries who may benefit from an accumulation distribution:

- **Young beneficiaries.** Instead of letting the IRS dictate when your beneficiary receives money from your retirement account, you can provide your own instructions and age limits for when your beneficiary can access the money.

- **Disabled beneficiaries.** By accumulating withdrawn money in an account inside the trust and using it only for specific, permitted purposes, you can provide financial help to your disabled beneficiaries without causing them to lose their government benefits.

- **Irresponsible beneficiaries.** Using money responsibly is a skill that some struggle to learn. If you have irresponsible beneficiaries, you can accumulate money in a trust and choose someone to manage the money, distributing it to your beneficiary according to your instructions.

- **Beneficiaries with marital problems or creditor problems.** If you are worried that your beneficiaries will someday go through divorce, bankruptcy, or other creditor problems, then you may consider accumulating the money and providing your beneficiaries with additional protections, rather than giving money to them outright.

How you handle retirement accounts in your estate plan has the potential to provide your beneficiaries with a supportive structure while attaining your goals. When ignored, however, this facet of estate planning can result in disappointing and unintended consequences. Have a discussion with your estate planning attorney to determine if a standalone retirement distribution trust will help accomplish your wishes.

Rebecca Mackie focuses her client-centered practice on educating clients and helping them choose the best plan for their unique circumstances while minimizing emotional and financial costs.

Rebecca Mackie

60

Remarriage Protection and Retirement Trusts

By Maribeth Berlin and Jeffrey Kabbe (Naperville, Illinois)

I f you have retirement accounts and are married, you likely designated your spouse as the primary beneficiary on the accounts without giving it a second thought. If you have children, you probably named your children, either individually or through a trust, as the secondary beneficiaries. You may feel confident that your wishes will be carried out after you are gone, but in fact, you are leaving a lot to chance.

If you are the first spouse to pass away, your surviving spouse becomes the owner of your retirement accounts, which is likely what you intended when you named them as your primary beneficiary. But consider what happens—or could happen—from that point forward.

YOUR SPOUSE, AS BENEFICIARY, HAS FULL CONTROL

If you name your spouse as the primary beneficiary of your retirement account, the account will likely be rolled over to their own account upon your death. At that point, they are in full control.

As the new owner of the account, your spouse will need to name a new primary beneficiary, and they can name anyone they choose. The secondary beneficiaries that you originally listed—your children—do not automatically carry over. At this point, your children could be accidentally, or even intentionally, disinherited. Such risks are even greater in a blended family where you and your spouse do not share the same children.

Let's assume that your spouse follows your wishes and names your children as the new primary beneficiaries on the account. Then, years later, your spouse remarries. They may choose to name their new spouse as the primary beneficiary on their retirement accounts **and yours.** There is now a significant chance of your children being disinherited from your retirement assets. If your surviving spouse passes away before their new spouse, the new spouse will have all the retirement accounts in their name and under their control. The new spouse will then designate new primary beneficiaries who may not be your children. The new spouse might name their own children or other family members instead.

Even if your surviving spouse does not name their new spouse as beneficiary, the new spouse may have a right under the laws of some states to claim an elective share of your surviving spouse's estate whether or not your children are the designated beneficiaries.

At this point, it is even more likely that your children will be disinherited—certainly not the outcome you intended. The good news is that you and your spouse can eliminate these risks with some smart, yet straightforward, estate planning.

USING RETIREMENT TRUSTS FOR REMARRIAGE PROTECTION

You can design a retirement trust to receive your retirement accounts upon your death and pass them on to your spouse as your primary beneficiary while, at the same time, guarding against the risks outlined above. You can design the same retirement trust to continue, passing your retirement accounts to your children or grandchildren when the surviving spouse passes away.

Imagine the situation described above, except that you name your retirement trust as the primary beneficiary of your retirement accounts. Your spouse, and then your children, are the beneficiaries within the trust.

If you are the first spouse to pass away, your retirement accounts go directly into your trust. Designating new account beneficiaries is unnecessary because the trust controls the beneficiaries now, and they are locked in. Your retirement trust becomes irrevocable at your death, and no one can change your retirement assets' current or secondary beneficiaries.

If, in this new scenario, your surviving spouse remarries, they do not have the option of naming their new spouse as the beneficiary of your retirement accounts. Your trust can even require a prenuptial agreement between your surviving spouse and their new spouse to provide further protection against the new spouse trying to claim your retirement accounts if your surviving spouse passes away or later divorces their new spouse.

When your spouse passes away, the remainder of your retirement accounts goes to your chosen beneficiaries, such as children and grandchildren, through the trust.

HOW A RETIREMENT TRUST WORKS

A standalone retirement trust can be a simple, yet effective, addition to your existing estate plan. The retirement trust is revocable, and you can update it at any time during your lifetime.

When you pass away, your spouse becomes the beneficiary of your retirement trust. Assuming the trust includes the necessary provisions, during your spouse's lifetime, they will receive the annual required minimum distributions from your retirement accounts. The required minimum distributions are based on your surviving spouse's life expectancy, and tax rules require withdrawal of a certain amount (and payment of income taxes) each year. Your spouse can also receive additional, discretionary distributions if needed.

Your spouse can be the sole trustee of your retirement trust after your death and have significant control over distributions. You have the option of naming a co-trustee, such as an adult child, to manage the trust with your spouse. On the other hand, you can name your spouse as trustee to begin with but require a co-trustee if your spouse remarries or reaches a certain age. A co-trusteeship requires both trustees to agree on distributions to your spouse. Alternatively, you can name just a child or someone else entirely as trustee.

After the second spouse's death, your children can be the next beneficiaries of the retirement trust. Each beneficiary can receive their share of your remaining retirement assets in an ongoing beneficiary trust, a subtrust within your retirement trust that safeguards the beneficiary's inherited assets from their potential liabilities, such as a divorcing spouse, bankruptcy, creditors, and lawsuits. Your child, or someone else, can be the beneficiary trust's trustee. The beneficiary trust can include a requirement that your child reach a certain age or other benchmark before they can manage their trust and be their own trustee.

RETIREMENT TRUSTS AND ESTATE TAX PLANNING

Even if remarriage is not a concern, a retirement trust can be essential if you have a taxable estate. Your estate is taxable if its total value (including life insurance and real estate) exceeds state and federal estate tax thresholds. Estates are usually exempt if their value is under a certain amount.

Spouses with taxable estates often use a credit shelter or bypass trust to leave assets to their spouse in a way that prevents the assets from being taxed at the surviving spouse's death, which is when estate taxes become due.

If you name your spouse as beneficiary of your retirement accounts, the accounts will pass directly to them, and they will become the owner. Your retirement accounts will then be part of their estate when they pass away. For the calculation of estate tax, your spouse's estate's value will include their own assets **plus** the retirement assets they inherited from you. By naming your spouse individually as beneficiary on your retirement accounts, you increase the value of their estate.

Instead, if you leave your retirement assets in a bypass trust for your surviving spouse, they have access to the accounts during their lifetime, but the remaining value is not included in their estate. An estate planning attorney can draft a standalone retirement trust to include a bypass trust for your surviving spouse so that your retirement assets remain part of your estate tax planning strategy.

Retirement accounts also have income tax consequences, which depend in part on the identities of the beneficiaries. Retirement benefits received by a trust for your spouse have different tax implications from benefits received by your spouse as an individual. Your estate planning attorney can help you weigh your options and craft the optimal standalone retirement trust for your family.

The attorneys at Kabbe Law Group focus their practice on helping families transfer wealth and protect their loved ones, giving clients the peace of mind that comes with comprehensive and personalized planning.

Maribeth Berlin   *Jeffrey Kabbe*

61

Overview of Estate Planning for Small Business Owners

By Victoria and Tyler Lannom (Cookeville, Tennessee)

Estate planning is all about transition. As a small business owner, you may have never considered establishing an estate plan that addresses your business. You may be too busy with the day-to-day operations of your business. Or perhaps you believe that estate planning is only for the ultra-wealthy, or that a business succession plan is only for large corporations. Regardless of your reason, an estate plan is crucial for the long-term success of every business.

Well-coordinated estate plans can prevent taxation of your business assets upon your death. In addition, proper business estate plans can control how and when your business assets are distributed and provide your loved ones with the foundation and stability to carry on your business after you are gone. The way your business is taxed, administered, or wound down after you pass away can have tremendous implications for your loved ones and beneficiaries.

For example, let's say Alice co-owns a local donut shop with Ben. Alice is a widow, but has one child, Darcy. Alice plans to leave all of her assets to Darcy when she passes away. Ben is married to Edith and has two children, Francis and Garland. Ben plans

x

to divide his assets equally between Edith, Francis, and Garland when he passes away. Neither Alice nor Ben wants to co-own and run the donut shop with the other's beneficiaries. However, if Alice and Ben do not set up estate plans or business succession plans for their donut shop, they will likely have to run the donut shop with the other's beneficiaries, which could lead to chaos and the failure of the business.

BUSINESS SUCCESSION PLANNING

Business succession plans outline what business owners want to happen when key individuals in a business—often the owners—pass away, become incapacitated, or retire. When you create a business succession plan, you must identify the ideal successor to take over your business in these circumstances. Once you make that decision, you must determine the best way to transfer or sell your business to that successor.

One effective method of funding a buy-sell agreement (an agreement governing the transfer of ownership upon certain triggering events) is to create an irrevocable life insurance trust (ILIT) and fund the trust with life insurance purchased by the trust on the life of each business owner to provide the necessary liquidity to purchase each owner's share in the business.

How Does It Work?

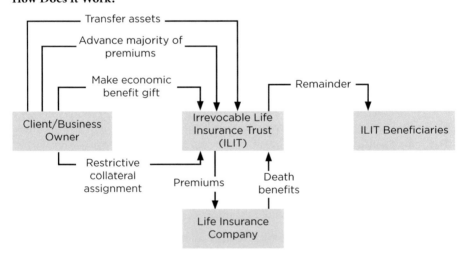

Business succession planning is critical to the health and longevity of your business. Succession planning should be considered when the business is initially formed. It is important to remember that every business is different, and therefore, every business succession plan will differ. For instance, when establishing a business succession plan, you must consider the following: Do you have a family member who is capable of running your business and wants to succeed you after you pass away? Is there management within your business that can steer the ship and support new ownership as your business continues to grow? Is the current management prepared to take over your company, and do they have the money to buy the company from your beneficiaries?

Whoever is set to succeed you needs to be actively involved in the transition process. If your plan is for your beneficiaries to sell your business to a third party after you pass away, it is important to understand the local market and what similarly situated businesses are selling for. A certified public accountant (CPA) or other tax professional can assist in establishing a general valuation for your business. If you do not currently have a formal business succession plan in place, work with your trusted financial advisor and estate planning attorney to begin the process.

TRUSTS FOR SMALL BUSINESS OWNERS

A revocable living trust (RLT) is an excellent estate planning tool that allows assets to be held and managed for beneficiaries during the trust creator's life. RLTs also allow assets to pass to your beneficiaries upon your death in private, without a cumbersome public probate proceeding. Business assets may be held in an RLT and managed by a trustee.

A great benefit of establishing an RLT for your business assets is that you, as the trust creator, can serve as the trustee during your life and can alter, amend, and add to the RLT at any time. An RLT allows you to maintain control of your business assets during your life; upon your death, your business assets pass directly to the RLT beneficiaries. With a business succession plan in place and estate assets held in trust, you can ensure that your business operations will continue without interruption.

How Does It Work?

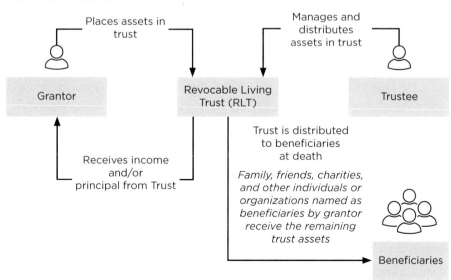

Trusts can also be a useful tool in your business tax planning strategy. For instance, if your business is structured as an S corporation, a grantor retained annuity trust (GRAT) can be utilized to transfer business assets before your death. Importantly, these appreciating assets are not subject to estate taxes in most situations. A GRAT provides an annuity to the trust creator (grantor), which is a fixed amount of money from the trust. It is important for the assets in the trust to generate enough income to fund the annuity, as this particular type of trust is irrevocable and cannot be altered. Common interests transferred into a GRAT include business shares, mutual funds, bonds, stocks, and other assets that are expected to appreciate. A GRAT can provide the trust creator and their family with substantial savings in estate taxes down the road.

There are other irrevocable trusts, such as the charitable remainder trust (CRT), that also allow the trust creator to plan ahead to minimize taxes and the erosion of family wealth. In a CRT, assets are placed into trust, and the beneficiaries receive payments for a specified period. Once the time period is over, the remaining assets are transferred to a tax-exempt charity. If a business is placed in the CRT and then sold, capital gains taxes that would have resulted from a sale by the individual owner may be avoided.

Consult with your financial advisor, tax professional, and estate planning attorney to determine whether a trust would benefit your small business estate plan.

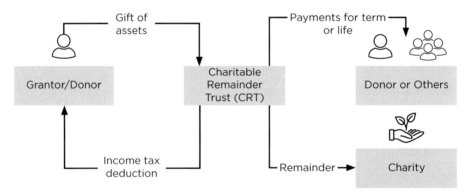

DURABLE POWER OF ATTORNEY

A durable financial power of attorney allows a trusted agent to make decisions for you in the event you become incapacitated. It is critical that your durable financial power of attorney document outline the requisite powers that will allow your agent to ensure there is no gap in the oversight and management of your business operations should something unforeseen happen to you. This foundational document is essential in any estate plan and should never be overlooked.

If you are a small business owner, estate planning should be part of the long-term plan for your business. It is very important that you meet with an experienced business and estate planning attorney to discuss your business needs and determine how you will establish your business legacy for generations to come.

Victoria Lannom   *Tyler Lannom*

Lannom Law LLC is an estate planning, elder law, and business development firm located in Tennessee. Our goal is to help our clients effectively manage their wealth throughout their lifetime and beyond.

62

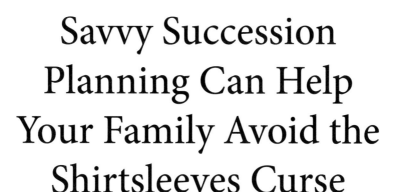

Savvy Succession Planning Can Help Your Family Avoid the Shirtsleeves Curse

By Benjamin Brickweg (Conifer, Colorado)

I have bad news. Someday you are going to die. Sorry for the unflinching dose of reality. But here is some good news: if you own a business, it does not have to die with you. That is likely to be good news for more than just you. Does your family rely on your business's income to support their lifestyle? If so, a succession plan is a must-have to help protect your loved ones from your inevitable absence.

The statistics are ugly. Two-thirds of family businesses do not survive the death of the founder. The saying "from shirtsleeves to shirtsleeves in three generations" reflects how hard it is to build a successful, profitable business and pass it on to family members who are as qualified as you are to run it—and as passionate as you are to keep it going for another generation.

Over 90 percent of business owners believe they should have a written succession plan, but you probably will not be shocked to learn that only one out of three entrepreneurs have put such a plan into writing. More than half of business owners leave their company because of an unforeseen event such as death or disability. That is why succession planning should be part of estate planning for every entrepreneur. If you have no idea what will happen to your business if you are not in the picture and that thought gives you pause, continue reading.

WHAT IS A SUCCESSION PLAN?

A succession plan is a written document that outlines how your business will continue to operate after your departure (whether you leave the business in a hearse or on a yacht). A succession plan protects the processes and protocols that enabled your business to reach its present level of success. It hands the reins to your chosen successors and preserves the institutional knowledge the new owners will need to keep the business humming, producing income for your family, and providing jobs for your employees.

COMPONENTS OF THE SUCCESSION PLANNING PROCESS

The business succession planning process can be divided into four components:

1. Personal and legacy goals
2. Business value and sellability
3. Business continuity
4. Family contingency and estate planning

FOUR COMPONENTS OF A SMARTEXIT ROADMAP[SM]

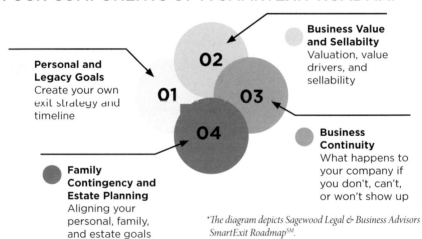

Business Value and Sellabilty
Valuation, value drivers, and sellability

Personal and Legacy Goals
Create your own exit strategy and timeline

Business Continuity
What happens to your company if you don't, can't, or won't show up

Family Contingency and Estate Planning
Aligning your personal, family, and estate goals

The diagram depicts Sagewood Legal & Business Advisors SmartExit Roadmap[SM].
© 2022 Sagewood Legal & Business Advisors | gosagewood.com

PERSONAL AND LEGACY GOALS

Figure out why and when you want to exit your company. You may love working in your business and intend to die in the saddle. Or perhaps you would rather create a valuable stream of cash flow today and then sell at peak value when you are ready to put yourself out to pasture. There is no wrong answer. Your succession plan should be based on your individual situation and goals. At my firm, Sagewood Legal & Business Advisors, we define ultimate freedom as owning a lifestyle business that creates a valuable stream of cash flow, runs without your daily involvement, and is sellable when the time is right.

Pick your exit type and postexit role. Passing your business down to your family is not the only exit strategy. You can create a succession plan to facilitate this strategy. However, assuming you are the sole owner, it will occur by default if you do not have a plan in place: you die, and your business falls into your family's lap. They may or may not be able to salvage the business if they inherit it without adequate preparation.

Other exit strategies include a merger with or acquisition by another company; a co-owner, management, or employee buyout; or going public with an IPO. If you do not care whether your company continues to operate or if you need quick cash, liquidation may be the answer.

A properly engineered succession plan takes your lifestyle, retirement, charitable, and business goals into account. For example, if you pass the business on to new owners while you are still able to work, do you want to stay on in some kind of advisory or mentorship role? Those who will take the reins when you step away may appreciate having you around during the transition. A good succession planning process, led by a third-party advisor with no skin in the game, can help you determine the exit strategy that is right for you.

BUSINESS VALUE AND SELLABILITY

Learn what your business is worth and how buyers will see it. Even if selling your business is not your exit strategy of choice, you need to know how much it is worth. Business valuation is part of your succession planning process, and it should be examined regularly. We suggest that our clients proactively review valuations every quarter.

Unfortunately, business valuation is an inexact science. There are several methods of valuation, and the complexity of the process often puts it far outside the wheelhouse of the average business owner. A quality analysis of your business value needs to include an overview of how sellable your business is and how your target buyers perceive your company. Sellability is a function of your company's financial performance, growth potential, cash position, and recurring revenue, along with intangible factors such as how differentiated the company is and how involved you are as an owner.

Enhance the value of your business. One of the biggest benefits of succession planning is the chance to increase the value of your business while you are still around to reap the benefits. Consider hiring an advisor experienced in leading business transactions to identify value-building opportunities you may have overlooked.

For example, your business will be a lot more attractive to buyers if your internal processes are thoroughly documented. A growing, increasingly profitable business may be more valuable than a stagnant one. High customer satisfaction scores and customer loyalty tell a buyer that the business will come with a happy customer base. A plan for retaining key employees gives a buyer peace of mind that they can maintain continuity. That is all worth paying for.

BUSINESS CONTINUITY

Create your short- and long-term business continuity plan. Your continuity plan needs to address the following aspects of your business: short- and long-term control, overall legal status, documentation, financial resources, owner involvement areas, and retention of employees, customers, and vendors. The plan should reflect the strategy you have developed, not determine it. That is why drafting your continuity documents should occur after you have worked with business valuation and exit strategy experts to craft your exit.

FAMILY CONTINGENCY AND ESTATE PLANNING

Set up a trust-based estate plan. The right strategy can help you protect your family, money, business value (or future), and end-of-life dignity. An effective estate plan will include options for your death and disability—the critical elements relating to both your planned and unplanned exit from your business. It avoids probate while protecting your money and your business from nursing home expenses, medical bills, and other unforeseen issues. A solid estate plan prevents your family from being forced to sell your business when you die.

Take action before the last roundup. One hundred percent of today's business owners will stop being owners at some point. Do not settle for a cookie-cutter succession plan template, or worse, no plan at all. A proactive transition planning process can help savvy business owners design an exit that achieves your own unique retirement and life goals. What's more, with the right advisor on your side, you can be sure to protect your friends, family, employees, and vendors, while also protecting your legacy from unnecessary taxes and fees.

Benjamin J. Brickweg, Esq., MBA, is the founder of Lodgepole Law, a boutique firm located in the mountains overlooking Denver that works with family-owned businesses seeking advanced estate planning and exit strategy solutions.

Benjamin Brickweg

63

Estate Planning, Business
Succession Planning,
and Exit Planning: How
Do They Fit Together?

By Cherish De la Cruz (Atlanta, Georgia)

In 2020, the number of small businesses in the United States reached 31.7 million, making up nearly all (99.9 percent) of US businesses. Consequently, it is important that small business owners recognize that their business may be their most valuable asset and plan for it accordingly.

A business owner's illness, incapacity, or death can severely impact their business. Since a business owner's net worth is intimately connected to their business, a family who relies on the business's income can face serious hardship if the owner dies, becomes incapacitated, or is otherwise unable to run the business. To avoid such a situation, the business owner should proactively involve their family members in creating a plan to ensure the business's continued success and avoid an interruption in the family's income at the owner's death or incapacity.

Business owners are sometimes so busy with the business's day-to-day operations that they fail to realize that their personal and business goals are not aligned. Business owners should look at their estate plans from both a personal and business perspective: their business and personal goals are distinct, but they should both be integrated into the estate plan.

KEY ESTATE PLANNING STEPS TO PROTECT YOUR BUSINESS AND LOVED ONES

Business owners should consider the following when contemplating their estate plan:

- providing for a spouse and other family members if the business owner becomes disabled or passes away
- issues that arise as a business owner ages, such as retirement and long-term health-care costs
- asset protection and business growth
- exiting the business

Depending on the size of the business, owners should also consider the implications of estate, gift, and generation-skipping transfer taxes.

KEY STEPS TO PROTECT THE BUSINESS: BUSINESS SUCCESSION AND EXIT PLANNING

To ensure a smooth business transition, an owner should have three key foundational documents in place: a will or trust, a medical directive, and a durable power of attorney. These legal documents should address not only the owner's personal assets and circumstances but also the business's assets and circumstances. They should specify how the business should be handled in the event of the owner's incapacity or death. Planning for the business owner's departure is called a *business succession plan.*

Business owners should ask themselves one of the following key questions as they begin the process: "Whom do I trust to sell my business?" or "Whom do I transfer my business to?" An ideal business succession plan begins with the end goal in mind and involves key proactive, strategic, legal, and financial decisions about who will take over the business upon the owner's retirement, death, or disability. Think of the business succession plan as a legal roadmap for the owner to follow when exiting the business. If the owner has not planned ahead for such scenarios by creating a business succession plan, the court could ultimately become involved, and the business's hasty sale or closure could potentially deprive the owner's family or beneficiaries of significant value.

FIVE TYPICAL SCENARIOS FOR TRANSFERRING OWNERSHIP INTEREST IN A BUSINESS

Example 1. Tom has a family-owned business, Ace Construction. Tom's sons, Rich and Harry, also work in the business. Tom's goal is to retire and transfer his shares to Rich and Harry over a five-year period.

Example 2. Bill and Ted co-own a restaurant. Bill plans to retire and sell his share of the business to Ted. Bill has a buy-sell agreement that addresses this retirement scenario.

Example 3. Alvin owns Good Sounds, a music production company, with Simon and Theodore. Alvin plans to retire, selling his shares to the business, which will then redistribute them to Simon and Theodore.

Example 4. Wayne owns A-1 Construction. None of Wayne's family members can take over his role in the business. Garth, a key employee, has a significant role in the company's day-to-day operations. A-1 Construction has purchased life insurance, and the proceeds will allow Garth to pay Wayne's wife so Garth can take over A-1 Construction when Wayne passes away or if he becomes disabled.

Example 5. Tommy's company, Callahan Auto, has been significantly profitable. Zalinsky Auto, a competitor, has approached Tommy with an offer to purchase Callahan Auto. Buy-Out Equity, a private equity firm, has also approached Tommy with an offer to purchase the business and repackage it in three years for other investors.

Generally, a buy-sell agreement is the ideal legal vehicle for a business owner to use for selecting the individuals or company they would like to transfer the business to. A buy-sell agreement is a contract that can require a successor/purchaser to purchase a business upon the occurrence of certain triggering events, such as incapacity, retirement, bankruptcy, and death.

A buy-sell agreement's benefit is that control of the business can remain with the individuals involved in its operation. The agreement provides the successor/purchaser with a mechanism and roadmap to follow if one of the triggering events occurs. For family businesses, this agreement may mean that heirs or other family members not **actively** involved in the business's day-to-day operations can sell their interests to the other owners, preserving family harmony.

Do not think of **exit planning** and **business succession planning** as separate processes. Rather, a successful exit plan encompasses all the essential components of a well-thought-out business succession plan. An exit plan's purpose is to proactively outline a business owner's strategic and successful exit. The goal is to facilitate the successful transition of the business to the next owner by avoiding the need for hasty decisions in an emergency situation.

There are various forms of exit plans. An exit strategy can involve

- a sale,
- listing with brokers,
- family succession,
- management buy-in or an employee stock option plan, and
- private equity.

Ideally, a business owner should develop a well-crafted exit plan in the beginning stages of their business and reevaluate the plan from time to time as the business grows. At a minimum, implementing an effective exit plan should start eighteen months before the desired exit date. However, the ideal time frame to begin executing the plan is three years in advance, so the business owner can implement effective tax strategies.

Because of the various considerations involved in business succession planning, it is important for a business owner to have the right team in place. At a minimum, the team should include a financial advisor, a certified public accountant, an estate planning attorney, a business attorney, and an insurance/risk advisor. Collaboration is key to coordinating all aspects of the business owner's interrelated personal, business, and financial goals. The owner should consult such professionals when forming the business to help prepare all interested parties: co-owners, family members, and key employees. In some scenarios, additional guidance from other professionals, for example, a mergers-and-acquisitions attorney, a valuation specialist, or an exit strategist, may also be useful when an owner is exiting their business.

De la Cruz Law was founded to provide seamless support to families and small business owners, and specializes in estate planning, probate, elder, and small business law.

Cherish De la Cruz

64

Why a Buy-Sell Agreement Is a Critical Piece of a Business Owner's Estate Plan

By Brittany Littleton (Tulsa, Oklahoma)

Y ou have poured your energy and resources into building a successful business that not only provides a valuable service to your customers but also supports your family, your partners, and your employees. But what happens to the company or the people you care about if you become incapacitated or die? It will be almost impossible for both your business and your family to continue to prosper if you do not plan proactively. A proper plan can ensure that your legacy continues long beyond your lifetime. A buy-sell agreement is a critical component of that plan.

THE OBJECTIVES OF A BUY-SELL AGREEMENT

If you own a family business or a closely held business with partners, you need a buy-sell agreement. A buy-sell agreement is a contract that specifies what rights and obligations you or a co-owner have if either of you leave the company. The terms of your buy-sell agreement will vary depending on your goals, but the agreement should achieve both your business planning and personal estate planning objectives by answering these critical questions:

- Who can own an interest in the business?

- Who can control the business?

- What happens upon a triggering event (e.g., retirement, divorce, bankruptcy, incapacity, death)?

- What price and payment terms will be paid by the company or remaining owners?

- How much money will you or your heirs receive?

The primary *business purpose* of a buy-sell agreement is to define the legal rights or obligations you and your partners have upon a triggering event, such as your death. In the agreement, you can restrict future control of the company to specified individuals, such as the remaining owners, agreed-upon family members, or key employees. This will be important to you and your partners in a variety of circumstances. For example, if you die and your business interest is inherited by your spouse, your spouse and partners are likely to have different interests in key business decisions such as distribution of profits, equity contributions, or day-to-day management. Your spouse may lack the knowledge or experience needed to step into your role as an active member of the company, and your partners may be unwilling to consider your spouse's opinion. A buy-sell agreement circumvents this potential conflict by establishing a fair price for your ownership interest that is then paid to your spouse (or other designated heirs) upon your death.

You may want to hire a qualified appraiser to determine the value of the company for purposes of negotiating the initial agreement. You and your partners can periodically agree to an updated value as the company grows. This allows you to ensure that the price payable for your business interest is fair and adequate, as you are likely to have a more informed opinion than your heirs or the executor of your estate. Absent a buy-sell agreement setting a fair market price, the Internal Revenue Service may audit your business records to independently determine the estate tax value of your business interest at your death. However, if your buy-sell agreement establishes an agreed-upon fair market purchase price, then that amount may be used instead. This not only helps the company and your estate avoid costly appraisals and valuation disputes, but also creates predictability that will allow you to determine what other advanced estate planning strategies may be beneficial to you.

The primary *estate planning purpose* of a buy-sell agreement is to ensure that purchase funds are available to pay your estate for your ownership interest upon your death (or other triggering events, such as incapacity or retirement). If you are like most business owners, your net worth is largely tied to your interest in your company. As a result, your estate may not have the liquidity needed to satisfy estate tax liability or other administrative expenses. Your business may also not have the cash to pay your estate the purchase price. If you qualify for affordable premiums, life insurance can be an ideal solution to provide the company or partners with purchase money upon your death without cash-strapping the business.

A common alternative to life insurance is to agree in advance to the terms of a secured promissory note that will go into effect upon the triggering event. This method may have the benefit of deferring income tax liability under the installment sale method of tax accounting. Another option is for the company to fund an investment that will be earmarked for purposes of fulfilling the buy-sell agreement. This strategy can be particularly effective with a buy-sell agreement triggered at your retirement, as you can use these funds as deferred compensation or purchase funds for a key employee you intend to be the business successor.

A buy-sell agreement can be mandatory or optional, depending on your goals. The buy-sell agreement can be structured several ways:

- **Redemption agreement:** The company purchases the departing owner's interest.

- **Cross-purchase agreement:** The remaining partners purchase the departing owner's interest.

- **Hybrid agreement:** The company has a first right of refusal to purchase the departing owner's interest, but if it declines, the remaining owners can purchase the interest (or vice versa).

You should consult with your attorney and CPA about which structure makes the most sense for you, as there are both legal and tax implications depending on how your business is organized and how the purchase price will be funded.

PLANNING FOR YOUR INCAPACITY AND DEATH BEYOND THE BUY-SELL AGREEMENT

While a buy-sell agreement addresses the contractual obligations that you, your partners, and your company have in the event of your incapacity or death, it alone does not avoid court interference. Guardianship and probate proceedings are unnecessary and expensive delays that can jeopardize both business continuity and the efficient administration of your estate. You can prevent these problems by completing a comprehensive personal estate plan.

If there are company decisions that require your vote during your incapacity, it may be necessary for a court-appointed guardian or conservator to vote on your behalf. A simple way to escape this unnecessary complication is to proactively designate a decision maker in a durable power of attorney. Make sure that you select an agent who understands your business and that the durable power of attorney includes express powers related to business management or ownership.

If you own your business interest in your individual name, then proceeds from any contractual obligation to purchase your share of the company arising from the buy-sell agreement will likely be payable to your estate. In most cases, this will require that your estate is administered in probate court, even if you have a last will and testament. In most states, probate is time-consuming, expensive, and publicly invites your creditors to make claims against your estate and other interested parties to contest your estate plan. However, you can avoid probate by owning your business interest in a revocable living trust. Before you assign your business interest to a trust, you should review your operating agreement or bylaws to confirm that the transfer is authorized. You should also confirm with your estate planning attorney that your trust is drafted to empower your successor trustee to make business decisions and, if applicable, includes necessary S corporation language.

If there is no buy-sell agreement or other governing document that addresses business succession upon your death, your business partners and heirs must rely on the default rules under state law. This could result in the liquidation and dissolution of the company. The assets and profits that remain after company debts are paid will be incorporated into your interest and then distributed to your heirs through your estate plan or probate proceedings, depending on how your ownership interest is owned.

THE BENEFIT OF ACTING NOW

It is common for business owners to procrastinate developing a business succession plan because there is inherent tension between what you want for your business, what you want for your family, and what your business partners and heirs may want once you are gone. Implementing a comprehensive estate plan and business succession plan requires foresight, effort, and challenging conversations with your family and business partners. However, the time and resources that you spend now will more than pay for themselves when a triggering event occurs. A thoughtful plan can minimize conflict, mitigate taxes, ensure business continuity, and protect your family's interest. After all the work you have done to build a thriving business, you deserve the peace of mind that comes from planning now.

Brittany Littleton is the founder of Littleton Legal PLLC, a boutique estate planning and business law firm serving Oklahoma families and entrepreneurs. Littleton Legal helps closely held businesses minimize conflict and plan for successful futures by creating thoughtful succession plans designed to maintain a thriving business while achieving multi-generational goals.

Brittany Littleton

65

Use a Directed Trustee to Save a Family Business

By Roger McClure (Fairfax, Virginia)

It is a common tragedy when a prosperous family business that provides employment and income for family members and long-time dedicated employees collapses shortly after the business founder's death. Overnight, family members and loyal employees are out of a job, and the family goes from being millionaires to potentially facing poverty.

Consider the following scenario in which a business owner uses a directed trustee to protect the family business. For twenty-five years Julie built a successful insurance agency that provides property, casualty, and life insurance to its customers. She has thirty employees, and the business is worth $12 million. Julie's son Alan works in the business. Her eighteen-year-old daughter, Michele, is in college and wants to become a doctor. Her seventeen-year-old son, Harry, is the quarterback of his high school football team. Julie has been divorced for ten years, and her former husband plays no role in the family or the business.

Julie does not want Alan to have complete control of her trust and estate. Alan's wife, Veronica Franco, is a gold digger who successfully pressured Alan to buy a huge eight-bedroom house on a golf course. She has elaborate parties and wears flashy jewelry. Julie often has to bail Alan out of financial troubles caused by Veronica's demands. Julie insists that her estate be managed by an independent trustee that will control Alan's—and Veronica's—spending. She does, however, trust Alan to run and expand the business.

Julie also owns a strip shopping center through a separate limited liability company (LLC). Her insurance agency occupies one of the six retail units.

Julie has implemented procedures, programs, and policies in her insurance agency that enable it to run very efficiently. As a result, the agency has record-breaking sales and profits whether or not she is in the office. Julie's agency is operated as an LLC, which avoids the double taxation that can occur with C corporations but provides asset protection for her.

Julie tells her WealthCounsel estate planning attorney that she wants to leave all her estate to her children in equal shares, allow Alan to run the insurance agency, and appoint an independent trustee to manage what will probably be a $15 million estate.

Trustees of an inheritance trust perform three general functions: managing assets, financial reporting, and preparing and filing the trust's tax returns. For asset management, licensed trust companies retain qualified professionals knowledgeable about managing stocks, bonds, and a broad range of financial instruments. However, these trust professionals usually have little expertise in real estate or running a business. Given their lack of in-house expertise about real estate and businesses, most trust companies will not accept real estate or businesses as trust assets unless the trust company has the legal right to sell them when it takes over the estate.

Unless the trust company is a directed trustee, it will likely sell the insurance agency and strip shopping center when she dies. Julie wants the highly profitable agency to continue operating to provide employment for her loyal and hardworking staff and a substantial inheritance and income for her children.

The WealthCounsel attorney structures the Julie Living Trust so that Julie will be in charge of her business and real estate while she is alive and competent. Upon Julie's disability or death, the trustees of her trust will be Alan and a directed trustee, and the trust will own the LLCs that own the insurance agency and strip shopping center.

Julie dies. At the time of her death, she had not been regularly participating in the business. Alan has been successfully running and expanding the agency. Michele is in her residency at a local hospital, and Harry is an NFL star. Her $15 million estate is to be divided into three equal shares for her children. Alan has the unilateral right to buy out his siblings for the estate-appraised value of their shares of the insurance agency.

State law determines whether using a directed trustee is allowed. The Julie Living Trust requires that the trust be administered in a state that allows directed trustees. Approximately thirty-two states have enacted versions of the Uniform Trust Code that allow directed trustees. Delaware, Nevada, South Dakota, and Alaska are prominent states with favorable trust laws that permit directed trustees. If your situation is like Julie's and your state does not permit directed trustees, you should set up your trust in a state that does.

Julie's estate planning attorney negotiates with a trust company in Delaware that accepts the appointment as a directed trustee to serve as a co-trustee with Alan. The attorney sets up an LLC in Delaware and transfers all the membership interests in the insurance and real estate LLCs to the Delaware LLC, and in exchange, the Julie Living Trust is the sole member of the Delaware LLC. There are separate share subtrusts for Alan, Harry, and Michele under the Julie Living Trust.

Alan is the manager of the Delaware LLC and the LLCs that hold the insurance agency and the real estate, and he oversees running the businesses. Alan instructs the Delaware directed trustee to hold one hundred percent of the membership interests of the Delaware LLC as trust assets. The directed trustee must follow Alan's direction on trust asset investment and, under state law, should have no liability to the beneficiaries or the trust instrument for following those directions.

All the net income of the agency and the real estate flows into the directed trustee's bank accounts in Delaware. Under each of the trusts for Alan, Harry, and Michele, the trustee has the discretionary power to make distributions for their health, education, and maintenance. The directed trustee also takes care of the trust accounting and tax reporting.

The directed trustee surveys Alan, Harry, and Michele annually to determine their ongoing needs and arrive at a distribution plan for that year. Alan and the directed trustee agree on the distribution amounts. Veronica pressures Alan for a new four-carat diamond ring, but Alan tells her the directed trustee denied her request.

A family accountant, lawyer, or friend may be a directed trustee. The directed trustee may also be guided regarding distributions. The family can have the trust's tax return prepared by their own accountant but reviewed, approved, signed, and filed by the directed trustee in any appropriate state. A trustmaker can shop for services and trustee fees. Even though a directed trustee is not liable for failure of investments, if the trust owns gold in an overseas vault, highly speculative securities, or high-risk investments, a directed trustee may get nervous and resign.

As a result of using a directed trustee and Alan's management expertise, Julie's business survives her death and grows to be one the largest insurance agencies in her state. With the inheritances she provided in good hands, each of her children is launched on a successful career, and Veronica can't stick her hand into the family pot of gold.

Roger McClure has over forty years' experience in business and estate planning, has published many articles in national publications, and is a sought-after national speaker. He provides very practical and useful advice to family-owned businesses, from basic to very advanced planning.

Roger McClure

66

A New Perspective on Employee Stock Ownership Plans: Using ESOPs for Intergenerational Estate Plans

By Brian A. Eagle and Scott J. Linneweber (Indianapolis, Indiana)

Proper business succession planning allows you to address the effects of the business's transition on your family, the company, and your community. Employee stock ownership plans (ESOPs) are unique qualified retirement plans used to facilitate the transfer of equity in privately-held businesses to the employees. Business succession planning using ESOPs is ideal for business owners who have twenty or more employees and at least $1,000,000 in earnings before interest, taxes, depreciation, and amortization (EBITDA) who desire to

- transition the business to their family,
- purchase minority family-owned interests,

- keep their business in the current community,

- reward their employees,

- diversify their portfolio, and

- reduce or eliminate estate taxes.

This strategy is designed to transition a business to family members or allow for its purchase from family members who own a minority interest in a company. The owner uses an ESOP to purchase a partial interest in the business for the benefit of the employees. The remaining interest is retained by the owner or family members. When the transaction is complete, the ESOP's ownership in the equity of the company is allocated to the participants (i.e., eligible employees) over time.

The company loans money to the ESOP for the purchase. To provide the loan, the company arranges for financing from a bank or negotiates with the owners to provide seller notes. The company then loans the funds to the ESOP in exchange for a note. The ESOP pays back the loan using annual tax-deductible contributions received from the company and uses the proceeds of the loan to purchase the partial interest in the company.

S corporations (S corps) and C corporations (C corps) are eligible to implement ESOPs, but limited liability companies taxed as partnerships and other partnerships are not. Unlike S corps, C corps can create multiple classes of securities. However, S corps may have voting and nonvoting shares. For business owners who want to transfer control of the business to their descendants, a C corp ESOP transaction provides some advantages compared to an S corp transaction. The two primary advantages are the ability to indefinitely defer or eliminate capital gain taxes under Internal Revenue Code (IRC) section 1042 and the ability to use super voting common stock (greater voting rights per share) for the ESOP transaction, which benefits multiple parties.

Chronologically, the ESOP transaction should precede sale or gift transactions. The ESOP transaction could be preceded by corporate transactions such as an S corp election revocation, accumulated adjustments account distributions, recapitalization wherein a second class of stock is created, and a stock split.

The stock sold to the ESOP must be an *employer security* as defined in the IRC. Simply stated, the security must have the highest dividend and voting rights.

ESTATE PLANNING EXAMPLE

Suppose a family with four children owns an S corp business worth $10,000,000. There is very little net worth outside of the business due to the depreciation of real estate and the need to use the operating cash flow of the business to fund growth. The parents own retirement accounts; however, these accounts are expected to be depleted before the parents' passing. One son and one daughter are active in the management of the business, and the two other children are not involved in the business.

Mom and Dad are willing to transfer the entire $10,000,000 during their lifetimes, relying on the assets in their retirement accounts and consulting fees and wages paid from the business pursuant to employment and consulting agreements to maintain their desired lifestyle.

The parents would like an equal distribution for each child. The parents are open to gifting strategies and creating trusts or family partnerships.

ESOP STRATEGY

Using an ESOP strategy, the parents would revoke the S corp election and recapitalize the company into two classes: common stock and super voting common stock. The super voting common stock, if structured correctly, would carry a valuation premium of 20 to 30 percent over the common stock; hence, the parents could sell less of the equity to gain the desired funds to diversify their net worth. If structured appropriately, all funds could be paid without tax consequences. Further, the company will initially receive cumulative tax deductions equal to the price of the ESOP transaction. In short, the company would pay the bank loan in pre-tax dollars instead of after-tax dollars and receive an income tax deduction because of the contributions to the ESOP, which is a qualified retirement plan under ERISA.

Finally, the common stock would be reduced in value due to the loan to finance the ESOP transaction and the shift of dividend rights to the newly created super voting common stock.

In summary, the ESOP transaction in this scenario would create millions of dollars in cumulative tax deductions, increasing the aggregate family wealth and lowering the value of the common stock to be transferred to family members who will control the business when Mom and Dad are no longer with them. The ESOP transaction would also mitigate gift and estate taxes and allow more shares to be transferred during Mom and Dad's lifetime using advanced estate planning strategies, such as sales to grantor trusts or grantor retained annuity trusts. In addition, cash generated from the sale of the super voting common stock to the ESOP could be used by Mom and Dad to equal-ize the estate distributions and for the purchase of substantial life insurance to provide for the children not involved in the business, potentially free of estate and gift tax. On the other hand, the family would share the equity with the employees and would no longer maintain 100 percent ownership.

The inception of an ESOP calls for modest formalization of corporate governance. However, in the hypothetical scenario, the family maintains control of both day-to-day operations and strategic direction and decisions.

CONCLUSION

ESOPs can be used to create more robust estate plans when the family's primary objective is the transfer of equity control to successor generations.

Clients may also consider a wealth replacement trust that holds a second-to-die life insurance policy to equalize distributions between the children working in the company and the children not involved in the business and to reduce estate taxes.

Brian Eagle

Scott Linneweber

The law firm of Eagle & Fein, P.C., celebrating 30 years of serving clients in 2022, inspires families to plan to meet their goals and objectives based on a unique process that focuses on the definition of proper planning. Our philosophy is to make the complex simple by taking the time to understand our clients' concerns, identify potential problems, and seek advantageous solutions.

67

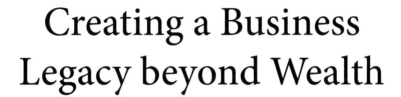

Creating a Business Legacy beyond Wealth

By Michael G. Stuart (Schaumburg, Illinois)

When my wife and I married in May 2019, her children and grandchildren lovingly accepted me as "Pappou Michael." Then when my oldest daughter and son-in-law blessed us with our first grandson in June 2020, I was overjoyed. Being a grandfather has been one of the most rewarding experiences of my life. Watching grandchildren grow and begin to participate in the family is amazing and energizing. It caused me to wonder what their lives will be like when they grow up. What can I do to make sure they know about their heritage after I am gone?

Life can change unexpectedly, and I want to make sure my grandchildren know how our family came to be. My dad passed when I was young, so I never really got to know him or learn about his dreams. As I built my practice, I realized that communicating my vision and purpose was as important as the legal documents I used to set it up. It was then that I began to help clients define their legacies so that their families could understand the passion behind the creation of their wealth. When working with business owners, I have taken a similar approach, encouraging them to include family members, close business associates, and employees in their vision for the business's continuation. Circumstances and finances may change over time, but a written legacy provides guidance to help those who are carrying it forward stay on track.

The legal definition of *legacy* is "a gift of property by will or testament."[1] The traditional concept of estate planning usually reflects the desire to control your property while you are alive and plan for yourself and your loved ones if you become disabled. It also enables you to leave what you have to whomever you want, whenever you want, and how you want, with the added benefit of minimizing costs to yourself and those you love. But I feel that there is a key component missing in the traditional approach: defining the **vision** you want to leave behind.

In this context, legacy has a broader meaning than its limited legal definition. It does not necessarily require great feats or accomplishments during your lifetime. Everyone has a story to tell, and they hope it will have an impact on those who come after them. If you had the opportunity to share your dreams, visions, and wisdom with your children, what would you say?

LEGACY IN BUSINESS

For many professionals and entrepreneurs, the business they have spent a lifetime building may be one of the largest assets in their estate. It also represents an investment of time spent away from the family for the family's benefit. In that respect, all businesses are family businesses. When considering retirement, many business owners consider only logistical and operational transitions to reach their goals when they decide to make that leap. But the exit planning process contemplates more than mere retirement. For example, you should clarify your personal goals to ensure that they will be met: Do you want the business to provide a benefit to the public beyond your involvement? Do you want family members or future generations to benefit from the business? How can you prevent family wealth from being lost over time?

Ask yourself the following questions:

- Who will keep the business running if you become disabled?
- If you have partners, do you have a comprehensive agreement that is current and in line with your goals?
- Will your family be protected if you do not make it to your planned exit so they can reap the benefits of the asset you have spent a lifetime building?
- Who are your current advisors that your family or partners should contact for guidance?
- Do you have regular family meetings to discuss such issues and prepare in case something happens to you?
- What is your long-term vision for the business?

---

1   *Legacy,* Britannica, https://www.britannica.com/topic/legacy (last visited Oct. 2, 2021).

LEGACY STORIES AND INTENTIONS

People relate to stories because they are personal histories, and that is what makes a legacy lasting. A legacy is the way you share your personal history, the way others relate to you, and the way your loved ones will remember you. A true legacy can immortalize the contributions, achievements, life lessons, and generosity you cultivated during your lifetime. It can make a meaningful difference in the lives of the younger generations and help them better understand the intention behind the wealth. It is in these ways that adding your story to your planning will ensure that your values and vision—in addition to your financial wealth—will enhance the lives of those you love.

In addition to sharing your story, sharing your intentions with your family can offer clarity and foster good decision-making. Because legal documents last beyond our lifetimes, capturing your legacy and vision will help future generations understand the love and hard work that went into building the wealth in the first place. Think about the wisdom and guidance you can offer future generations to help them deal with the issues of their day. Further, think about communicating the legacy to children who are too young to appreciate the wealth or business that you are passing on to them so they can better comprehend the impact as they mature.

This is where designated helpers come in. You should make sure that you or your designated helpers have control in times of crisis. However, most legal documents do not include specific guidance to assist such helpers during a critical time. In times of crisis, memories of prior discussions fade and emotions may become overwhelming. I generally recommend that clients write a letter or record an audio or video message to memorialize their wishes so that there is no confusion. In our practice, we call them legacy letters, which underscores their important role in the overall estate plan. You are the best person to share these details because, without your first-person experience, succeeding generations may be unable to offer the same inflection needed to realize your vision, desires, and goals.

CONNECTION THROUGH LEGACY

Discussions about important issues that would otherwise be lost or overlooked also bring families closer together. Family meetings are critical for understanding the parents' rationale and intention for certain actions and decisions.

We use technology that allows us to incorporate clients' mission, vision, values, and goals into their legal documents while retaining the importance of the document and avoiding confusion during a crisis. To support our focus on legacy communication, we intentionally work with other like-minded organizations, such as Legacy Foundry, because it is vitally important. In our collaboration with Legacy Foundry, we have discovered the perfect vehicle to foster communication between family members and others on the following subjects:

- medical desires if you are hospitalized
- rehabilitation in a nursing facility or home healthcare, or with the help of family members
- the history and meaning behind the wealth
- guidance for younger generations about how the wealth was built
- open discussions among the generations so each one can understand the others' viewpoints
- understanding the estate administration process
- avoiding family conflict
- understanding family goals

Legacy Foundry's interactive platform enables the conversation to occur in a nonthreatening forum where all generations can be heard. Each generation certainly has different values, and this forum is a way to open the dialogue calmly and equitably.

Both exit and estate planning are vitally important for every business owner. They are among the most significant financial and emotional events of your life, and integrating true legacy components can help increase their impact and longevity. By obtaining proper counsel about the issues involved, you can gain peace of mind that the business you have spent a lifetime building will achieve your goals and provide for you and your family as you intended. So establish your team of advisors, share and memorialize your legacy stories and intentions, select your helpers, and build a foundation that will enrich the lives of many generations to come.

In addition to his estate planning practice, Michael conducts one-on-one and group training for attorneys, helping them grow, maintain, and transition, and create lasting, purposeful legacies.

Michael Stuart

68

Estate Planning for Gun Owners

By David Duringer (Morro Bay, California)

state planning is not merely about protecting assets. Fundamentally, it is about protecting your family. But let us begin with protecting your assets, and suppose those assets include guns.

Your guns may be worth more than you think. Guns already outnumber people in the United States, but demand for guns keeps rising and so does the price. From an estate preservation standpoint, you do not want whomever is handling your estate to waste assets by selling them for a song. Worse, a survivor who is afraid of guns may just surrender the guns for destruction by a local police department. Instead, to avoid waste, plan to have your guns handled by someone knowledgeable whom you appoint as a special trustee for guns under your main trust or separate gun trust. It is generally advisable to use a trust to avoid probate court fees, delay, and making information about your guns public.

A gun-wise trustee can better avoid accidental felonies and other criminal liability. Possession and transfer of guns and ammunition are highly regulated under state and federal law. The strictest penalties are under the National Firearms Act (NFA), which applies to certain limited classes of firearms and other items such as suppressors (silencers) and explosives. You can go to prison for a long time and pay a very steep fine just for possessing one of these items without proper registration and payment of tax.

Nevertheless, they are somewhat common in many states. It is not necessary to create a specially drafted NFA trust in order to acquire an NFA item. But having such a trust may help in some states, for example, to eliminate the possibility that a family member may be criminally liable just for living under the same roof. NFA violations are strict liability crimes, meaning the government need not prove intent.

While most gun owners are not directly affected by the NFA now, there are proposals to expand the NFA to include all semiautomatic firearms. Those who may be at a disadvantage using manually loaded weapons, such as women or the elderly, may opt to comply with the NFA to obtain or retain autoloaders, which may be easier (or at least quicker) for them to operate in self-defense. Again, in many states, it may be beneficial to hold NFA firearms in an NFA trust specially drafted for that purpose.

Other state and federal gun laws are harsh, yet not quite as harsh because unlike the NFA, these laws require the government to prove some type of intent. They include prohibitions on transfer and possession of certain types of weapons. They also include prohibitions on transfer to and possession by certain types of people, called *prohibited persons.* In addition to the federal government, each state has its own categories of people considered prohibited persons. A beneficiary or a trustee might be a prohibited person even if they never had any criminal conviction. For example, perhaps they smoke marijuana, are subject to a protective order, renounced their US citizenship, or were dishonorably discharged. Those are just a few examples. It is very important that no beneficiary or trustee possess guns if they are a prohibited person. Also, there may be state-level requirements for firearm safety education in order to lawfully possess guns and other transfer requirements such as going through a federal firearms licensee (FFL, also known as a dealer) or registering the firearm with the state. State laws vary; while using a dealer is not always required, it is often recommended because it involves a background check.

In addition to jail time, violation of state and federal gun laws can lead to massive fines that may be chargeable to your estate. There is also the potential for massive tort liability in the event guns are mishandled and injury or death results.

So, at a minimum, if you simply own guns and care about the orderly settlement of your estate, then you will benefit from carefully choosing someone with firearm expertise who will handle those guns for you to avoid waste and potential civil and criminal liability. That individual may act as a special trustee for guns placed in your revocable trust, or you may decide to set up a separate gun trust. This person should also be the agent under your power of attorney, at least for handling guns.

Remember, estate planning is also about planning for incapacity. Although "from my cold dead hands" is a rallying cry for gun owners, the reality is that many of us may become incapacitated at some point, spelling an early end to our gunslinging days. Also, if you regain capacity, you may want to reacquire your firearms. You must plan for incapacity under both your trust and power of attorney to determine this process for yourself. Handle incapacity before it handles you!

Depending on your relationships with your guns and with your family, the above may be all the planning you need. Perhaps you just want the guns sold at the highest price. Perhaps you want to give a gun outright and do not care whether the beneficiary keeps it or sells it. For example, if you are a collector and no one else in your family has an interest in guns, you may want the collection sold or donated to charity.

It is your relationship with your guns that primarily determines the level of gun planning you need.

Some families have a long tradition of hunting, which can be a basis for a firearm legacy; but hunting is not as common as it once was due to urbanization and agriculture.

Other families put the focus on defensive training, even for minor children. There are quite a few cases of kids using firearms to defend themselves and their families.

I had a very poor relationship with my first guns. The only training I had was the bare minimum the state required. I did not know what I did not know. Later on, as a young dad, I took some high-level defensive training, got hooked, and became a concealed-carry instructor. I now have a different relationship with guns.

Most gun owners, even those with a carry permit or ex-military or law enforcement, do not regularly engage in high-level firearm training and competition. You probably will not be interested in the next level of gun planning—the ultimate in family protection, leaving a legacy of firearm training for generations—unless you experience such training at a local range or one of the megaschools. Without it, you will not have the perspective to know what is possible in terms of training your family under time pressure with objective, immutable performance criteria, and training them to train others.

So, get trained! Then, as you continue to train with your family, get to work adding language to your main trust or separate dynastic gun trust, incentivizing defensive gun handling, instructorship, gunsmithing, manufacture, reloading, and any other firearm activities you want to encourage for generations. You can also incentivize other values. For example, many families consider a relationship with God highly complementary to a relationship with guns. You can also incentivize career, charity, financial mentorship, estate planning, and the maintenance of family relationships—any values you deem important for family protection.

David R. Duringer, JD, LLM (Tax), Protective Law Corporation (LawNews.TV), located on California's Central Coast, helps families grow their power by transmitting life, fortune, and honor to succeeding generations.

David Duringer

Special Needs and
Public Benefits Planning

69

Elder Law Concepts

By Daniel Surprenant and Michelle Beneski
(New Bedford, Massachusetts)

Within the larger subject of estate planning is the concept of elder law. Essentially, elder law is estate planning that deals with issues more common among the senior population. Because they regularly address these issues, elder law attorneys are not only proficient in the substantive law in this area, but are also familiar with the challenges, characteristics, and joys of regularly serving elders. An elder law attorney is better equipped to analyze and counsel clients as they plan for and experience issues such as dementia and Alzheimer's disease, loss of mobility, family conflicts, as well as in-home and facility-based care options.

The *Elder Law Answer Book* explains elder law in this way:

> Usually elder law attorneys focus their practices in a handful of areas. Those focus areas typically include long-term care planning, guardianship and conservatorship, advance medical directives, and the more traditional trust and estate planning. Other elder law attorneys spend considerable time dealing with Medicare and other government benefits; abuse, neglect, and exploitation issues; age discrimination; charitable giving; probate administration; and a host of other practice areas.[1]

As an elder law client, you may be concerned with issues such as protecting your

---

1   Robert Fleming and Lisa Nachmias Davis, The Elder Law Answer Book (Aspen Publishers, 3rd ed., 2013).

home and other assets from the high cost of long-term care, minimizing estate taxes, and protecting your child's inheritance from their own potential divorce or creditors' claims. You may also be concerned about avoiding the cost and delay of probate court proceedings when you pass or naming the person you would like to make your medical decisions if you cannot.

In Massachusetts, the state in which I practice, private payment for nursing home care can easily reach $14,000 per month or $168,000 per year. That is a scary number for many clients. A good elder law attorney will walk you through whether, and how, you may be able to protect assets and qualify for Medicaid to pay for your care, legally and in compliance with the complex Medicaid regulations.

An elder law attorney will also guide you in deciding and formalizing who will make your medical and legal decisions when you are no longer able to do so, and help you incorporate flexibility into your plan in case life's circumstances change. There is no one-size-fits-all solution. Your plan should be driven first by your goals, as well as your assets, circumstances, family, health, and other considerations.

Two clients that appear identical because they have the same assets may have very different estate plans because their goals are very different. Let's consider the situation of Jack and Betty Holmes, who are seventy-one and sixty-nine years old, respectively. They are in good health with three children and five grandchildren. They own a home worth $450,000 and have other assets valued at roughly $500,000.

When their elder law attorney asked about their goals, Jack and Betty expressed concern about protecting their home and assets from the cost of long-term care. They also wanted to avoid the cost and delay of probate, which takes over a year to complete in their state and costs several thousand dollars. Lastly, they wanted to make sure that if one of their children passes, even after their own deaths, the child's inheritance will go to the child's children, not to an in-law.

An elder law attorney will review various foundational documents, such as a will, durable power of attorney, healthcare proxy, living will, and Health Insurance Portability and Accountability Act (HIPAA) release. Also, the attorney will explain options to protect their home, including trusts, life estate deeds, and outright gifting.

After considering their options, Jack and Betty gravitated toward an irrevocable trust to protect their home from long-term care costs, which, in their state, enabled them to continue to live in the property, sell the property, change trustees, and change beneficiaries (those who will receive the home when they pass). Jack and Betty were surprised at the flexibility that the planning offered.

Additionally, in their case, the trust was structured to last for the lifetimes of their children so that if a child passed, the trust's assets will be transferred to the child's children rather than to the child's spouse. Lastly, the trust will avoid probate at the death of both Jack and Betty and their children.

In creating their plan, Jack and Betty gained the peace of mind of knowing that (1) they had chosen a trustee who will make important legal and financial decisions if they cannot, (2) the assets in the trust will be protected after Medicaid's five-year lookback period, (3) their money will stay in the family, and (4) their family will likely avoid guardianship, conservatorship, and probate court proceedings. Their estate plan will enable them to save and protect potentially hundreds of thousands of dollars and ensure that their personal wishes will be followed.

As they say, "timing is everything." Better results are usually achieved by planning early, rather than late. None of us knows when we may pass, become disabled, need long-term care, or lose a loved one. There are many estate planning and elder law strategies that require formalization well before they are needed. Typically, your plan must be in place for five years—the current look-back period in most states—prior to applying for Medicaid for your home to be protected from the cost of long-term care. Of course, there are exceptions that a good elder law attorney can explain. Some other examples of time-sensitive planning include the use of both spouses' estate tax exemption for married couples or the removal of life insurance from your taxable estate. To accomplish these objectives, estate planning documents and strategies must be put in place well before you need them.

The good news is that you can take action to achieve your estate planning goals. An experienced elder law attorney is well versed in the issues and solutions available for seniors. You will be happy to find that the cost of planning is far outweighed by the savings and protection you provide for your loved ones, not to mention your own peace of mind.

Daniel Surprenant & Michelle Beneski

Surprenant & Beneski, P.C. focuses on achieving client goals in the areas of estate planning, elder law, and special needs planning. Our managing partners are certified elder law attorneys (CELAs) and are perennially listed on Boston Magazine's list of Super Lawyers for estate planning and elder law.

70

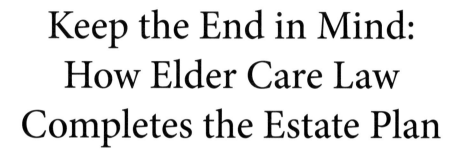

Keep the End in Mind: How Elder Care Law Completes the Estate Plan

By Brian Andrew Tully (Melville, New York)

A comprehensive estate plan can, upon your passing, help minimize estate taxes, avoid probate, establish family trusts that benefit your children and grandchildren, and even protect your accumulated wealth from the risks of divorce, addiction, and misuse. This is all critical, and we should each have a complete estate plan in place before we pass.

However, an estate plan that does not fully explore the needs and options for what happens *between* the date of the signing of your estate planning documents and the future date of your passing is neglecting a very serious aspect of life: aging. Your net worth and extensive irrevocable grantor trust probably will not be the first thing on your mind if your doctor tells you that you have Parkinson's or Alzheimer's disease. Every estate plan—both those designed to minimize taxation for generations and those that simply leave the family home to the children—must address the reality of elder care.

The US Department of Health and Human Services reports that people aged sixty-five and older have a 70 percent chance of needing long-term care.[1] This is a significant number of people that will need help due to a functional or cognitive decline. These are people that you and I know; they may be members of our families or perhaps even ourselves. The fact that such a significant number of people will need elder care translates into one thing: we must plan for not only our estates but also for our care.

I have been helping families plan for their estates and care for over twenty-three years. I can attest to you that those who focus only on the estate plan may be struck with an elder care crisis that impacts not only their physical and cognitive care but also the stress levels, emotions, and dynamics of their immediate family. In addition, for some, the financial impact will be devastating: home care in New York can be as high as $10,000 per month and nursing facility care can reach $20,000 per month. Elder care will always be stressful, emotional, and expensive, but those who plan for this likely scenario will be prepared to avoid a crisis.

A typical estate plan does not entirely ignore the possibility of physical and cognitive decline, as it includes a durable power of attorney and healthcare advance directives that appoint decision makers should you be unable to make financial, legal, or healthcare decisions. These documents are essential, but they do not address the care aspect of aging. Elder care should be an integral part of your estate plan: it can impact your financial assets as much as taxes and probate can, and it can impact your family as much as your death can. As such, to properly complete your estate plan, be sure to address the following elder care topics during your estate planning consultation.

First, understand that Medicare does not pay for long-term care. There are two types of care as we age: medical and long-term. Medical care is care that involves doctors, hospitals, and rehabilitation centers and is generally covered under your medical insurance or Medicare. Then, there is care that is long-term but not medical in nature. This is when a person requires assistance with either functional needs or cognitive needs. Functional needs are known as the activities of daily living and include essential tasks such as walking, bathing, and toileting. Cognitive needs include the instrumental activities of daily living such as shopping, driving, cooking, and cleaning. Long-term care is at the heart of elder care law.

Second, where will you receive your long-term care? You can receive long-term care in various types of residential settings, and it will all depend on your level of care. For example, will you be able to receive the care you need in your home? Or in your child's home? Will you be able to reside in, and afford, an assisted living facility or a

---

1 *How Much Care Will You Need?*, U.S. Dep't of Health and Hum. Servs., Admin. for Community Living, https://acl.gov/ltc/basic-needs/how-much-care-will-you-need (Feb. 18, 2020).

continuing care retirement community? Perhaps your needs will be significant, and a nursing home will be the safest setting. This issue cannot be resolved before the need arises; however, it is important to be aware of your options, as each one has different criteria and varies in cost.

Third, how will you pay for the care you need in the setting that you want? There are three ways to pay for long-term care: private pay, long-term care insurance, and Medicaid. Paying privately for the care is not possible for many, as the cost can range from $100 per day to nearly $700 per day depending on the city in which you live, the level of care, and the residential setting. However, if paying privately is the plan, and it is for many wealthy families, the focus is more on the care planning and not the Medicaid planning. For this client, the goal is singular: get the best care possible wherever you are.

If you choose to purchase long-term care insurance, you must qualify health-wise and obtain sufficient coverage to pay for the care in your region in the residential setting you desire. Unfortunately, many do not qualify for coverage or they do not purchase sufficient benefits to pay for the daily care, with the result being that they still need to privately pay or pursue the Medicaid option.

Finally, a significant number of families, even those with substantial assets, rely on Medicaid despite its eligibility requirements, as they plan for asset protection as part of their estate planning. An *elder care protection plan,* for example, encompasses the necessary estate planning, the appropriate level of Medicaid eligibility planning, and helps the client prepare for care as they age. When completed in advance of the statutory look-back periods, protected assets are shielded from Medicaid liens and state recovery, thereby saving them for a surviving spouse or as inheritance for the children. For this client, the goal is to shelter as many assets as possible and receive the best care possible.

Regardless of your financial status, an estate planning consultation that encompasses elder care issues may better serve you and your family because you will be doing your part to avoid a crisis. A crisis, as I share with my clients daily, occurs when there has been no planning or preparation. If a crisis does occur, the costs will always be greater, the options will be limited, and there will always be more stress. Elder care is certainly the great equalizer: The need for it will strike most of us, whether you have millions in the bank or just thousands—so it is wise to be prepared and do what you can to avoid the crisis.

Do not fret if you already have an estate plan in place and these aging issues were not discussed. Simply seek out an experienced elder care law attorney to address the above issues.

Estate planning and elder care are two points along the same line in our lives. When we are planning our estates, regardless of our age and our net worth, we need to always keep the end in mind.

Brian Andrew Tully, JD, CELA, has been certified as an elder law attorney since 2003 and is the founder of Tully Law Group, PC, an elder care law firm.

Brian Tully

71

Medicaid Eligibility for Nursing Home Care

By Kevin Pillion and Jada Terreros (Sarasota, Florida)

G iven the rising costs of long-term care, clients often ask about using Medicaid to cover nursing home care. There are a number of rules, pitfalls, and strategies for getting Medicaid to pay for nursing home care. The following are your seven takeaways from this chapter:

1. Medicaid is the single largest payer for nursing home care in the United States.

2. Nursing home costs often exceed $10,000 per month.

3. Numerous Americans will need nursing home care during their lifetime.

4. The rules for receiving Medicaid are complex and state specific.

5. The exceptions and pitfalls to the rules for Medicaid eligibility vary widely.

6. Consult a qualified elder law attorney to learn more about Medicaid eligibility in your state.

7. You can find an elder law attorney online at www.naela.org or www.nelf.org.

MEDICAID AND ITS IMPORTANCE IN PAYING FOR NURSING HOME CARE

Medicaid is a **joint federal-state public benefit program** that provides healthcare and long-term care coverage (among other things) to millions of Americans. In fact, Medicaid is the single largest payer for nursing home care in the United States. Each state runs its own Medicaid program; however, all states must follow federal law to receive federal money, which pays for at least half of each state's Medicaid costs. In some states, Medicaid goes by different names, such as MassHealth in Massachusetts, Medi-Cal in California, and TennCare in Tennessee.

Medicaid pays for room and board (called custodial care) in a nursing home, which often costs more than $10,000 per month. Most nursing home residents are elderly and lack the financial means to pay for their long-term care, especially given that the average stay for nursing home residents is more than two years. The cost can be particularly onerous for a married couple because the healthy spouse (also called the community spouse) may be left impoverished if the couple's joint income and assets are depleted to pay for the ill spouse's care in a nursing home.

Medicaid is different from Medicare. Medicare is health insurance; it does not pay for custodial care in a nursing home. Rather, Medicare pays only for skilled care during the first one hundred days in a nursing home if they were preceded by a qualifying hospital stay of more than three consecutive days.

RULES FOR MEDICAID ELIGIBILITY

There are two general criteria for getting Medicaid to pay for nursing home care.

- **Financial eligibility.** You must have limited income and assets to qualify for Medicaid. In 2022, in many states, Medicaid applicants must have less than $2,523 of monthly gross income. In addition, in many states, Medicaid applicants may keep only $2,000 of countable assets, while their community spouses may have up to $137,400 of countable assets in 2022. Typically, the Medicaid applicant's monthly income limit and the community spouse's countable asset limit amounts increase annually, but the $2,000 countable asset limit for the Medicaid applicant remains the same in many states.

- **Nonfinancial eligibility.** To be eligible for Medicaid, you must be a resident of your state and a US national, citizen, or permanent resident or a documented alien in need of a nursing-home level of care. You must also meet certain other conditions, for example, be blind, disabled, or sixty-five years of age or older.

However, the myriad exceptions to the general criteria complicate Medicaid eligibility. Examples of exceptions to the financial eligibility rules include the following:

- Income from the US Department of Veterans Affairs Aid and Attendance program does not count for Medicaid eligibility purposes.

- Some states exclude retirement assets (e.g., 401(k), 403(b), and individual retirement accounts) if certain conditions are met.

- Some states exclude the applicant's primary residence as a countable asset while the Medicaid recipient is living.

PITFALLS TO MEDICAID ELIGIBILITY

Navigating unforeseen pitfalls further complicates Medicaid eligibility. Actions taken by the Medicaid applicant or community spouse prior to filing a Medicaid application can delay eligibility or disqualify the applicant. Failing to take certain actions is even more perilous because it may negatively impact not only the applicant while they are living but also their family after the recipient's death. Beware of the following three common pitfalls:

- **Gifting.** Generally, Medicaid applicants and their spouses cannot make gifts to certain persons within sixty months (in most states) of applying for Medicaid (called the *lookback period*), even though Internal Revenue Service rules allow gifting. Go figure: two government agencies at odds. Gifts made within this lookback period render Medicaid applicants ineligible for Medicaid coverage for a specified number of months (called the *penalty period*).

- **Poorly drafted or no legal documents.** Your Medicaid eligibility may be delayed or denied if you have poorly drafted or no legal documents. Poorly drafted documents lack specific authority for Medicaid eligibility strategies. Unfortunately, some online do-it-yourself, and even attorney-prepared, legal documents (especially durable financial powers of attorney and trusts) are ineffective for Medicaid eligibility planning, even though such documents are otherwise legally valid. Consider making an appointment with a qualified elder law attorney to review your legal documents and make sure they are compatible with Medicaid eligibility.

- **Medicaid estate recovery and liens at death.** Federal law requires that a state recover Medicaid expenditures made on a recipient's behalf by filing a claim in probate court against the recipient's estate after they die (called *Medicaid estate recovery*). Many states will put a Medicaid lien on the home of a deceased Medicaid recipient for estate recovery purposes, even though the home was properly excluded as an asset on the Medicaid application. Some states even place the lien on the home while the recipient is living. This issue underscores the importance of proper planning.

STRATEGIES FOR GETTING MEDICAID

There are several strategies for getting Medicaid to pay for nursing home care. These strategies fall into two groups: *income planning strategies* and asset planning strategies. Because Medicaid law is state specific, not all strategies are effective in every state.

Income planning strategies are available when Medicaid applicants make too much income. The three primary income planning strategies are

- using a qualified income trust (also called a *Miller* trust) in states known as "income-cap" states,

- spending down your income on medical expenses in states known as "medically needy" states, and

- using Medicaid's spousal impoverishment rules (called *minimum monthly maintenance needs allowan*ce an*d monthly income allowan*ce) to transfer part or all of the Medicaid applicant's monthly income to the community spouse.

Asset planning strategies are available when the countable assets of Medicaid applicants (plus their spouses if married) exceed the asset limit rules. Some basic strategies include

- paying down the mortgage on your primary residence,

- making improvements to your primary residence,

- buying a car, and

- purchasing a Medicaid-compliant annuity.

More complex asset planning strategies are available for Medicaid eligibility planning; however, they require in-depth planning with the help of a qualified elder law attorney. For example, the elder law attorney may advise you to

- enter into a personal services contract with a nonspouse caregiver,

- lend money to a family member under a Medicaid compliant promissory note, or

- establish a qualified Medicaid trust (whether self-settled or pooled).

All the strategies discussed in this chapter are legally permissible. There is nothing unethical in planning for Medicaid eligibility as long as you comply with federal and state laws. However, Medicaid was not meant for wealthy individuals or to be exploited by the children of Medicaid applicants.

If your Medicaid strategy fails, the consequences are severe. Indeed, you will need to pay privately for your nursing home care until your penalty lookback period expires or your Medicaid application is approved. Because Medicaid rules are extremely complicated and differ in each state, misinformation about Medicaid eligibility is widespread, especially on the internet. Therefore, consider hiring a qualified elder law attorney instead of an unlicensed Medicaid planner or nonlawyer at the beginning of your Medicaid eligibility process.

Kevin Pillion

Jada Terreros

Kevin Pillion is a certified elder law attorney (CELA) and a graduate of Georgetown University Law Center. Jada Terreros is a Florida licensed attorney and graduate of the William S. Boyd School of Law at the University of Nevada, Las Vegas. Their email addresses are kevin@lifelawfirm.com and jada@lifelawfirm.com, respectively.

72

Special Needs Trusts: Protecting Beneficiaries with Special Needs

By Natalie Gilbert (Edmond, Oklahoma)

When you are deciding how each of your children or other beneficiaries should receive inherited assets at your death, there is no one-size-fits-all distribution scheme that works for everyone. A primary consideration as you are creating your plan is whether any of your beneficiaries have special needs. For each beneficiary, determine the following:

1. How old is the beneficiary?

2. Is the beneficiary able to handle money responsibly?

3. Has it been determined that the beneficiary has a disability, serious illness, or special need?

4. Is the beneficiary receiving government benefits or public assistance of any kind?

Three ways that you can leave funds to a beneficiary after your death are 1) outright and free of trust, 2) utilizing a general needs trust, and 3) utilizing a special needs trust. Distributions of inherited funds outright and free of trust go directly to the beneficiary with no restrictions. A general needs trust typically allows the beneficiary to receive distributions necessary to provide for their health, education, maintenance, and support and may allow access to additional funds upon the occurrence of certain milestones or ages. The trust may even allow the beneficiary to gain full control of the general needs trust upon reaching a certain age.

Regardless of your answers to questions 1 and 2 above, if you answered yes to questions 3 and 4, then you should consider creating a special needs trust for your beneficiary.

WHY A SPECIAL NEEDS TRUST?

A special needs trust (SNT) is also known as a supplemental needs trust, a disability trust, or a qualifying trust. The essential purpose of an SNT is to improve the quality of a beneficiary's life without disqualifying them or reducing their eligibility for government benefits. The SNT provides a framework for care and management of assets for the beneficiary, protects assets from creditors, and extends the life of the assets for the beneficiary.

The SNT protects a disabled or special needs beneficiary's eligibility for any government benefits or public assistance they are receiving or may receive such as Medicaid, Social Security Disability Insurance (SSDI), Supplemental Security Income (SSI), or other federal means-tested government benefits for which eligibility is based on income, resources, gainful activities, or financial need. The goal of the SNT is to supplement the funds available for the care of the beneficiary without being considered a resource or income available to the beneficiary in their qualification for government benefits.

It is important to note that the SNT cannot provide basic support (food, shelter, cash on hand) because that is the type of support the beneficiary would receive from government benefits, such as Medicaid or SSI. Distributions for these purposes would likely reduce the amount of government benefits granted to the beneficiary. The SNT funds can be used for supplemental items, such as vehicles, education, cable, telephone and internet services, entertainment, travel, furniture, clothing, hygiene care, medical care beyond what is considered a necessity, and other areas that enhance the beneficiary's life without impacting their access to important government benefits.

Because the assets are held in an SNT, they are also protected from anyone seeking to take advantage of your loved one. Your beneficiary will not have unfettered access to the funds. Instead, the trustee will apply the funds directly towards the needs of the beneficiary that qualify according to the instructions provided in the SNT document.

Unlike a general needs trust, an SNT neither allows the beneficiary to directly receive inherited assets nor to control the SNT. The SNT beneficiary should never be given any control over the distribution of the trust assets and should not have the ability to revoke or modify the trust in any way. This ensures that the beneficiary is provided financial security and prevents them from being disqualified from continuing to receive their current benefits or benefits they may receive in the future.

If you do not have an estate plan and one of your beneficiaries has special needs, the state laws of inheritance may require that a portion of your estate assets pass to your special needs child, sibling, parent, or other loved one at your death. If such inheritance exceeds the level of assets that the beneficiary is allowed to have to qualify for SSI or Medicaid (levels vary from state to state), they will be disqualified from receiving valuable benefits that could pay for medical, therapeutic, and support needs. The same can be said for large monetary gifts that are provided during your lifetime to a loved one with special needs. The purpose of a trust or a gift is to *help* your loved ones, not to hurt them—which is where an SNT comes into play.

TWO TYPES OF SPECIAL NEEDS TRUSTS

There are two primary types of SNTs: the third-party SNT and the first-party SNT. A third-party SNT is typically created by the parent of a special needs child, but could also be created by a grandparent, sibling, aunt, uncle, or other loved one. The SNT could be included in the third party's last will and testament or living trust to avoid the often lengthy and expensive probate process. The trust could also be drafted as a standalone SNT. The third-party SNT is most commonly funded upon the death of the individual (parent, grandparent, sibling, etc.) who established the SNT, with assets that never belonged to the beneficiary. However, multiple individuals could contribute to a standalone SNT for the benefit of the special needs beneficiary.

First-party SNTs are created for individuals with disabilities or special needs who either inherit assets outright, already own a substantial amount of assets, or receive a court settlement. The downside of a first-party SNT is that any funds left in the trust at the beneficiary's death must be used to repay the Medicaid programs, even to the extent of exhausting all remaining trust funds. In contrast, the creator of a third-party SNT can designate who is to receive any remaining assets in the trust at the beneficiary's death and the remaining assets are not required to be used to repay any Medicaid programs. Thus, if possible, it is incredibly beneficial to establish the SNT for the disabled beneficiary before they receive any assets.

WHO MANAGES THE SPECIAL NEEDS TRUST?

A successor trustee must be chosen to manage, invest, and distribute the SNT assets. You can choose the successor trustee who will serve in this capacity at your death. The ideal trustee should understand public benefits, have sound financial skills and knowledge, keep detailed books and records, and be trusted to make decisions in the best interest of the special needs beneficiary. The trustee can be an individual or a corporate entity. Examples of those who could serve as an individual trustee are a trusted family member or a friend who knows your family and the beneficiary. Conversely, a corporate trustee may be a bank or a trust company with a team of professionals well-versed in SNTs.

The trustee has a fiduciary duty to administer the trust according to the instructions in the trust document and to properly manage and distribute the funds to align with the rules and regulations of the government benefits so as not to cause disqualification. It is important to choose a person or entity that you trust for this job. Your estate planning attorney will assist you in making this decision.

Parents, grandparents, or other loved ones often assume that another family member will provide for the individual with special needs and do not create a plan. Establishing a special needs trust sets up your special needs loved one for success and enables a trusted individual or entity to manage the funds on their behalf. Talk to your estate planning attorney to determine if special needs planning should be considered for your loved one.

Natalie Gilbert is a senior attorney with Evans & Davis, a law firm committed to providing estate planning, business planning, trust administration services, and probate on a personal level while building long-standing relationships with each of their clients and their families.

Natalie Gilbert

SECTION 8

Creditor Protection

73

Domestic Asset Protection Trusts

By Ted Gudorf (Dayton, Ohio)

If you have worked hard to provide security for your family, you do not want to see the fruits of your labor drained by a creditor's claims. The most burdensome claims often stem from a judgment in a lawsuit, which can total hundreds of thousands of dollars or more. While anyone may be sued, you are especially vulnerable if you are a professional with significant assets and personal exposure to malpractice or breach of contract claims, for example, a physician, attorney, business owner, or farmer.

One way to shift assets out of the reach of most potential future creditors is to place them in a domestic asset protection trust (DAPT). What is a DAPT, and how does it provide asset protection? A DAPT is a self-settled, irrevocable, discretionary trust of which the settlor (trust creator) may be—but is not required to be—the sole beneficiary. Let's unpack what that means in layman's terms.

HOW DOMESTIC ASSET PROTECTION TRUSTS WORK

Self-settled means that the settlor puts their own assets into the trust. *Irrevocable* means that once the settlor creates the trust, they cannot revoke it. And *discretionary* means that distributions of income or assets from the trust are made in the sole discretion of the trustee who manages the trust. The trustee of a DAPT is independent of the settlor. However, the settlor can usually designate the person or entity who will serve as trustee, such as a financial institution, attorney, or even a family member.

The settlor of the trust is or may be added as a beneficiary of the trust but has no control over the trust assets: the beneficiary cannot demand or force a distribution. DAPTs must also contain a spendthrift provision that prevents the beneficiary from borrowing against trust assets and prevents creditors from reaching those assets. A wide variety of assets can be used to fund a DAPT, including cash, securities, real estate, business assets, vehicles, boats and aircraft, artwork and collectibles, intellectual property, and limited liability companies (LLCs) that own any such assets.

In general, a beneficiary's creditor can only assert a claim against trust assets to which the beneficiary has a right. Because the beneficiary of a DAPT cannot revoke the trust to reclaim its assets and is not entitled to distributions, the creditor cannot reach those assets or income—at least until a distribution is made or promised to the beneficiary.

Example: Assume you are a forty-five-year-old surgeon who owns lucrative rental properties in three states and has a stock portfolio worth more than $1 million. You have medical malpractice insurance, of course, but you know that 85 percent of surgeons are eventually sued, and you want to protect your assets in case a claim ever exceeds your policy limits. You have enough income from employment that you will remain solvent even without the income from your rental properties or stocks.

Your attorney recommends that you create LLCs in each state in which you own rental property and transfer ownership of the property to the LLCs. Your attorney forms a management company LLC to own the other LLCs. He also forms a DAPT that will own both the management company LLC and the stock portfolio. The trustee is a bank.

The assets are not in your name, and you have also given up all control over them. The trustee of the DAPT controls whether and when you receive income from the trust, according to the terms of the trust document. The downside, of course, is that you cannot demand access to the assets. The upside is that your creditors also cannot demand access to them.

Let's change the scenario a little bit. Assume that you have the job and assets described above, but you have already been sued by a patient before creating the LLCs and DAPT. Can you still use the DAPT to protect your assets from the lawsuit? No—not from this potential creditor. If you create a trust with the intent to defraud a creditor, a court will probably find it to be void. Most states that allow DAPTs will void a trust if there was clear and convincing evidence that it was created with the intention to defraud a creditor. In other words, you will probably be able to use a DAPT only to protect against possible future claims that have not yet arisen.

PROTECTIONS FOR CREDITORS UNDER DOMESTIC ASSET PROTECTION TRUST LAWS

All fifty states permit the creation of a hybrid DAPT (which is a DAPT of which the trustmaker is not a beneficiary but can be added as one), as long as the trustmaker does not actually become a beneficiary of the trust. However, most states do not allow for the creation of a DAPT if the trustmaker is a beneficiary. These trusts are controversial because of the possibility that a settlor could try to use a DAPT to shield assets from recovery by a legitimate creditor. As of this writing, nineteen states (Alaska, Connecticut, Delaware, Hawaii, Indiana, Michigan, Mississippi, Missouri, Nevada, New Hampshire, Ohio, Oklahoma, Rhode Island, South Dakota, Tennessee, Utah, Virginia, West Virginia, and Wyoming) have statutes that permit the creation of these types of DAPTs. Also, if you live in a state that does not allow the creation of DAPTs, you may still be able to create a DAPT in a state that does, but you may have to transfer the property to that state if it is possible to do so.

States that allow the creation of DAPTs typically have measures in place to protect creditors. As mentioned above, you cannot use a DAPT to defraud an existing creditor. A DAPT will generally not allow you to shield assets from a claim that has arisen or may arise from events that have already taken place. States that allow DAPTs have statutes of limitations that allow preexisting creditors or future creditors to file claims for a specified period after the creation of the trust.

Most states also do not allow a DAPT to shield assets from every type of creditor. For instance, most states make exceptions for claims of divorcing spouses, child support, alimony, or some combination of these. You also cannot render yourself insolvent by pouring all of your assets into a DAPT. Many states that allow DAPTs require you to sign an affidavit of solvency with every transfer of an asset into the trust.

REQUIREMENTS OF A DOMESTIC ASSET PROTECTION TRUST

If you want to protect your assets from creditors using a DAPT, your trust must fulfill the following requirements:

- The trust must be irrevocable.

- As settlor of the trust, you may be—but are not required to be—the sole or primary beneficiary, but you may not serve as trustee; you must not have control of the assets in the trust.

- The trust must have a spendthrift provision.

- Distribution of trust income or assets must be entirely within the trustee's control.

- At least one trustee of the trust must be a resident of the state under whose laws the trust was created, and at least some of the trust's administration must take place in that state.

- DAPTs are considerably more complicated than most trusts. If you are interested in a DAPT, be sure to work with an attorney who is experienced with this asset protection tool.

Ted Gudorf is an AV-rated, Ohio-based estate planning and elder care lawyer located in Dayton, Ohio. The firm is licensed in Ohio and Wyoming. Most attorneys are board certified by the Ohio State Bar Association.

Ted Gudorf

74

LLCs for Estate Planning and Asset Protection

By Roger McClure (Fairfax, Virginia)

Bob and Mari Mori are in their sixties and have three children, Ellen, Latha, and Bob Jr. Both Ellen and Latha are married, have children, and are doing well financially. Ellen has plans to move overseas with her family. Bob Jr. has a disability, is only able to work part-time, and still lives with his parents at the age of forty-two. Bob and Mari are concerned that someone will need to care for Bob Jr. when they die.

Bob is an executive with a stable Fortune 500 company. Mari has her own dental practice. They have a house worth $800,000, retirement savings and financial assets of $1.5 million, life insurance with a death benefit of $500,000, and two rental properties with total equity of $400,000.

They consult a WealthCounsel attorney for estate planning and asset protection. Their goals are to avoid probate and federal estate taxes, take care of their children, manage their retirement accounts, and protect themselves from rental property lawsuits.

To accomplish their goals, their attorney recommends that they establish a joint living trust, healthcare powers of attorney and directives, general powers of attorney for their retirement and other nontrust assets, and pour-over wills. In addition, their attorney advises them to form limited liability companies (LLCs) for ownership of their rental properties as well as their investments in stocks and bonds. The attorney explains that although LLCs can be formed in any state, there are many factors to consider when selecting the appropriate one, and it often makes sense to form an LLC in the state where the assets the LLC will own are located. The Moris decide to form the LLCs in their home state of Texas, which has favorable LLC laws and is also where their rental properties are located.

ESTATE PLANNING WITH LLCS

Although a living trust with a backup pour-over will is one of the premier legal instruments for avoiding probate, saving on federal estate taxes, and simplifying the administration of an estate for the heirs, an LLC may be the preferred estate planning tool under certain circumstances. Specifically, LLCs can be helpful in estate planning for families with heirs or property located in other countries.

In the United States, trusts are based on state common law, which is derived from English law. Trusts that people set up while they are living or upon their death are permitted in all fifty states and the District of Columbia. However, in Central and South America, Europe, and most of Asia, the majority of countries have a legal system that differs dramatically from English common law and may not recognize trusts.

As a result, if Ellen and her family move permanently to Germany, for example, and she receives her inheritance that is owned by an American trust, she may have to pay higher taxes and will have difficulty opening and managing trust accounts. To avoid these issues, Bob and Mari may want to use an LLC as the primary estate planning tool for their heirs and property located outside the United States.

ASSET PROTECTION WITH LLCS

Many people think that when they set up a living trust and transfer property to that trust, the assets held in the trust will be protected from creditors. This is not true in any US state for a typical revocable living trust in which the parents who established the trust are named as trustees. Approximately seventeen states have laws that allow you to set up an asset protection trust that names an outside trustee to protect the assets. But many people do not want to use asset protection trusts because they often must give up control of their assets to someone outside the family.

In contrast, an LLC allows you to maintain control of your assets while benefiting from substantial asset protection. LLCs provide business owners with limited liability for business operations. Entrepreneurs put only the money they invest in the business at risk. In other words, if there are lawsuits filed against the business, the owners risk losing only the money they have invested in their business, while their home, savings, and retirement accounts are protected. Corporations provide similar protection, but general partnerships do not. If you form an LLC, however, you are still at risk for any personal guarantees of mortgages on rental properties and for injuries to people for which you are at fault.

In a minority of states, LLCs provide a second layer of protection—protection for the assets owned by the LLC. If none of Bob and Mari's assets are owned by an LLC and Bob is held liable for $2 million as a result of an auto accident he caused, and his auto insurance will only cover $500,000, then he will owe the person who sued him $1.5 million dollars. Bob's $1.5 million creditor may be able to take his home, his rental properties, the cash value of his life insurance, and his life savings to satisfy the judgment.

However, in a minority of states, if Bob and Mari transfer their rental properties or investments to a properly created LLC, they can protect the properties and financial assets from personal creditors whose claims arise from events such as auto accidents or defaults on personal loans. In those states, state law does not permit a creditor to obtain a court order requiring an LLC owner to sell LLC property to pay non-LLC debts. This type of protection is called "limitations on charging orders" and is provided under current law in states such as Texas, Delaware, Virginia, Nevada, and Florida. It is not available in New York, California, Maryland, or other states that have passed the uniform law for LLCs drafted by the Uniform Law Commission. It is important to keep this in mind because, as mentioned above, you can choose the state where you set up your LLC.

No asset protection strategy provides a bulletproof shield of protection, however. If you do something morally reprehensible that causes harm, you will likely be held liable for damages caused by your actions.

To protect their assets, Bob and Mari decide to set up two Texas LLCs: one to own their two rental properties located in Texas and the other to own their stocks and bonds. Bob, Mari, Ellen, and Latha are the managers of the LLCs, but Ellen, Bob Jr. and Latha do not have membership interests. Rather, Bob and Mari own 100 percent of the membership interests in the LLCs. Upon Bob's and Mari's passing, their estate plan comprising the two LLCs and a joint revocable trust will enable their rental properties and financial assets to pass automatically to the trusts set up for their children in their joint revocable trust.

Using LLCs in addition to other estate planning tools, Bob and Mari's estate plan is set up to avoid probate, prevent fights among their children upon their deaths, allocate their properties the way they want, take advantage of any exemptions from federal estate and capital gains taxes, shield their retirement accounts, prevent their rental houses from causing them financial ruin as a result of future events, and protect their rental houses and finances from greedy personal creditors.

Roger McClure has over forty years of experience in business and estate planning, has published many articles in national publications, and is a sought-after national speaker. He provides very practical and useful advice to family-owned businesses, from basic to very advanced planning.

Roger McClure

75

Multiple Business Entities as an Asset Protection Tool

Rodney Gregory (Jacksonville, Florida)

A multiple business entity strategy (MBES) involves establishing separate business entities to hold business assets in order to protect them against creditors' claims and lawsuits. Utilizing multiple limited liability companies (LLCs) or corporations can insulate the assets held in each one from undue risk if financial or legal issues arise involving assets held by one of the other entities.

MULTIPLE BUSINESS ENTITY STRATEGY

An MBES involves at least two entities: a holding company (sometimes known as a parent company) and an operating company.

THE HOLDING COMPANY

The holding company, or parent company, does not own, manufacture, produce, or sell any products or services. The purpose of the holding company is to own and oversee the subsidiary operating companies. This strategy provides both capital-raising and risk-management benefits. A holding company can own all or part of a subsidiary. However, to maintain control, a holding company must generally own 51 percent of a subsidiary (or have the largest ownership interest if there are many owners).

THE OPERATING COMPANY

The operating company (or companies) manufactures, produces, and/or sells products or services. Operating companies hold and operate the business's assets. The best way to protect a company's assets is to form as many operating companies as necessary to protect each asset. Forming a separate LLC to own each of the assets may seem excessive, but it is the best way to protect each asset. The operating companies can do business with one another: for example, your leasing company LLC can lease property owned by another LLC or lease its office space from an LLC formed to own the office building.

Example: Seeleg owns two plots of land and a leasing company that leases the land and other assets. Currently, Seeleg's business, Seeleg LLC, owns and operates all of these assets. If someone were injured on one of the plots of land owned by Seeleg LLC, all of the assets it owns would be at risk if a lawsuit were filed. This could lead to financial devastation if the assets were pursued to satisfy a judgment. Instead, Seeleg should create separate business entities to hold each asset. Using multiple business entities protects the asset held in each entity from liabilities arising from the assets held by the other entities. The following graphs illustrate the two strategies:

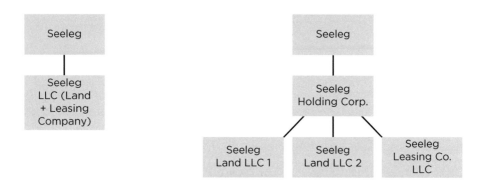

An MBES is also beneficial for raising capital.

Example: Assume Seeleg owns a single building. He forms an operating LLC to own the building and a holding LLC that owns the operating LLC. This provides Seeleg with the option to sell a portion of the holding LLC to raise capital to expand the business or cash out part of his business without having to decrease the business's ownership interest in the building.

TYPES OF BUSINESS ENTITIES

A variety of different business entities can be used as holding and operating companies. The most common are LLCs and C corporations. In terms of risk management, LLCs and C corporations offer similar asset protection. Each type of entity has advantages and disadvantages. There is no definitive best structure; rather, the decision about which to use is dependent on the relevant facts and circumstances.

LLCS

LLCs are generally a simpler business entity than corporations. They typically cost less to create and maintain than other types of entities. Owners are generally not liable for the business's debts and liabilities. One of the primary reasons to choose an LLC over a C corporation is that LLCs are not taxed at the company level. All profits from the LLC are included as ordinary income on the owner's income tax return. This also means that losses pass through to the owner and can offset the owner's other gains. LLCs provide other tax benefits, including for start-up capitalization, transfers of assets, and distributions of appreciated property.

C CORPORATIONS

C corporations are more complex than LLCs, and therefore, they often cost more to create and maintain. C corporation owners (called stockholders) enjoy limited liability similar to LLC owners (called members). C corporations provide a variety of unique tax benefits and capital-raising opportunities. However, C corporations are subject to double taxation: they are taxed at the corporate level on earnings and again at the shareholder level on distributions of earnings and profits.

SHOULD YOU EMPLOY AN MBES?

Almost all companies, regardless of size or complexity, should implement a multiple business entity strategy. The reason is simple: asset protection. By creating a holding company, risk is insulated at the operational level. Seek advice and counsel from a competent lawyer experienced in MBES to determine the best strategies for owning business assets to properly manage risk and protect them from creditors and lawsuits.[1]

Rodney G. Gregory, the American Barrister, has an LLM in advanced civil litigation from Nottingham Trent University and a JD from Washington and Lee University School of Law. He represents individuals and families in wealth planning.

Rodney Gregory

1   Arya Salehi, my esteemed senior law clerk and a 3L at Washington and Lee University School of Law, provided invaluable assistance in the preparation of this chapter.

SECTION 9

Charitable Giving

76

Lions, Tigers, and Bears, Oh My! Three Types of Charitable Vehicles

By Rodney Gregory (Jacksonville, Florida)

This chapter describes key differences and similarities between private foundations, public charities, and trusts for charitably inclined clients. Contributions to these charitable vehicles enable you to fulfill philanthropic goals, benefit from a charitable tax deduction, and reduce estate and income taxes because you no longer own the contributed property.

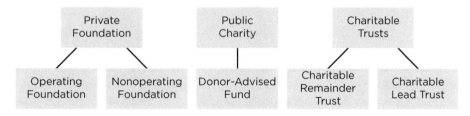

The distinguishing features of these charitable vehicles have tax, operational and other implications. Some of the primary characteristics of each vehicle are described below.

PRIVATE FOUNDATION

A private foundation is a 501(c)(3) tax-exempt independent legal entity established for charitable purposes, whose funding typically comes from a single individual, a family, or a corporation. The donor can have a significant degree of control over the private foundation and typically determines its mission, the members of its board, its investments, and its distributions. The degree of control, particularly over how charitable funds are applied, is generally unavailable through other vehicles. Private foundations also afford donors an opportunity to establish a philanthropic legacy by involving younger generations in governance and eventually relinquishing control to them. However, because of the many rules and compliance requirements to which private foundations are subject, including many anti-abuse rules and possible excise taxes, they are expensive and onerous to establish and maintain.

There are two types of private foundations: nonoperating foundations and operating foundations. Nonoperating foundations are more common. Their philanthropy typically involves making grants to public charities. A nonoperating foundation must generally distribute 5 percent of its net investment assets annually. Donations to most nonoperating foundations are deductible for income tax purposes up to 30 percent of adjusted gross income (AGI) for cash contributions and up to 20 percent of AGI for certain appreciated property. By contrast, operating foundations usually do not make grants to other charitable organizations but focus instead on maintaining their own programs on a continuing and sustained basis. Operating foundations are required to spend at least 85 percent of their adjusted net income or their minimum investment return, whichever is less, on their charitable operations. Donations to an operating foundation are generally deductible up to 50 percent of AGI for cash[1] and up to 30 percent for certain appreciated assets.

Because establishing and maintaining a private foundation is complex, private foundations are usually only a good fit when control or fostering philanthropy in younger generations is paramount to the donor and the donor's contribution to the foundation will exceed $2 million.

PUBLIC CHARITY

A public charity is a 501(c)(3) tax-exempt independent legal entity that is established solely for charitable purposes and is exempt from treatment as a private foundation, typically because it relies primarily on funding from the general public to support its activities. Public charities are governed by a diversified board of directors, a majority of whom are not related by marriage or blood.

Public charities typically conduct charitable activities and provide services for their

---

1   Until 2026, the 50 percent limit is increased to 60 percent under certain circumstances.

own projects. They are generally dependent upon financial support from the public and may solicit donations or grants from individuals, corporations, private foundations, and the government. Most public charities must verify substantial support from the general public to maintain their tax-exempt status with the Internal Revenue Service.

Establishing and maintaining a public charity can be time-consuming and difficult, particularly if the charity needs to meet the public support test to qualify as a public charity. Contributing to an existing public charity, however, can be very easy—and tax-advantageous. Contributions to public charities can usually be made by check or even credit card, and they are generally deductible for income tax purposes up to 50 percent for cash and up to 30 percent for certain appreciated assets. However, donors to public charities, even those making significant contributions, generally do not have much say in how their funds are used. Even where a charity agrees to accept a contribution subject to conditions, the donor typically will not have the extent of oversight or control a private foundation affords.

DONOR-ADVISED FUND

A donor-advised fund (DAF) is a special account created and maintained within a sponsoring public charity. It is an asset account, similar to a bank account, owned by the sponsoring charity rather than the donor, that holds investments and makes distributions to other charities, potentially according to the donor's recommendations. In general, donations to DAFs are treated the same as donations to a public charity under current law. The applicable current-year charitable income tax deduction is up to 50 percent of AGI for cash and up to 30 percent for certain appreciated assets. Contributions to the DAF are deductible when made, even if the funds are not immediately distributed to a charity.

DAFs are popular charitable giving vehicles for good reason: a DAF can be established at several major financial institutions without the assistance of an attorney, may have low initial contribution requirements (e.g., $5,000), affords the donor a voice regarding the further disposition of the funds, can be used to involve younger generations in the donor's philanthropy, and is not burdensome to maintain.

CHARITABLE TRUSTS

When people refer to charitable trusts, they are usually referring to charitable split-interest trusts. In a charitable split-interest trust, the beneficial interests can be split between charitable and noncharitable beneficiaries, within parameters set forth in the tax laws. The charity can be the lead beneficiary, making the trust a charitable lead trust (CLT), or it can be the remainder beneficiary, making the trust a charitable remainder trust (CRT). The ability to provide for both charitable and noncharitable beneficiaries while still receiving a tax deduction for contributions distinguishes charitable split-interest trusts from the other charitable giving vehicles discussed in this chapter, as the funds of private foundations, public charities, and DAFs generally cannot be distributed to noncharitable beneficiaries.

CHARITABLE REMAINDER TRUST (CRT)

After the term of a CRT expires, the remaining assets pass to a charity chosen by the donor, such as the family's private foundation or DAF. When a donor establishes and contributes assets to a CRT during their lifetime, they get an income tax deduction in the year of the contribution of up to 50 percent of AGI for cash and up to 30 percent for certain appreciated assets. The deduction is not for the entire value of the trust; rather, it is calculated based on several factors, such as the amount contributed, interest rates, and terms of the trust. In addition to the income tax deduction, the donor receives a gift tax charitable deduction for part of the value of the contribution to the trust, and that deduction may offset the potential gift tax consequences of naming a noncharitable beneficiary other than the donor or the donor's spouse to receive the payments during the term.

CRTs are typically structured so that the assets are not part of the donor's estate for estate tax purposes. A CRT is not subject to income tax and therefore does not pay capital gains tax when it sells appreciated assets, though portions of the distributions to the noncharitable beneficiary will be treated as capital gain. This effectively enables the donor to defer and spread out a potentially significant capital gains tax. CRTs are commonly used when a donor wishes to provide for charity and also receive a stream of payments into the future, provide a stream of payments to someone else, sell a highly appreciated asset without incurring a large capital gains tax immediately, or fund a private foundation.

CHARITABLE LEAD TRUST (CLT)

When a CLT is funded during a donor's lifetime, the CLT makes distributions to one or more charitable organizations chosen by the donor, such as a DAF, for a fixed term of years or for the lives of one or more individuals. Those distributions are usually guaranteed annual payments or payments of the trust's income. Unlike a CRT, a CLT is not an income tax-exempt entity; however, a CLT may receive a charitable deduction for all or portions of the distributions it makes to charities. After the end of the term, the remaining assets pass to the noncharitable beneficiaries selected by the donor (e.g., the donor's children).

Unlike with a CRT, when a donor contributes assets to a typical CLT (i.e., a nongrantor CLT), the donor generally does not receive an income tax deduction. However, the trust's income is no longer part of the grantor's income, which may be the functional equivalent of a deduction. The donor can receive a gift tax charitable deduction either when the trust is funded or when distributions are made from the trust to charities, depending on how the trust is structured. That gift tax deduction may zero out an otherwise taxable gift of the remainder interest to the noncharitable beneficiaries. CLTs are typically structured so that the assets are not part of the donor's estate for estate tax purposes.

CLTs are often used by donors who wish to provide for charity and also transfer potentially significant wealth to noncharitable beneficiaries at a reduced (or potentially zero) gift and estate tax cost. CLTs are most effective at transferring wealth at a low tax cost when interest rates are low.

CONCLUSION

Donors can provide for charities or accomplish their charitable objectives using a variety of different vehicles. Many of those vehicles are complex, but they can be very worthwhile to establish for the right donor. A qualified estate planning attorney can analyze a potential donor's circumstances and goals and advise as to which vehicles might be best for that donor. That attorney may also be able to assist the donor in establishing the foundation, trust, or other vehicle. There are multiple companies that can provide invaluable assistance in determining worthy charities, such as Charity Navigator, a well-regarded nonprofit evaluator that provides free access to data, tools, and resources to guide philanthropic decision-making. As an additional resource, Foundation Source is a company that will work with your estate planning attorney to establish and support private foundations for individuals and families by providing administrative services, online tools, and expert guidance.[2]

Rodney G. Gregory, the American Barrister, has an LLM in advanced civil litigation from Nottingham Trent University and a JD from Washington and Lee School of Law. Mr. Gregory represents individuals and families in wealth planning.

Rodney Gregory

---

2   Arya Salehi, my esteemed senior law clerk and a 3L at Washington and Lee School of Law, provided invaluable research and scrivener assistance in preparation of this chapter.

.

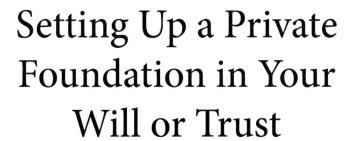

77

Setting Up a Private Foundation in Your Will or Trust

By Christine C. Weiner (Irvine, California)

Since the founding of our country, Americans have had charitable intentions. Families who have achieved a measure of success often wish to help others who are less fortunate and to give back to their community to benefit youth, educational institutions, houses of worship, artistic endeavors, scientific research, and social causes. Over the past century, the private foundation has become a popular tool for contributing to a favorite cause.

With today's increased life expectancy, you may want to ensure that you have enough assets to live comfortably in your retirement years and provide a legacy for your children before charitably sharing your wealth. By establishing a private foundation in your will or trust, you can fulfill your charitable goals after your death.

WHY SET UP A PRIVATE FOUNDATION IN YOUR WILL OR TRUST?

In addition to fulfilling charitable goals, setting up a private foundation may provide tax savings. No one has a crystal ball to show what the level of our wealth will be when we pass away. Individuals concerned about minimizing potential federal estate taxes can include a flexible formula in their will or trust that allows the executor or trustee to determine whether the value of the assets requires that a private foundation be set up to offset estate taxes after the individual's death. For 2022, the exemption from federal estate taxes is $12.06 million per person or $24.12 million per married couple. However, the current exemption amount is set to expire on December 31, 2025. Because the current exemption amount is very high, some individuals or families may be exempt from federal estate taxes right now, so establishing a private foundation to minimize taxes may not seem necessary. However, by the time they pass away, their wealth may have increased, or the current generous exemption from federal estate taxes may have changed or reverted to the previous exemption amount of $5 million per person or $10 million per married couple (indexed for inflation).

Provisions in a will or trust that direct the creation of a private foundation allow families who may encounter this dilemma the opportunity to adopt a wait-and-see approach. For example, a formula clause could specify that the allocation to the private foundation should be the percentage of assets that will reduce the federal estate tax (and state death taxes, if applicable) to zero. It can also give the executor or trustee the option not to fund the private foundation if the assets are insufficient to do so.

Flexibility may also be important if an individual or family has not made a final decision regarding the important purposes of the private foundation and the public charities or purposes that it should support. In general, a private foundation must operate for public purposes; that is, exclusively for religious, charitable, scientific, literary, or educational purposes. However, within this broad range of activities, the individual or family may designate specific types of activities for the private foundation to support, such as scholarships; youth camps; specific charities in their community; their own alma mater; their religious group; specific art museums, musical groups, or scientific research, etc. As long as the individual has testamentary capacity, they can amend their will or trust to change, add, or delete specific types of philanthropic activities.

REQUIREMENTS FOR A PRIVATE FOUNDATION

In general, a private foundation that complies with the requirements of federal law is exempt from income tax, and contributions to it are deductible for income, gift, and estate tax purposes. As mentioned, federal law requires that a private foundation be operated for public purposes, and the will or trust must contain a purpose clause that includes this information. Further, the individual or family may more narrowly define the specific purposes of their private foundation, as discussed above.

There are distinct differences between a public charity and a private foundation. First, contributions to a public charity are eligible for a higher income tax deduction than contributions to a private foundation. When a donor contributes to a public charity, they receive an income tax deduction in that year of an amount not exceeding 50 percent of their adjusted gross income. Any unused charitable income tax deduction can be carried over for the next five years. In contrast, when a donor contributes to a typical private foundation, the amount of cash donations may be deducted in the year of contribution to the extent of 30 percent of the donor's adjusted gross income. The unused portion can be carried forward for five more years, but the deduction is limited to 30 percent of each year's adjusted gross income.

Another difference relates to special requirements and excise taxes imposed by Internal Revenue Code (I.R.C.) §§ 4940–4945, as amended. Because the the Internal Revenue Service (IRS) perceived abuse of private foundations' tax-exempt statuses, Congress enacted a system of alternative penalty taxes that can be imposed on private foundations. The penalty taxes are designed to ensure that the earnings of private foundations will not inure to the benefit of any private shareholder or individual.

Many of the rules applicable to establishing a private foundation do not apply to public charities. Individuals and families who wish to set up a private foundation need to be aware of these rules to avoid running afoul of them and incurring unexpected penalties or taxes.

When establishing a private foundation, the donor or family should carefully consider who should serve as the proposed foundation's manager and on its board to ensure that its governance will comply with the applicable rules and regulations. If family members are not well-suited for these roles, the donor or family should choose and prepare other individuals to step into them. After they have chosen the manager and board of directors, the donor or family can name the proposed administrators in the relevant provisions in their will or trust.

OPTIMUM SIZE OF GIFT OR PHILANTHROPIC ENTITY

Because of the administrative requirements for tax filings, record-keeping, and board governance, a private foundation's initial funding should be at least $3 million. If the founding contribution is less than $3 million, the administrative requirements may become too burdensome, and the tax benefits will be insufficient to offset the effort needed to maintain the foundation as a viable entity.

WHAT SPECIAL ADVANTAGES DO PRIVATE FOUNDATIONS PROVIDE?

Private foundations provide a number of principal advantages, including the following:

- Expanded opportunities to give

Charitable recipients authorized to receive a grant from a private foundation and receive a deduction for grantmaking include

> » public charities in the United States,

> » international charities that are recognized in the United States,

> » international organizations not recognized in the United States for charitable purposes, and

> » individuals, for charitable purposes.

- Control of decision making

The primary advantage of a private foundation is control. The donor or family controls the foundation's board and distributions and may select grant allocation to one organization, one sector, or one geographic location. This sweeping control, limited only by IRS rules and regulations, is the chief reason that donors or families choose a private foundation over other types of charitable entities or organizations.

- Family engagement

Private foundations offer a number of opportunities for families to become involved in charitable giving by

> » involving family members in philanthropic decisions;

> » institutionalizing philanthropy for generations;

> » teaching children about philanthropy; and

> » paying appropriate salaries to family members as officers, directors, or service providers.

- Tax benefits and deductions

> » **Maximize lifetime giving.** As mentioned, if a person makes a lifetime gift of cash to most private foundations, the tax deduction is limited to 30 percent of their adjusted gross income in that year, with a carryover option of five additional years, with each subsequent year limited to 30 percent of adjusted gross income for that year. If a person makes a lifetime gift of real property or stock to a typical private foundation, the tax deduction is limited to 20 percent of their adjusted gross income in that year, with a carryover option of five additional years, with each subsequent year limited to 20 percent of adjusted gross income for that year.

> » **Estate tax benefit.** There is a charitable estate tax deduction for private foundations formed by will or trust at death. The rules are complicated, and therefore individuals or families desiring to set up a private foundation by will or trust should consult a tax and estate planning attorney, a certified public accountant, and their other financial advisers to determine how to establish the proposed private foundation and the clauses that they must include in their will or trust for the foundation to be respected for tax purposes. Adher-

ing to the requirements ensures that establishing the private foundation in a will or trust will result in the desired charitable tax deduction percentage or dollar amount.

CONCLUSION

An advantage of including a private foundation in a will or trust is that the donor can amend the instrument up to the date of death as long as they have testamentary capacity. This advantage allows the donor to determine who is suitable to train to serve as manager or on the board of directors; the types of charities they want to benefit; and the readiness of adult children to understand the rules and be trained to participate in its management. While a private foundation is an effective way to accomplish charitable and tax-savings goals, the rules and requirements for establishing and maintaining a foundation are onerous. Consult an experienced estate planning attorney to ensure that you take the proper steps to achieve your objectives.

Christine C. Weiner practices in Irvine and Palm Desert, California, in the areas of tax, asset protection, business planning, and estate planning, and is certified as a specialist in estate planning.

Christine Weiner

Appendix

Felicia A. Acosta-Steiner, JD
Legacy Legal, LLC
8100 E 22nd St N
Suite 1400-2
Wichita, KS 67226
felicia@legacylegalllc.com
316-202-2067

Yasmin Wardie Adamy, Esq.
Adamy Law, PLLC
2850 Isabella Blvd
Suite 10
Jacksonville Beach, FL 32250
yaz@adamylaw.com
904-947-4890

Meghan M. Avila, Esq.
Celaya Law
1455 First Street, Suite 216
Napa, CA 94559
firm@celayalaw.com
707-492-3112

Brett J. Barthelmeh, Esq., AEP
Squillace & Associates, P.C.
20 Park Plaza
Suite 1115
Boston, MA 02116
brett@squillace-law.com
617-716-0300

Joel R. Beck
Peach State Wills & Trusts | The Beck
Law Firm, LLC
2090 Sugarloaf Pkwy
Suite 135
Lawrenceville, GA 30045
678-344-5342

Michelle D. Beneski, Esq.
Surprenant & Beneski, P.C.
MyFamilyEstatePlanning.com
Hyannis, MA
508-994-5200

Michelle A. Booge, Esq.
Dyer Bregman & Ferris, PLLC
3411 N 5th Ave
Suite 300
Phoenix, AZ 85013
602-254-6008

Megan E. Bray, JD
Bray Law Office
9393 W. 110th St. Suite 500
Overland Park, KS 66210
megan@mbraylaw.com
www.mbraylaw.com
913-451-6936

Benjamin J. Brickweg
Lodgepole Law
PO Box 889
Conifer, CO 80433
hello@lodgepolelaw.com
303-592-9950

C. Dennis Brislawn Jr., JD
Oseran Hahn P.S.
11225 SE 6th St, Suite 100
Bellevue, WA 98004
dbrislawn@ohswlaw.com
425-455-3900

Marty Burbank, JD, LLM
OC Elder Law
619 N Harbor Blvd.
Fullerton, CA 92832
info@OCElderLaw.com

Linda A. Burrows, JD, LLM (Tax)
Claritas Law, APC
info@claritaslaw.com

Glenn Busch, BSBA Accounting, JD, LLM (Tax)
Law Office of Glenn Busch P.C.
260 Madison Avenue
21st Floor
Manhattan
New York, NY 10016
Gbusch@Buschlegal.com
212-661-3600

Anthony G. Celaya, Esq.
Celaya Law
1455 First Street, Suite 216
Napa, CA 94559
firm@celayalaw.com
707-492-3112

Rosanna Chenette, JD
Law Offices of Rosanna Chenette, P.C.
250 Bel Marin Keys Blvd
Building A, Suite 1
Novato, CA 94949
415-895-8544

Becky Cholewka, JD
Cholewka Law
4365 E Pecos Rd
Suite 104
Gilbert, AZ, 85295
Becky@GilbertLawOffice.com
480-497-3770

Jerry D. Clinch, JD
Clinch Law Firm, LLC
209 E 6th Street
York, NE 68467
jerry.clinchlawfirm@gmail.com
402-908-5699

Doug Coe
Legacy Legal, LLC
8100 E 22nd St N #1400-2
Wichita, KS 67226
316-202-2067

Patricia De Fonte, JD, LLM
De Fonte Law PC - Estate Planning With Heart
4104 24th Street
Suite 212
San Francisco, CA 94114
info@defontelaw.com
415-735-6959

David R. Duringer, JD, LLM (Tax)
Protective Law Corporation
895 Napa Ave Suite B4
Morro Bay, CA 93442
info@lawnews.tv
805-225-5105

Jennifer Elliott, JD
San Clemente Estate Law, P.C.
100 S Ola Vista, Suite A
San Clemente, CA 92672
Jennifer@SanClementeEstateLaw.com
949-420-0025

Anthony R. Fantini
Fantini Law Firm, P.C.
661 Andersen Drive, Suite 220
Seven Foster Plaza
Pittsburgh, PA 15220-2700
Info@FantiniLaw.com
412-928-9200

Danielle R. Feller
Daly Mills Family Law
111 W Broad St
Statesville, NC 28677
drfeller@dalyfamilylaw.com
704-878-2365

Shawn D. Garner, JD
Deason Garner & Hansen
6024 E 32nd St
Yuma, AZ 85365
shawn@deasongarnerlaw.com
928-783-4466

Natalie J. Gilbert, JD
Evans & Davis PLLC
natalie@evansdavis.com
866-708-2335

Douglas G. Goldberg, Esq.
Goldberg Law Center, P.C.
4003 N Weber St
Building G
Colorado Springs, CO 80907
Doug@GoldbergLawCenter.com
719-200-5416

Ted Gudorf, JD, LLM
Gudorf Law Group, LLC
8153 N Main St
Dayton, OH 45415
tgudorf@gudorflaw.com
937-898-5583

Adam Hansen, JD
Deason Garner & Hansen
6024 E 32nd St
Yuma, AZ 85365
adam@deasongarnerlaw.com
928-783-4466

Rodney J. Hatley, Esq., LLM (Tax)
Hatley Law Group, A P.C.
12636 High Bluff Dr.
Suite 400
San Diego, CA 92130-2071
rod@hatleylawgroup.com
858-465-8001

Gregory Herman-Giddens, JD, LLM, TEP, CFP
999 Vanderbilt Beach Road
Suite 509
Naples, FL 34108-3507
gherman-giddens@galbraith.law
239-260-3045

Mark Ignacio, Esq.
Mark Ignacio Law APC
7317 El Cajon Blvd.
Suite 101
La Mesa, CA 91942
mark@ignaciolaw.com
619-810-4644

Erin Johnson
Erin Johnson Attorney at Law LLC
PO Box 189
Rico, CO 81332-0189
erin@fone.net
303-588-2695

Riley Carbone Kern, JD
Tallgrass Estate Planning, LLP
7377 S Sleepy Hollow Dr
Tulsa, OK, 74136
riley@tallgrassestateplanning.com
918-770-8940

Jeffrey L. Knapp, JD, EPLS, AEP®, CFP®, CLA, CTC, APM
The Knapp Law Firm LLC
The Wealth Strategies Center
11 S Finley Ave.
Basking Ridge, NJ 07920
jknapp@knapplaw.net
908-696-0011

S. Victoria Lannom, JD, LLM
Lannom Law LLC
640 N Dixie Ave
Cookeville, TN 38501
931-651-1900

Tyler W. Lannom, JD, LLM
Lannom Law LLC
640 N Dixie Ave
Cookeville, TN 38501
931-651-1900

Brittany Littleton, JD
Littleton Legal PLLC
2604 W Kenosha
Suite 100
Broken Arrow, OK 74012
brittany@littletonlegal.com
918-608-1836

Attorney Rebecca M. Mackie
Kohls & Associates, LLC
6041 Monona Dr Suite 100
Monona, WI 53716
rmackie@kohlslaw.com
608-221-8000

Kevin C. Martin, JD, LLM, MBA
Kevin C. Martin, Attorney at Law, PLLC
700 K St NW
3rd Floor
Washington, DC 20001
kevin@kevinmartinlaw.com
202-549-2588

Roger McClure
Washington Wealth Counsellors PC
10511 Judicial Dr
Fairfax, VA 22030
roger@wealthcounsellors.com
571-633-0330

Courtney Medina
C Medina Law, Inc.
1317 W Foothill Blvd
Upland, CA 91786
courtney@cmedinalaw.com
909-921-6343

J. David Meredith, MA, JD
Meredith Law Firm, PC
8505 Technology Forest Pl
Suite 604
The Woodlands, TX 77381
david@meredith-law.com
832-246-8481

Carla M. Miramontes, Esq.
Dyer Bregman & Ferris, PLLC
3411 N 5th Ave
Suite 300
Phoenix, AZ 85013
602-254-6008

Michael Monteforte Jr., Esq.
Monteforte Law P.C.
300 Trade Center
Suite 5640
Woburn, MA 01801
mike@montefortelaw.com
978-657-7437

Sheena M. Moran
S. M. Moran Law Office, P.C.
5104 S Field Street
Unit B
Littleton, CO 80123
sheena@smmoranlawoffice.com
720-460-1476

Sarah L. Ostahowski, JD
Sarah's Law Firm
502 N McEwan St
Clare, MI 48617
sarah@sarahslawfirm.com
989-567-2100

Christopher C. Papin
Papin Law, PLLC
1424 S Fretz Ave
Edmond, OK 73003
chris@papinlaw.com
405-531-9196

Heather L. Parker, Esq.
The Parker Law Office, LLC
6640 E Baseline Road
Suite 103
Mesa, AZ 85206
HP@ParkerLawAZ.com
480-264-5177

Arthur J. Pauly, Jr., JD, Esq.
Attorney at Law
Roseville, CA 95661
916-207-7526

Kevin Pillion, Esq., CELA
Life Planning Law Firm, P.A.
1671 Mound Street
Sarasota, FL 34236
kevin@lifelawfirm.com
941-914-6000

Heather Bartel Reid, Esq.
Squillace & Associates, P.C.
20 Park Plaza
Suite 1115
Boston, MA 02116
heather@squillace-law.com
617-716-0300

Clifford J. Rice
Rice & Rice Attorneys
100 Lincoln Way
Suite 1
Valparaiso, IN 46383
www.riceandrice.com
219-462-0809

Chris Rippy, JD
Rippy, Stepps, & Associates, P.A.
1237 Front St
Conway, AR 72032
Chris@Rippylawfirm.com
501-428-9139

Ashley E. Sharek, Esquire
Sharek Law Office, LLC
Box 130
Bradford Woods, PA 15015
contact@shareklaw.com
412-347-1731

H. Van Smith, Esq.
Smith Strong, PLC
3111 Northside Ave
Suite 102
Richmond, VA 23228
hvansmith@smithstrong.com
804-325-1245

Linda A. Sommers
Sommers Law Group, LLC
390 Union Blvd
Suite 280
Lakewood, CO 80228
linda@5280EstatePlanner.com
303-984-9900

Ashley Ryan Sorgen, JD, LLM
Edmonds Sorgen, LLC
807 E. Washington Street
Suite 200
Medina, OH 44256
330-725-5297

Benjamin J. Sowards, Esq.
Sowards Law Firm, APC
2542 S Bascom Ave
Suite 210
Campbell, CA, 95008
info@sowardslawfirm.com
408-371-6000

Michael G. Stuart, JD, CPA
Pavone Law Group, PC
255 E Lake St
Bloomingdale, IL, 60108
mstuart@pavonelawgroup.com
630-424-1100

Daniel M. Surprenant, Esq.
Surprenant & Beneski, P.C.
MyFamilyEstatePlanning.com
Easton and New Bedford, MA
508-994-5200

Nicole Ramos Takemoto
Candelaria PC
1981 N Broadway
Suite 440
Walnut Creek, CA 94596
nicole@candelarialawoffices.com
925-233-6222
800-303-7423

Jada W. Terreros, Esq.
Life Planning Law Firm, P.A.
1671 Mound Street
Sarasota, FL 34236
jada@lifelawfirm.com
941-914-6000

Jeanne Vatterott-Gale, JD
Hunt and Gale
256 S 2nd Ave Suite E
Yuma, AZ 85364
receptionist@azyumalaw.com
928-783-0103

Jim Voeller
The Voeller Law Firm
19311 FM 2252, Suite 103
San Antonio, TX 78266
jvoeller@voellerlaw.com
210-651-3851

Nicole D. Warmerdam
Law Office of Nicole Warmerdam
951 Mariners Island Blvd
Suite 300
San Mateo, CA 94404
nicole@nw-trust.com
650-689-7169

Christine C. Weiner, JD, TEP, CEPA
Christine C. Weiner, A Professional
Law Corp
18111 Von Karman Avenue
Suite 460
Irvine, CA, 92612-7152
cweiner@EstateTrustLawyer.com
949-300-7800

Wayne M. Zell, JD, CPA
Zell Law, PLLC
11718 Bowman Green Dr
Suite 100
Reston, VA 20190
wayne@zelllaw.com
571-203-9355